THE
GREAT
WHITE
HOPES

THE
GREAT
WHITE
HOPES

THE QUEST TO DEFEAT JACK JOHNSON

GRAEME KENT

FOREWORD BY HARRY CARPENTER

SUTTON PUBLISHING

First published in the United Kingdom in 2005 by
Sutton Publishing Limited · Phoenix Mill
Thrupp · Stroud · Gloucestershire · GL5 2BU

British Library Cataloguing in Publication Data
A catalogue record for this book is available from the British Library.

ISBN 0-7509-3892-7

Typeset in 11/13.5pt Sabon.
Typesetting and origination by
Sutton Publishing Limited.
Printed and bound in England by
J.H. Haynes & Co. Ltd, Sparkford.

CONTENTS

FOREWORD
by Harry Carpenter

This book is about envy: white envy of black talent. The talent belongs to Jack Johnson, the first black man to win the world heavyweight championship. Because he was black, and successful, he was reviled in the USA by white men. Mind you, he didn't help his cause. He was saucy, he smiled a lot (this was interpreted as a sneer), he flaunted his wealth with fast cars and sprauncy clothes, and, oh, the horror of it, he married two white women and formed a liaison with a third, which led to a criminal charge and exile from the States. In the seven years of his reign as champion, the world of boxing was determined to get him beaten.

Before we get too high-minded about what seems to us now an insane chase for a white Sir Galahad, let's remember that other sports dragged their feet when it came to recognising black talent. Jackie Robinson was the first black player allowed to participate in major league US baseball, and that didn't come about until the late 1940s, some thirty years after Jack Johnson had left the world stage.

In Britain black (or coloured, as we had to say then) boxers were denied the right to fight for a British title until 1948. The first man to break the colour bar was Dick Turpin, elder brother of Randolph. Hasn't there always been a white edginess about black success and doesn't it still exist? For evidence of that I give you some members of football crowds.

I never met Jack Johnson (he died in 1946), but in the 1950s I went to Texas, Johnson's home state, where segregation still existed. Black people couldn't stay in white hotels, couldn't eat in white restaurants and, when they got on a bus, were banished to the back seats. In those surroundings it wasn't too difficult to understand how the impact of Johnson's boxing supremacy must have felt.

The American white hatred of Jack Johnson in those early years of the twentieth century was mirrored when Muhammad Ali came on the scene in the 1960s. Here was a modern-day Johnson: voluble, smiling, taunting, boasting and blessed with a boxing talent such as had not been seen before, or since. The US press immediately pinned the bad-boy label on him. He had too much lip, he was arrogant, he answered back and his unpopularity with white people increased a thousand-fold when he refused to swear the oath of allegiance to the US flag, which meant he wouldn't go to Vietnam ('them Viet Cong never called me nigger'). The fate of Jack Johnson now befell Muhammad Ali. He faced a criminal charge and, although he wasn't forced to leave the States, he was exiled from boxing for more than three years. When he was allowed back, his first opponent, Jerry Quarry, was a white man.

Graeme Kent is a painstaking researcher and writer. You will find plenty in this book you didn't know before. I thought I knew a bit about Victor McLaglen. I was wrong. I didn't know the half of it. There are two levels at which Mr Kent's book is important. It adds considerably to our knowledge of the heavyweight championship and it lays bare a fascinating slice of social history. Graeme Kent has pulled off a fine double.

Harry Carpenter
March 2005

ACKNOWLEDGEMENTS

I have received much help from many people in the writing of this book, and I would like to express my thanks to them. For information on Victor McLaglen's service in the Life Guards at the turn of the century I am indebted to K.C. Hughes, Assistant Curator of the Household Cavalry Museum, while details of other aspects of McLaglen's rather mysterious wartime military career were supplied by Major (retd) J.E.H. Ellis, Curator of the Cheshire Military Museum, Major (retd) J. Rogerson, Curator of the Prince of Wales Royal Regiment and Queen's Military Museum, and Amanda Moreno, Curator of the Regimental Museum of the Royal Irish Fusiliers.

Patti Wotherspoon of the Vancouver Public Library's Research and Information Centre provided background information on Jack Johnson's sojourn in Canada, while closer to home Helen Wallder of the Doncaster Local Studies Library discovered a great deal of material on local heavyweight 'Iron' Hague. Tracey Booth of the Local Studies Library, Kingston upon Hull, found information about the early life of Con O'Kelly. Malcolm Matthews of the Local and Naval Studies Section of the Plymouth Library Service provided information about the White Hopes campaign in the West of England. My friend, the late Bob Hartley, was able to supply a great deal of first-hand information about life on the boxing booths and the career of the American heavyweight George Christian. I am indebted to Barry Hugman, Editor of *The British Boxing Board of Control Yearbook*, for his permission to reprint some of the material on Victor McLaglen that was first published in his annual. I am grateful to Dr Sandra Salin for her meticulous translations of French sporting journals and magazines from the opening decades of the twentieth century.

Acknowledgements

I am deeply indebted to Harry Shaffer for allowing me access to many old newspaper clippings from his magnificent collection in Archives of Antiquities of the Prize Ring – antekprizering.com.

The only other book published on the subject of the White Hopes is *White Hope* by Oswald Frederick (the late Fred Snelling, doyen of British boxing writers). This is a small paperback published in the 1940s. Fred, with typical modesty, claimed that he wrote it in a few weeks while fire-watching during the London bombing raids. Fred was very kind to me when as a young man I first wrote about boxing in the 1950s, and I hope that I may have done some justice to the topic that is rightfully his.

Finally, I would like to express my gratitude to my editor Sarah Bryce, for her unflagging enthusiasm and support for the project and her dedication and conscientiousness in seeing it through to its conclusion.

Graeme Kent
Lincolnshire, March 2005

INTRODUCTION

The worldwide search between 1908 and 1915 to find a white fighter who could defeat the unpopular black champion Jack Johnson is one of the most unusual yet little-known stories in the annals of world sport. This is the first full-length book to deal with the history of the White Hopes.

Carrying out the research has occupied many years in a number of different countries. A great deal has been written about the charismatic and controversial Johnson, but hardly anything has been said about his Caucasian challengers. Apart from the film actor Victor McLaglen, none of the White Hopes wrote a book about his experiences, and even McLaglen's autobiography hardly touched upon his ring career. Much of this investigation necessarily has been conducted with the aid of yellowing press cuttings and dusty contemporary accounts of court proceedings between 1908 and 1915, along with other public records and private reminiscences, published and unpublished.

During the bizarre hunt, hundreds of ambitious young men came forward all over the world to challenge Jack Johnson, and thirty or forty of them proved good enough or determined enough to have been classified, no matter how briefly, as a White Hope. Their stories are told, often for the first time, in these pages.

The optimistic Hopes came from different countries and varied backgrounds. Victor McLaglen was the English son of a South African bishop. Oklahoman railway fireman Carl Morris was sponsored by an oil millionaire, failed as a scientific boxer and reinvented himself under the billing of the world's dirtiest fighter.

Luther McCarty ran away from a tent show where he was selling snake oil dressed as a Native American. George Rodel's manager claimed that his South African heavyweight had been a Boer War hero, until the unforgiving press discovered that the fighter had only been a child when the war ended. French Hope Georges Carpentier was a genuinely decorated war hero, but was so small that he seldom dared to be photographed next to potential opponents. Handsome, philandering Frank Moran was the boyfriend of silent-film stars Mary Pickford and Pearl White and was stranded penniless in wartime Paris by a heartless manager. There were many others, all with their own fascinating stories.

Their heyday was a brief one, less than seven years in duration, and when it was over the fall from grace for many of them was equally swift. Sandy Ferguson and Jim Barry were both killed in barroom brawls. Al Palzer was shot to death by his own father. Iron Hague was gassed on the Somme and never fought again. Luther McCarty was killed in the ring.

The saga of the White Hopes was played out against a background of vicious racial prejudice and unrest. Only twelve years before Jack Johnson took the title, the US Supreme Court's decision in *Plessy* v. *Ferguson* had upheld the principle of racial segregation. Jack Johnson was feared by many whites as 'a bad nigger', the term traditionally applied to slaves who had had the courage to rebel against their masters. To have such a proud and independent man as heavyweight champion, a position Eldridge Cleaver, spokesman for the militant Black Panthers movement, has called 'the ultimate focus of masculinity in America', was regarded by many whites as an affront to white supremacy, to be rectified quickly.

The era of the White Hopes was a fascinating one and deserves to be remembered. It is hoped that this account will present a true picture of an unusual and long-departed age.

1

'THERE WAS NO FIGHT!'

It was several minutes past midday on the afternoon of 26 December 1908. The first World Heavyweight Championship under the Marquess of Queensberry rules between a white and a black boxer was about to end. In the fourteenth round, Tommy Burns, the totally outclassed Canadian heavyweight champion of the world, had been smashed to the canvas for a count of eight. As the fighter staggered to his feet, bleeding from the nose and mouth, Superintendent Mitchell, in charge of the 250-strong police contingent at the ringside in the open-air stadium at Rushcutters Bay, just outside Sydney in Australia, climbed into the ring.

Unable to make himself heard above the noise of the crowd, the inspector indicated to the referee, Hugh D. McIntosh, who was also the promoter of the contest, that he should stop the fight. McIntosh nodded and moved forward to do so. Ignoring him, Jack Johnson, the black American challenger, advanced to finish off the reeling Burns.

Sam Fitzpatrick, Johnson's manager, and his seconds, terrified that their man would be disqualified, screamed at Johnson to step back. Their cries rose to the cloudless skies; unable to borrow enough wood to complete the stadium, McIntosh had built it without a roof. The black heavyweight saw his handlers' wild gesticulations and hesitated. McIntosh shouted, 'Stop, Johnson!', and placed his hand on the black man's shoulder as an indication that he was the winner and new champion.

Realising what was happening, Tommy Burns turned on Superintendent Mitchell, who had instigated the stoppage, and swore luridly at him, demanding that he be allowed to fight on. Pat O'Keefe, a British middleweight boxer and Burns's chief second, hurried across the ring and led the still shouting and struggling former champion back to his corner. Burns was $30,000 richer, the highest sum ever paid to a boxer up to that time, compared to Johnson's $5,000, but his championship had passed out of his hands.

Towards the end of his life the Canadian would always deny vehemently that he had been outclassed by Johnson. He claimed that the police had intervened mainly because Rudy Unholtz, a German-born South African boxer on Johnson's payroll, had crept under the elevated ring as early as the tenth round. From here, Burns declared indignantly, Unholtz had kept screaming, 'Stop the fight!', thus influencing the police at ringside. Few spectators backed Burns's claim.

In the immediate aftermath of the Rushcutters Bay championship bout, Burns stayed on in Australia and lost much of his purse money at the races. He took his losses philosophically. A shrewd businessman but a pragmatist, he had been paid one dollar and twenty-five cents for his first fight, against Fred Thornton in Detroit in 1900, and he had once journeyed all the way to the Yukon to inspect a gold mine he had won in a poker game. Finding it to be worthless, he had earned his passage back by fighting the local champion, Klondike Mike Mahoney.

For some time Johnson had been pursuing Burns halfway across the world in search of a title shot. Over a nine-year period, he had defeated all the major black contenders and those white heavyweights who would fight him, and now he was 30. He had scraped a living across the USA, working as a sponge fisherman, stable boy, porter, dock labourer and sparring partner. He had ridden the rails as an itinerant wanderer and lived and fought in hobo jungles. Before he had been lucky enough to embark upon an organised boxing career, he had taken part in the horrific 'Battles Royal', where half a dozen or more black youths were pitched into a ring at the same time and forced to fight for the delectation of a largely white audience until only one was left standing. It was the right sort of background to produce a tough, bitter and fearless man.

After years in the doldrums, boxing was undergoing a worldwide resurgence, although there was little legislation anywhere to control the sport. There were no national controlling bodies and there was little organisation, just fights everywhere before huge crowds. Even

President Theodore Roosevelt in the White House had his own resident fisticuffs trainer in 'Professor' Mike Donovan, a grizzled former bare-knuckle fighter and veteran of General Sherman's Civil War march through Georgia.

Taking advantage of the general enthusiasm for boxing, Johnson decided temporarily to remain in Australia, though definitely not in Sydney. A goodwill visit by a fleet of sixteen US battleships, which had occurred before the title fight, had aroused alarm and anti-black resentment in the city. Many citizens feared that the warships would be crewed almost exclusively by black seamen, who might not take kindly to the prevailing 'White Australia' policy. This had caused *The Age*, a Melbourne newspaper, to state reassuringly, 'It is not at all probable, however, that a very large proportion of the crews will be found to be coloured. There will be some on the battleships, but they will not be nearly as numerous as rumour is suggesting just now.'

Hugh D. McIntosh had relied on sailors from the fleet to support the Burns–Johnson contest. In fact the Americans showed very little interest in the bout, causing the promoter to remark, possibly with some exaggeration, 'Australians supported it. I had counted on American sailors for a possible sellout. Exactly two appeared in uniform. They started fighting and had to be evicted.'

Before the fleet had left to sail home, the Australian Defence Minister, Mr Ewing, had urged the departing Americans to tell their fellow-countrymen that they had seen for themselves that Australia was emphatically a white-man's country and would remain so.

The 'White Australia' policy had been sparked off in the 1850s to combat the influx of over 50,000 Chinese immigrants who came to join in the gold rushes. Not only were the new labourers distinctive in their appearance, maintaining their own social customs, they toiled hard and cheaply. Soon they became very unpopular with Australian workers in the goldfields. By 1888, legislation had banned any more Chinese from entering the country. It was not long before the policy was applied tacitly to all non-whites. This was emphasised in 1903, when a trading vessel was wrecked off the coast at Point Nepean. The survivors were taken to Melbourne by a rescuing tugboat, but only the white officers and crew-members were allowed ashore. The non-whites were put on a Japanese mail ship and conducted to Hong Kong. Within another five years, by the time that Burns fought Johnson, most of the South Sea Islanders who had been recruited in the nineteenth century to work in the cane fields of the north had been sent back home.

So how did a black boxer become heavyweight champion of the world on Australian soil? White Australians loved their sport and were becoming increasingly good at it. The English cricket team which had toured the continent in 1907/08 had lost four of the five games it had played against the Australians, while at the 1908 Olympics the Wallabies had defeated England, the only other entrant for rugby football, 32–3.

In addition, boxing was immensely popular in Australia, and in Squires and Lang the country had just produced a pair of formidable heavyweight boxers of its own. So highly were these two regarded by their fellow-countrymen that the world's leading big men, Jack Johnson and Tommy Burns, had been imported in the hope that the favoured home-grown boxers would defeat them. Unfortunately, both Australians had been crushed by Burns, while Johnson had compounded the national disappointment by thrashing Lang. These impressive results had led to a public outcry for Burns to defend his title against the black challenger, and Johnson had been allowed to return to meet him.

The black fighter's subsequent victory was a watershed in the history of sport. For the first time, boxing left the sports pages and was featured all over the world in major news stories on the front pages of the contemporary tabloids and broadsheets alike. Typical was the *New York Evening Journal*, which published a picture of Johnson occupying most of the front page, unprecedented coverage for a sporting personality. Caucasian supremacy had been publicly challenged and humiliated. The fact that the breakthrough had occurred in the haphazard and often crooked world of professional boxing made matters even worse. What, people wondered, appalled, would happen to the established order with the scarcely known and unpredictable ogre Jack Johnson now bestriding the sport like a colossus, a figurehead for his oppressed race?

In the immediate aftermath of his victory the new champion felt that, under the circumstances, he would be more popular on a tour of the remoter areas of Australia than he would in the large cities. He cashed in on his new title by touring Western Australia, fighting exhibition contests and making public appearances. In the outback, with his outgoing personality, gold teeth, shaven head and colourful ring attire, he was a great success. By the end of his short small-hall tour of the Antipodes, he had almost doubled the money he had been paid for fighting Burns. If he had been self-confident before, Johnson was now positively ebullient.

An example of his strong self-worth and refusal to buckle under white pressure occurred in the gold-mining town of Kalgoorlie, when he stopped for a drink in the Palace Hotel. While he was there, one of his many new-found instant friends admired Johnson's superb defensive qualities but remarked that it would not have been much of a fight at Rushcutters Bay if Burns had not done most of the attacking. Johnson disagreed in lordly fashion, stating that his ability was such that he could force any opponent to lead, while picking him off with his devastating counter-punches. At this, a 61-year-old respectably dressed gentleman with luxuriant mutton-chop whiskers stepped forward from the back of the crowd and informed Jack Johnson crisply that never in a million years could the new champion force him to lead unless he wanted to.

A murmur of recognition went round the bar. The challenger was Larry Foley, the father of scientific Australian boxing, the man who had learnt his trade from Jem Mace, the Swaffham Gypsy, and who had passed it on in turn to such ring luminaries as Peter Jackson, Frank Slavin and Bob Fitzsimmons. Now a local politician, he was in Kalgoorlie for an assembly of state councillors.

Lazily, Johnson unpeeled himself from the bar to face his affronted elderly opponent. He raised his massive fists and started swaying gently, his feet planted firmly on the floor. For three minutes, by the watch of one onlooker, Charlie Rose, who described the odd confrontation in his autobiography, *Life's a Knockout*, Johnson feinted, punched the air and made fake attacks. It was all to no avail. The vastly experienced Foley just stood his ground stolidly, refusing to respond to any of the champion's overtures.

The crowd began to grow restless and jeer at Johnson. The black fighter was not disturbed. Suddenly he bent forward and murmured a scatological remark about Foley's parentage. The Australian veteran flushed, spat an oath at Johnson and lashed out with his right hand. Johnson deflected the blow easily by placing a massive hand across Foley's biceps at the crucial moment. Calmly he murmured to the still outraged councillor that the drinks were on Foley.

It was Johnson's first public exhibition as the champion of how he could always get under the skin of self-important members of the establishment. However, Jack Johnson knew that the big money lay back in the USA, and that, scarred by his experiences, confrontational, self-assured and afraid of no one, he was about to return and make the whites pay dearly if they wanted the title back.

All over the world writer after writer began to stress the fact that Johnson had been completely superior to his outweighed opponent, and declared that a white contender must be found to wrest the title back from the black man. Jack London, the novelist, who had witnessed the bout, led the way. 'There was no fight,' he wrote in a *New York Herald* article syndicated across the world. 'No Armenian massacre could compare with the hopeless slaughter that took place in the Sydney Stadium today.' Australian writer W.F. Corbett, also present, demanded despairingly, 'We now have a black champion of the world. Who will dethrone him?' The *Melbourne Herald* said of Johnson's victory, 'Already the insolent black's victory causes skin problems in Woolloomooloo . . . It is a bad day for Australia and not a good one for America. The United States has 90,000 citizens of Johnson's colour, and would be glad to get rid of them.'

The *New York Times* demanded the instant emergence of a white champion to undo what had happened in Australia and take the title back from Johnson. The black journal the *Colored American Magazine*, on the other hand, described the result of the bout simply as 'the zenith of Negro sport'. It was rumoured in the USA that President Teddy Roosevelt himself, a keen follower of boxing and smarting from recent public condemnation after the disciplining of a black regiment involved in an uprising in Texas, had expressed his concern that a black man had won the supreme crown of pugilism.

This was taking place at a time when blacks made up roughly 10 per cent of the population of the USA, and 89 per cent of the black population lived in the southern states. Only five months earlier there had been a major racial disturbance in Springfield, Illinois. A white man had died of razor wounds inflicted upon him by a black man, and a white woman had subsequently falsely accused a black man of raping her. In the riots that had ensued, businesses had been burnt to the ground, forty black men had been attacked and several killed. Armed militia had been called out and five white men had been shot and killed by the part-time soldiers. After matters had calmed down eighty people were indicted and brought to court. There had been only one minor conviction.

As Jack Johnson prepared to leave Australia for home, more and more newspapers in Europe and the USA joined in the campaign to find a Caucasian heavyweight who would bring the title back to the white race. Johnson was vilified as newspapers devoted hundreds of column inches to the search. Competitions for big men were held in halls all over the world. Managers began to scour the factories, farms, armed services and even prisons for a behemoth who would be their meal ticket in the lucrative scramble to dethrone the black champion. The White Hope campaign had started. It was to lead to seven years of trouble and madness.

2

THE FUTURE ASSISTANT PROVOST MARSHAL OF BAGHDAD

The first fighter that Johnson met after winning the title was probably one of the worst. He was also one of the most interesting and irrepressible. The name of the first White Hope was Victor McLaglen. He was a 22-year-old English soldier of fortune, the son of a South African bishop. For the previous five years, since 1904, he had been working his way optimistically around North America doing a variety of menial jobs. His fighting record was negligible. He was matched against Johnson as a last-minute substitute because the champion and his connections knew that the burly and willing youngster had no chance.

McLaglen claimed to have been born in Tunbridge Wells, Kent, in 1886, one of eight brothers and a sister, although his birth certificate gives the less salubrious East End of London as his birthplace. He had been brought up in South Africa, where his father became Bishop of Claremont. The family then returned to England in 1899, at the time of the Boer War. One of McLaglen's older brothers, Fred, joined the colours and left for Cape Town.

The 14-year-old McLaglen dearly wanted to follow him, but his father forbade it. McLaglen, who captained the Tower Hamlets schools' football team, was already tall and looked older than his years. He ran away from home, lied about his age and joined the Life Guards, in the anticipation of being sent to the war. The attestation book of the 1st Life Guards for this period records that he enlisted on 30 July 1901. He gave his age as 19, his trade as engineer, and claimed to have been born in Stepney, London. His complexion was dark and his eyes were hazel.

To his chagrin, Trooper McLaglen, instead of fighting the Boers, found himself spending most of his time on guard duty outside Windsor Castle. It was here that he first learnt to box and took part in his regimental heavyweight championships, fighting grown men when he was only 15 or 16.

For a future professional fighter McLaglen had joined the Army at just the right time. The first independent Army championships had been held only seven years earlier, in 1894. In the following year the sport was given an enormous fillip when Field Marshal Lord Wolsey, the Commander-in-Chief of all Britain's armed forces, attended the Guards' boxing competition at Chelsea Barracks and was so impressed by the fighting spirit he saw in the ring there that he declared that in future he wanted to see every soldier a boxer.

Wolsey was just the man to be impressed by a public display of aggression. As a young subaltern he had decided that the fastest, if riskiest, way to promotion was to place himself in harm's way at every conceivable opportunity. At a speech at the Brigade of Guards' championships in 1899, before a wildly cheering audience, he stressed the importance of boxing for soldiers: 'It is conducive to endurance and pluck, and makes men of them – the sort of men who alone can defend us against our foes.'

Efforts to make Army boxing socially acceptable, however, were less successful. When Colonel G.M. Fox, Inspector of Gymnasia at Aldershot, invited a number of ladies to attend the Army finals, the first contest they witnessed was such a bloody one that they swept out en masse, and the experiment was not repeated. But Wolsey's imprimatur was all that the sport needed in military circles. Officers everywhere did their best to accede to the field marshal's expressed wish, and placed boxing high on the agenda of training exercises. By 1900, there were 137 entries for the Army championships for other ranks. The officers had their own less-well-supported championships. In the championships for privates and NCOs, entries included seventeen sailors and a number of members of the part-time militia, an early form of the Territorial Army. They were allowed to enter because many of the militia were on standby to leave their civilian occupations to be shipped to South Africa.

The standard in Army boxing was quite high at this time. In one championship final, Private Ham of the Ninth Lancers, a former professional who had boxed under the name of the Bermondsey Boy, was outpointed over three rounds by Sergeant Collins of the Guards. Afterwards Ham protested indignantly that he could not get going in the limited time provided. With the connivance of his officers and the tacit approval of Lord Wolsey and the War Office, the soldiers were rematched over ten rounds at the National Sporting Club. This time Private Ham won.

Like many later boxers, McLaglen found that boxing was a passport to a relatively easy life in the Army. He was excused many of the fatigues that were the lot of his less athletic comrades. He was still only a boy, fighting men, and it was during this period that he began to accumulate some of the battered features which were to serve him well as a 'heavy' in his later Hollywood pictures.

The Boer War ended in 1902 without having needed McLaglen's services. After three years of home soldiering, bored and disillusioned and still, at 17, too young to serve, he was at last discovered by his father, who promptly informed the authorities that his wayward boy was still under age and would have to be discharged immediately. The Life Guards agreed and McLaglen was released. The official reason given was 'Discharged in consequence of him having made a mis-statement as to his age on enlistment'. McLaglen's service conduct summary was adjudged to have been very good.

Army service had not made McLaglen lose his taste for adventure. 'By this time, my brothers, all of whom were as tall as I, had scattered all over the world,' he recounted in a later newspaper interview. 'I decided I wanted to go to Canada.'

When he was 18, McLaglen crossed the Atlantic steerage and found work as a farmhand at ten dollars a month in Ontario in south-eastern Canada. He had not been there long when he heard of a silver strike at Cobalt, not too far away. McLaglen abandoned the farm at once and joined in the rush. Only seven years had passed since the famous Klondike gold rush in the Yukon had made wealthy men of some itinerants.

The silver had been discovered in 1903 when two men employed to find suitable timber for the construction of a railway line had instead discovered rocks containing metallic flakes as they scouted the edges of a remote lake. They sent samples of the rocks to be analysed and were told that the gleaming flakes were silver, assaying 4,000 ounces to the ton.

In the following year the two pioneers established a silver mine in the region. Any attempts they might have entertained of keeping their discovery to themselves were thwarted when a third man, a blacksmith called LaRose, also stumbled across the secret. Mining lore has it that one day, while working, he threw his heavy hammer at a fox which was annoying him. The hammer missed the animal but knocked a lump out of a piece of rock, disclosing signs of silver deposits. Whatever the truth of this, by 1904 it was known that there was silver in large and valuable quantities in the region of Lake Timiskaming. Even official reports emerging from the area were using such emotive descriptions as 'pieces of native silver as big as stove lids or cannon balls lying on the ground'.

It was essential to get there before the lakes and rivers froze over and isolated the region for the winter. There was a newly constructed railway line heading northwards from Toronto, but the majority of prospectors came through the passages between the hills in great convoys of humanity, packers carrying their equipment on dog sledges at ten cents a pound, while the hopeful fortune-hunters trudged behind. McLaglen was among the hundreds of hopefuls who arrived among the first wave.

There was nothing in the region but snow, ice and flat rock. Even so, the mining camp sprung up on every level surface that could be found. Cobalt, so named for the mineral found lying interleaved with the silver deposits in the ground, was known as that most cherished of institutions, a 'poor man's mining camp', because the silver veins lay so close to the surface, it could be mined with a pickaxe and shovel. A historian described the first shipments out as 'slabs of native metal stripped off the walls of the vein like boards from a barn'.

McLaglen joined up with several other prospectors and started digging some way from the centre of the region. Although he was still only 19, he had achieved his full growth, being a muscular 6ft 3in at a weight of just under 14 stone, and was fully able to hold his own with his companions at digging or fighting off potential claim-jumpers.

For months they toiled under conditions of great hardship. Eventually they found silver and started to pile it up. It was then that McLaglen encountered his first great setback. It was discovered that he had no right to the claim. He was always vague about the exact details. The most that he would later ever say about the event was, 'I was deliberately cheated out of my share of the silver after I had worked a year. We had found the ore but I had failed to sign certain papers that would have entitled me to my share.'

Whether or not McLaglen was defrauded by his partners is uncertain, although they would have been brave men to have attempted to cheat such a husky youngster. It is more likely that he fell foul of mining bureaucracy. A regulation was being widely enforced whereby a valuable mineral had to be found on the site before a claim could be registered. Many miners found that their claims did not belong to them because they had registered them before striking lucky, and this was probably McLaglen's misfortune.

Whatever the cause, in 1905 the disillusioned 19-year-old was broke and in urgent need of money. For shelter he built himself a wooden shack on the shores of Lake Timiskaming. By this time Cobalt had become a boom town. Major mining companies and syndicates were moving in to work alongside the fortune-hunters. At its peak, 10,000 people were living in the town.

The tough miners were in urgent need of forms of relaxation on which to spend the fortunes some of them were accruing almost overnight. Saloons and brothels flourished, taking in thousands of dollars a week. One popular form of entertainment was the arrival of battered but experienced professional boxers and wrestlers, willing to take on all comers for a price. These were familiar sights in mining camps.

The pioneer in this field had been the veteran Australian heavyweight Frank Slavin. A few years earlier he had toured the mines of the Klondike gold rush in Alaska, interspersing his own efforts at prospecting with fighting before enthusiastic crowds for enough money for another grubstake. Slavin was past 40 when in 1902 he had engaged in his last mining-camp bout, and his example had opened the door for many others.

In McLaglen's case it was a professional wrestler who arrived at the mining camp. The down-and-out McLaglen accepted the man's challenge and defeated him before a large audience of miners. He won only a few dollars, but many of the miners had bet on him to win, a sign that the young giant already had something of a reputation as a fighter. After McLaglen's success, the winning punters passed the hat for him, and he ended up with almost $500, more money than he had ever seen before.

For a man of his strength and size, fighting seemed an easier option than mining. McLaglen took the decision to become a professional – challenging anyone in the area at wrestling or fighting, either with the gloves or bare fists. Among the tough but untutored prospectors he proved a real handful, taking a share of the gate money for his bouts from any local entrepreneur who cared to make the arrangements.

Things were going so well that McLaglen sent for his brother Fred, the sibling who had fired his incipient wanderlust by going off to fight the Boers. By this time Fred had engaged in a few boxing matches himself and was able to impart such skills as he had to his brother and to act as his sparring partner. It was during this period that McLaglen developed his main training exercise. He would saw logs of wood at chest-height for long periods. He never became a skilful boxer, but he was strong and his exercise routines helped him to develop a fair right-hand punch. He also enjoyed boxing. 'I always loved the flicker of the gloves,' he once reminisced, 'the tap of feet on the canvas, the snort of breath as the punches beat home.'

For a time, he and Fred toured the thriving mining areas, challenging all comers at boxing or wrestling. When no one accepted their challenges they put on exhibitions of both sports. Fred soon tired of the rough-and-ready conditions of Ontario and decided to try his luck further south, in the USA, where he would fight as Fred McKay. Before he left, he saw McLaglen fixed up as a professional wrestler with a touring circus, where the young man accepted challenges from the audience, paying twenty-five dollars to anyone who could last three rounds with him. McLaglen's main venue was the Happy Land Park in Winnipeg. Here his most notorious and highly publicised stunt was to defeat an entire football team in the ring, taking its members on one at a time.

This job did not pay very well, and although it got him away from the dangers and hardships of the mining camps McLaglen soon became fed up with it. He quite liked the ambience and the relatively easy way of show-business life, but aspired to something a little higher up the evolutionary scale than the small circus with its cowed animal acts and unfunny slapstick clowns. At some time during this period he worked as a barman, then as a railway policeman driving hobos away from the sidings and dissuading them from 'riding the rods'.

Next, with a partner called Hume Duvel, he put together a physical culture and strongman act that entailed being clad in silver paint and involved displays of muscle-flexing and strength, including the lifting of impressive weights which were perhaps not quite as heavy as they looked. McLaglen's speciality at this point, and one he was rather proud of, was to lie in a wrestler's bridge on the stage with an anvil balanced on his chest, while his partner used a sledgehammer to break a rock placed on top of the anvil. The new act, calling itself the Great Romanos, was almost immediately successful once they started looking for work.

The two of them were booked for a tour of the Pantages circuit. This was a chain of vaudeville theatres running down the Pacific coast of the USA and Canada. When McLaglen joined it, the circuit had only been in operation for four or five years, but it had a good reputation. It was definitely to be preferred to the notorious 'Death Trail', another chain of Pacific seaboard halls, or, even worse, the Shitty circuit, as the underfunded east-coast Sheedy circuit was known to artistes unfortunate enough to be booked on it.

On the Pantages circuit there were between eight and ten acts on a typical bill, including acrobats, contortionists, comics, singers, dancers and speciality performers. Admission cost ten cents. Shows seldom lasted more than an hour, and in order to make the

15

maximum amount of money the next audience was shoehorned in just as the last one departed.

The Great Romanos was a so-called dumb act, meaning that the protagonists did not speak. Usually they were in the lowly regarded first or last positions on the bill, sometimes known as 'walk-in' or 'walk-out' acts, as spectators either arrived or departed during their performances. These spots notoriously went to the strongman and alley-oop, or acrobatic, artistes. They performed in front of the curtains while the scenery was set for the more expensive 'flash acts' involving a large number of performers. Bottom-of-the-bill acts like McLaglen's were lucky to earn twenty dollars a week and to work for thirty weeks in the year.

At least the bishop's son got to see more of North America as he moved round the country with the act. By now he was beginning to supplement his income by boxing in properly organised professional tournaments, usually picking up bouts in towns along the route of the circuit, or during weeks when he had no theatrical bookings. For a time he settled in Milwaukee and he is next recorded as engaging in three bouts in the Washington area during this period. He fought a no-contest bout with Phil Schlossberg, outpointed Emil Shock and knocked out Curley Carr, all of them little known. The fight manager Doc Kearns, who met McLaglen at this time, described him as 'a big-chested youngster with a booming laugh and he could fight like a tiger'.

The bout with Schlossberg, the Heavyweight Champion of the US Navy, occurred in Tacoma in 1908, where the English fighter's bad luck kicked in yet again. According to his own account, McLaglen had been holding his own up to the end of the fourth round. During the interval, however, an overexcited second, 'Longshoreman' Bill Burke, inadvertently administered the *coup de grâce* to his already exhausted fighter. Writing about the incident in the *Ring* magazine of January 1932, almost twenty-five years later, McLaglen's manager of the time, Biddy Bishop, described how McLaglen's second tried to administer water to the heavyweight: 'He raised the bottle with the same hand in which he was holding a smaller bottle of ammonia. Vic opened his mouth with the intention of taking a gulp of water,

16

and as he did so, the ammonia was spilled down his throat, and with a moan he sank to the floor, completely out.'

The referee declared the fight abandoned. The stricken McLaglen was carried back to his dressing room, where a doctor revived him. It was midnight before the heavyweight was fit enough to leave the stadium and return to his digs, where he was confined to his bed for a few days.

By 1908, he was firmly based at Tacoma in Washington and taking part in wrestling matches as well as boxing contests. Then, as now, wrestling was mostly a case of fixed, choreographed matches, and McLaglen was obviously already showing signs of latent thespian ability. On 4 November 1907, the *Tacoma Daily Ledger* reported, 'In the fiercest and at the same time very cleanest wrestling match ever seen in Tacoma, Dr B.F. Roller of Seattle last night twice pinned "Sharkey" McLaglen, the South African champion, to the mat and won the bout after a forty-two-minute struggle before an assembly of 800 appreciative lovers of sports at the Savoy Theater.'

During this part of his career, McLaglen sometimes claimed to be South African, although, having left the continent when he was a boy, there was no way in which he could have been the champion of that country. Ever the pragmatist, he was also billed as a Scottish heavyweight when fighting in cities with large Caledonian immigrant populations. He adopted the nickname of Sharkey in deference to a barrel-chested heavyweight challenger from a former era, Sailor Tom Sharkey.

Although he enjoyed fighting, the extroverted McLaglen never bothered to keep a complete record of his contests, a sign that he did not take boxing very seriously. He was a self-avowed 'pork-and-beaner', someone who often fought only for his next meal. When he could on his travels, on arrival at a new town he would challenge a local champion purely as a means of garnering publicity for his vaudeville act. This meant, of course, that he was always up against the district favourite, something that never particularly bothered him even though he was only just out of his teens: 'I always liked a mixed reception,' he claimed. 'The knowledge that some of the fans were against me always inspired me to do my best.'

The fight with Jack Johnson came out of the blue. McLaglen just happened to be available when the champion's original opponent, Denver Ed Martin, dropped out. The fact that Martin had been selected as an opponent in the first place was a sign that Johnson was not being fed with 'a live one' so early in his reign. Martin's recent record was spotty in the extreme. At one time he had been a leading heavyweight, noted for his footwork, but that had been a decade earlier.

Martin had already met Johnson twice. In 1903 in Los Angeles he had gone twenty rounds with the up-and-coming Galveston man for the so-called Coloured Heavyweight Championship, a synthetic title dreamt up by Californian sports writers. Martin had held his own with the younger man for the first ten rounds but had then been floored several times, leaving Johnson to run out an easy winner. A year later they had met again. By now Johnson had improved considerably, while Martin had deteriorated commensurately and was knocked out in the second round.

Since then, over a period of five years, Martin had almost drifted out of the game, fighting on average only once a year, with a solitary win to his name. He had been resurrected on this occasion merely to provide an easy opponent for Johnson, who had barely trained since winning the championship three months earlier, in December 1908. No reason was given for his late withdrawal from the exhibition; it was merely announced that Martin had been called away unexpectedly to Seattle.

When the black fighter pulled out of the fight, there was consternation in the Johnson camp. Every seat in the Vancouver Athletic Club had been sold and Johnson had already collected his share of the box-office receipts. They had to get someone to sit in the opposite corner. It did not matter who this was. In boxing parlance, the only stipulation was that the opponent should at least have a pulse.

It was then that Victor McLaglen appeared, swaggering, charismatic, capable of engendering his own headlines, with a few fights behind him and showing absolutely no sign of being able to bother Jack Johnson in the ring. He was made for the part and was quickly imported from his temporary home in Tacoma.

At the time, Johnson had other things on his mind. Arriving from Australia by way of Hawaii, because of his colour he had been refused admittance to half a dozen hotels in Victoria on Vancouver Island and was dossing down in a cheap lodging house on the waterfront. To make matters worse, he had decided in future to look after his own affairs and was in the messy process of dispensing with the services of his indignant manager, Sam Fitzpatrick, one of at least eight managers Johnson was to employ over the course of his career. The forthcoming fight was merely the beginning of a long process for Johnson of cashing in on his championship with a minimum of effort.

The bout was billed as a no-contest affair, which meant that McLaglen would have to knock Johnson out to win, a most unlikely eventuality. Because of this it was not billed as a world-championship defence. In fact, it was little more than a glorified exhibition match, designed to show Johnson off to the Canadian audience.

This meant nothing to the British heavyweight. Later in life, when he was a more-than-capable character actor in Hollywood, McLaglen was known for never turning down any role offered to him, no matter how unsuitable, as long as the money was right. Whatever his private reservations might have been about entering the ring with the most deadly heavyweight of the age, McLaglen jumped at the offer.

He was well aware that he had little or no chance against the champion, but not only would the money offered be useful, McLaglen knew that the fame that would follow would carry over into his show-business career. From now on, no matter what the result, he would always be known as the first man to fight Johnson after the latter became champion, an item which soon found its way into his billing matter for the halls. And anyway, there was always the chance, no matter how faint, that he might just manage to connect on Johnson with one lucky sucker punch.

Such was Johnson's fame, even this early in his career as a title-holder, that the fight was a sell-out. McLaglen recorded later that engrossed spectators were practically hanging from the rafters.

It mattered little that local newspapers were contemptuously dismissing the challenger as an unknown.

The evening's entertainment began with Johnson, resplendent in white tie and tails, being introduced to the enthusiastic audience from the ring. He made a short speech, complimenting the citizens of Vancouver for being fair-minded and good sports. He paid a tribute to Canadian former champion Tommy Burns as 'that great, game little fellow'. Johnson concluded his peroration by announcing that he was ready and waiting to meet ex-champion James J. Jeffries at any time, adding, 'No matter where or when I fight I will be trying, and if I am beaten it will be by a better man.'

Johnson then left to change into his fighting gear, while McLaglen entered the ring to wait for him. Nervous as he was at the time, years later McLaglen was able to describe vividly the preamble to the fight. Upon the champion's return, he recalled, Johnson was wearing bright blue trunks and received a warm welcome from the spectators. The champion's weight was announced as 15st 1lb, while McLaglen was almost a stone lighter at 14st 2lb.

The fight itself was to prove an anti-climax. Johnson felled McLaglen with almost the first punch he threw. The two men broke from an early clinch and Johnson shot a hard straight left to his opponent's body. Entering into the spirit of the event McLaglen had been smiling at the time, but the grin turned to a grimace of agony. The Englishman backed away slowly, then his legs buckled, he sank to his knees and his body doubled up, his forehead resting on the canvas. When he staggered to his feet at the count of nine, all the fight had already been knocked out of him.

The next day, Vancouver's *Daily Post* reported contemptuously the white heavyweight's reaction: 'For the rest of the bout he was looking for a soft spot to fall. As McLaglan [*sic*] had no business in the ring in the first place, not having the speed to cope with the shifty black, he made but a sorry showing thereafter.'

Onlookers were struck by Johnson's sheer strength in throwing around the burly McLaglen at will, and commented on the fact that the champion did not move his feet much, being content to occupy the centre of the ring and force McLaglen to circle warily around him. The champion impressed with his ability to tie up his opponent in a clinch, using only one hand, while walloping McLaglen with his free fist. Above all, Johnson's hand speed was marvelled at; when he delivered combinations of punches the effect was little more than a blur.

Satisfied that he had little to beat, Johnson toyed lazily with his big opponent throughout the rest of the bout and resorted to his custom of talking idly to ringsiders as he held off the sweating, swinging Englishman. The champion did not sit down between rounds and was heard idly discussing the latest fashions in male costume jewellery with an acquaintance seated close to the ring.

For his part, once the initial effects of Johnson's body punch had worn off, McLaglen did his best to land a haymaker, gaining slightly in confidence as the bout went on. 'I tried my best to rattle him in the last two rounds,' he wrote later in his autobiography, 'conscious of the immortality that would be mine were I lucky enough to slip him a sleeper.' Better men than McLaglen had tried unsuccessfully to do that and would continue to do so for the remainder of the champion's reign. Magnanimously, Johnson allowed McLaglen to last the six-round distance, and the official verdict was that of a no-decision.

After the exhibition, some forty representatives of the black community in Vancouver gave a dinner in Johnson's honour at the Bismarck Café in the city. Several white members of the Vancouver Athletic Club were also present. In a short, dignified speech Jack Johnson commented that he was glad to see members of both races sitting in amity at the long table. He repeated his intention to fight any challengers. 'Be my next opponent yellow, grizzly, gray or black,' he announced, 'I will fight him with the same courage and determination that I have shown in the past.'

The next afternoon, the world champion was seen off at the railway station by a large crowd of all colours. Johnson took the Canadian Pacific Railroad as far as Moose Jaw and caught a connection to Chicago, where he was to make his home for a few years.

The Vancouver fight made so little impression on the champion that, like the *Daily Post* reporter, he could not even spell McLaglen's name correctly and had forgotten that there had been no referee's decision when, years later, he mentioned the episode in his autobiography.

'Between stage appearances I had some minor ring affairs,' he wrote dismissively. 'One of these was with Victor MacLaghlen [*sic*] in Vancouver, 10 March 1909, which I won in six rounds.'

Victor McLaglen continued to box. After the Johnson bout he returned to the Pantages circuit with the Great Romanos, this time with his brother Arthur as his partner, performing in *tableaux vivants* clad in white body stockings and duplicating well-known Greek statues. When stage work dried up they would take work with circuses between engagements. McLaglen was never a top-of-the-bill act, but his unexpected six rounds with Jack Johnson had given him, as he had anticipated, a certain amount of fame in the sticks.

He was never shy of cashing in on the attendant publicity, giving interviews to local newspapers all along the Pantages route, not unexpectedly allowing himself the best of it for the press stories. What had in reality been an extremely one-sided exhibition bout was transmogrified for the public into a thrilling close encounter, with McLaglen, in his version, taking the champion to the wire.

His favourite publicity-seeking ploy for the act was to turn up at a gymnasium in whichever city he was appearing in that week, and noisily challenge the best-known local heavyweight to a bout. The fact that it would be almost impossible to arrange and stage such a contest in the seven days that he was in the vicinity was not lost on the strong man, but he usually managed to have a few journalists waiting in the gymnasium to take down the affronted reaction of the local hopeful.

In Springfield, Missouri, in 1911 it all went horribly wrong. The local fistic hero was a heavyweight called Joe Cox. In the hope of getting the customary headlines McLaglen swaggered along to the town gymnasium, accompanied by a coterie of reporters, and noisily challenged Cox.

Unfortunately for the Englishman, a wily local promoter called Billy McCarney had joined in the managerial scramble to find a White Hope. He had a secret prospect hidden away and was planning to match his hopeful with Cox in the near future. His heavyweight's name was Jess Willard, known as the Pottawatomie Giant, a man of 6ft 5in in height and weighing 18 stone. Willard was slow and clumsy and at this stage almost completely untutored in the fistic arts. However, he was terribly strong and the possessor of a hard and extremely long left jab. He had won a few contests, but so far he had been kept under wraps and the ingenuous McLaglen had not heard of him.

Knowing of McLaglen's inglorious fighting record, McCarney proposed, tongue-in-cheek, that McLaglen first fight a few rounds in the gym with Willard. If he acquitted himself well, promised the promoter, he would consider matching the Englishman against Joe Cox in a public contest.

It was not what McLaglen had been expecting, but he agreed to come back later and face Willard. As soon as the Englishman had left, McCarney spread the word that his giant was about to be let loose on a mug, albeit one who had fought the world champion only a couple of years earlier. When McLaglen returned, he found to his amazement that the gymnasium was packed to capacity. McCarney had charged fifty cents a head for eager locals to witness the slaughter. When he saw Willard for the first time, McLaglen must have wondered if he had been taken for a sucker. Willard, a former cowboy, had to duck his head to get through the door, and the breadth of his shoulders seemed to blot out the sunlight streaming in through the window.

Nevertheless, the bishop's son did his best. He bundled in gamely to Willard, only to discover that there seemed no way past the big man's telescopic left jab. When Willard finally unloaded a couple of devastating rights in the fourth round, McLaglen realised how badly he had been had. He quit on the spot and reeled bloodily away from the gymnasium, to the jeers of the spectators.

It was not quite the end of Victor McLaglen's boxing career. Over the next few years, whenever he was out of work, he would summon up his resolve and grimly return to the ring.

To his credit, one of McLaglen's victories was over a very useful second-rank heavyweight called Dan 'Porky' Flynn. During the course of a long career Flynn fought a number of the top White Hopes, including Carl Morris, Gunboat Smith, Boer Rodel and Battling Levinsky. He knocked out Rodel and went the distance with the others, so this victory by McLaglen was easily the Englishman's outstanding ring achievement.

In 1912, to Victor's great chagrin, another of the bishop's siblings tried to get in on the act. This was the 6ft-8in-tall Leopold McLaglen, a drifter like his brothers, but more of a chancer than the others. He turned up in Milwaukee, falsely claiming to be the heavyweight ju-jitsu champion of the world. Down on his luck, a condition not unfamiliar to the McLaglens, Leopold tried to drum up interest in his unsuccessful stage act by challenging any boxer or wrestler in the USA to meet him in the ring. In the meantime he was forced to earn a crust by working as a cinema doorman.

None of this would have bothered Victor in the slightest had it not been for the fact that in his advertising material Leopold was appropriating the forenames of his two better-known fighting brothers, calling himself Victor Fred McLaglen, and claiming to have been the member of the family who had gone six rounds with Jack Johnson. To make matters worse, Leopold's challenge was taken up by a very experienced heavyweight called Fireman Jim Flynn, who thrashed the inept Leopold McLaglen in a couple of rounds.

Victor was shocked by his brother's chicanery and the brazen manner in which Leopold had attempted to steal his thunder. Without mentioning his treacherous brother by name, he fired off an indignant letter to the *Milwaukee Free Press*, which was printed on 10 March.

Plaza Theater, San Antonio, Texas, 6 March 1912:
Sporting Editor, Free Press.

To my surprise today I take up a paper and in the sporting column I note that they are advertising a fighter in Milwaukee who is taking the name of Vic McLaghlen [*sic*] and claims to be the first man to have fought Jack Johnson after he won the championship from Tommy Burns.

Now I wish to say that this man is an imposter and that he is taking my name and that I was the party that fought Johnson in Vancouver, 10 March, 1909. I am now in vaudeville, playing the interstate circuit.

The idea is this: I get the credit of taking that awful licking from Flynn, when I am hundreds of miles from Milwaukee. You might recollect I played the Crystal Theater in your town last summer under the name of Romano, doing a statue act and showing the various punches of famous fighters. You would do the public and myself a lot of good if you expose this imposter.

Victor M'Laghlen (of Romano Brothers)

By now Victor was 26 and tiring of fighting. Counting his early Army days, he had been in the ring, on and off, for ten years and had got nowhere. His fighting pretensions were even being ridiculed in the press. Even his former home-town newspaper, the *Milwaukee Free Press*, took a sideswipe at him in its edition of 23 February 1913 while ostensibly denigrating another fighter: 'New York newspapers are acclaiming Greek Knockout Brown of Chicago as a coming world's middleweight champion. That's not surprising. They fell for Vic McLaughlin [*sic*] as a prospective white hope.'

The theatrical bookings were beginning to dry up as well. McLaglen and brother Arthur had had enough. 'We got tired of that,' he explained simply, 'so we shipped for Hawaii. From there we went to the Fiji islands, Tahiti and Australia.'

Attempts to dive for pearls in the South Sea Islands failed, so they moved on to Australia. Arthur McLaglen had been there before. In 1910, he had fought three two-round exhibition contests with former world heavyweight champion Bob Fitzsimmons. However, as soon as they landed they heard of a gold strike in the interior. Ignoring his unpleasant prospecting experiences in Canada, McLaglen promptly joined in the gold rush with his brother.

Still their luck did not turn. On one occasion they almost died of thirst and starvation. They next set sail for South Africa. By this time McLaglen was practically down and out. He and Arthur had made no money in Australia. They reached South Africa only to hear that war had broken out in Europe. The news did not displease the McLaglens. Neither of them was averse to fighting, and at least military life offered the prospect of regular meals and adventure. 'We left immediately for London to enlist and glad to get the chance,' Victor McLaglen said.

News of the war had brought home all the McLaglen brothers old enough to fight: Victor, Lewis, Leopold, Clifford, Arthur and Fred. They arrived, broke but optimistic, from such remote places as China, Canada and South Africa. They were all a little weary and shop-soiled.

Leopold, red-bearded, broad-shouldered and a towering 6ft 7in tall, had been appearing at the Cape Town music halls, still spuriously claiming to be the world's heavyweight ju-jitsu champion. He usually included a demonstration of hypnotism in his act. One night in Cape Town, when a member of the audience mutinously refused to fall under his influence, the exasperated Leopold had punched the man in the face. The assaulted South African had promptly fought back, driving the gigantic performer from the stage and causing his subsequent performances to be cancelled.

Fred had been fighting in the USA without a great deal of success. By the time he reached England again, Fred had opposed and been knocked out by such white heavyweight prospects as Dan Dailey, Al Reich, Carl Morris and Gunboat Smith. Doc Kearns had seen Fred fight during this period and had described him succinctly as a one-punch fighter: 'One punch on the whiskers and he folded.'

His great moment had come in 1912, when the *Milwaukee Free Press* of 9 December had written, 'Fred McKay, the Winnipeg giant, came a little closer into the limelight as a prominent white hope last night by knocking out Bill Tate at the Queensboro A.C.' Unfortunately, only two years later, after a run of defeats on McKay's part, on 27 October the same newspaper noted, 'Fred Mackay [*sic*] of Canada, who has been one of the noted divers in the boxing game, has quit the sport and is going into the saloon business in Canada.'

To make matters worse, Fred had to put up with a considerable amount of ribbing when he met up with Victor in London. In one of his final bouts in the USA, in January 1914, Fred had been knocked out in two rounds by Porky Flynn, one of Victor's occasional victims.

Fred's story had an unhappy ending. All six brothers enlisted, achieving some newspaper publicity as 'the Fighting Macs', and went off to fight. Five of them returned in 1918, but Fred was killed while serving in East Africa.

Victor McLaglen was commissioned and spent a few months as a recruiting officer in London, addressing huge audiences in Trafalgar Square. In 1915 he managed to squeeze in one more bout, defeating Dan McGoldrick on a technical knockout in five rounds. His military career after this is obscure. There are no traces of him in the military archives of the Cheshire and Middlesex regiments, or the Irish Fusiliers, three of the units in which he claimed to have served.

In interviews McLaglen also told reporters that he had been posted to the Middle East where he saw action against the Turks at Sind, Judalia and Sheikh Saad, and that he had been promoted to captain for bravery. Again there are no official records of his having been present at such engagements.

He does resurface briefly. At the end of the war, by virtue of his impressive size, battered face and fighting background, he was appointed Assistant Provost Marshal of Baghdad, responsible for the discipline of both the troops stationed in the town and the Arabs who lived there. The job was no sinecure. He was involved in a number of brawls, trying to separate fighting soldiers and Arabs, and claimed to have been stabbed twice and to have survived an attempt to kill him with poisoned dates.

In 1919 he was out of the Army, unemployed again, penniless and by this time married. He was also 32 years old, past it for most heavyweights, especially less able ones who had taken as many ring beatings as he had. Nevertheless, as he had done so many times before, McLaglen made one last effort to restore his fortunes by entering the ring.

He was matched with the up-and-coming Frank Goddard, a future British heavyweight champion, although his title tenure of only three weeks would set a British record for brevity. Goddard's other claim to fame was that he had been banned from one training camp because his language was too bad for the other boxers, and from another for throwing a plum pudding at a portrait of Queen Victoria hanging on the wall.

The former White Hope was billed as Captain Victor McLaglen, and much was made in the publicity build-up of his bout with Jack Johnson ten years before. McLaglen was no match for his younger opponent, who as a former humble trooper must have relished the prospect of hitting an officer with impunity, and he was knocked out in three rounds. It was one of his last fights.

It was during this period that McLaglen's fiery father, the Bishop of Claremont, caused a public stir. On 14 November 1919, the 68-year-old prelate offered to fight five rounds with anyone of his own age in aid of a fund for disabled troops. The Associated Press report went on: 'The bishop's offer was prompted apparently by his indignation at something the newspaper printed concerning his son. "Why", he asks, "is it astonishing that a man who chooses to fight in the ring for money should be the son of a bishop, or a man of considerable educational attainments? Neither is there anything contrary to Christianity in boxing. This is solely the nonsense of clergy who have forgotten that they are men, living in a world of men and not of Victorian old ladies."' Nobody responded to the Bishop's challenge.

Victor McLaglen made another appearance on the British boxing scene in 1919. Booming, larger than life and full of blarney, he turned up at a Plymouth boxing hall. Full of wild stories about his recent service in the Middle East and insisting on being addressed by his rank of captain, the heavyweight had embarked on yet another temporary career, that of boxing manager.

His protégé was a 15-year-old Arab boy, Hussein Ibn Abbass. McLaglen claimed that he had discovered the youth abandoned by his tribe in the desert and that he had taken him in as his batman and servant. He had given the youth boxing lessons, he asserted, and was now launching him on a fighting career which was sure to lead to a championship.

Hussein Ibn Abbass caused quite a stir in Plymouth by entering the ring in a turban and the flowing robes of an Arab. Unfortunately, he was knocked out in the eleventh round by Seaman George Harris and was seldom heard of in the boxing ring again. He also caused something of a stir at the local Royal Hotel that night by breaking a curfew imposed upon him by McLaglen, shinning down a drainpipe and running off to sample the nightlife of the city. Years later, McLaglen took Hussein Ibn Abbass to Hollywood with him, always referring to the youth as his adopted son.

3

THE PHILADELPHIA IRISHMAN AND
TWO WARM BODIES

Almost as soon as he had won the title, Johnson had signed up for a lucrative thirty-week stage tour. A month after his clash with Victor McLaglen in March 1909, he had already embarked on his stage appearances at the Gayety Theatre in Brooklyn, appearing between burlesque acts. His billing read:

> *During the Action of the Burlesque*
> *Jack Johnson*
> *The undisputed Champion of the World will appear in an Exhibition*
> *of Bag Punching, General training for the Prize Ring,*
> *and in a Three-Round Exhibition of Boxing in conjunction*
> *with his sparring partner, Kid Cutler.*

The trouble with Johnson was that his private life often seemed to be lived in public. He was dogged by reporters. Every unwise move or thoughtless remark was sure to be reflected in the headlines the following day. His first wife, who was black, had left him long since because of his infidelities. A long-term black girlfriend, Clara Kerr, ran away with Johnson's best friend. They took with them everything of Johnson's that had not been nailed down. A white, New York Irish consort, Hattie McClay, who had been with him at Rushcutters Bay, was fast becoming an alcoholic, causing even the pragmatic champion considerable embarrassment. Amid general horror and much sanctimonious hand-wringing from onlookers, he took up with other white women. One of these was Belle Schreiber, a 23-year-old white Milwaukee prostitute, a fact brought up eagerly in court when he was later arrested. He met

31

another white woman, Etta Duryea, who left her husband to live with the fighter.

He also bought his mother a fine house in Chicago and started to indulge his passion for fast and expensive motor cars. He dressed expensively and carried a gold-topped cane. A proud and defiant man, Johnson refused to conform to the white public's picture of the self-effacing manner in which a black man should conduct himself.

His attitude during the ring exhibitions he was fighting in this period also infuriated many white spectators, especially his habit of condescending to his opponents and talking back to ringsiders. Nevertheless, his physique and boxing ability were generally admired. The *New York Times* of 26 December 1908 said, 'Not since the days of James J. Corbett has the prize ring seen so perfect a looking boxer as Johnson. Long and lithe and graceful, he is as true as an arrow in placing his blows.'

Older fight followers were reminded of a former heavyweight champion, the rambunctious John L. Sullivan, who had been a considerably riotous liver and womaniser. But John L. had been white and his activities had been regarded with a tolerant eye. Jack Johnson was black and showing every sign of not knowing his place. It was a hard concept for the public to deal with. Other leading black heavyweight fighters of the time, like Sam Langford, Joe Jeanette and Sam McVey, were generally considered 'good niggers', humble in public and content to batter one another half to death for minuscule purses, leaving white fighters unscathed to be brought along gently by their managers. Johnson wanted to be treated as an equal.

Equality cost, and Johnson soon found himself in need of fresh fights to fund his lifestyle. By now the White Hope campaign was just getting under way, and there were big bucks to be made by entering the ring with some of the first batch. The champion knew that none of them stood any chance against him. He celebrated the fact by buying a new fast car – a 690 Thompson Flyer which he crashed at least once – and spent much time at the racetracks and in saloons and brothels. Even as a wealthy champion, however, it was later reported in one of Johnson's court cases that because of the colour of his skin the heavyweight was still denied admittance to the Everleigh Club, a luxurious house of ill repute.

Later, when he was on trial on a trumped-up charge of transporting a prostitute across state lines, witnesses gave detailed descriptions of the black champion's efforts to gatecrash the high-class brothel. The club was run by two sisters, Minna and Ada Everleigh, who had invested $35,000, inherited from their father, in a fifty-room mansion, which they transformed into a house of pleasure furnished with impeccable taste. The sisters served cordon bleu meals at fifty dollars a head, while the services of the decorous, well-mannered girls started at fifty dollars.

The Everleigh Club survived for eleven years, mainly because the sisters paid protection money to two corrupt Chicago politicians, 'Bathhouse' John Coughlin and 'Hinky Dink' Mike Kenna. So powerful were these ward leaders that not even Jack Johnson could break the club's colour bar, and he was forced to retreat from the door. Johnson did, however, score one minor victory over the club. He managed to entice away Belle Schreiber, one of the working girls there, and make her his mistress. He was aided in this endeavour by his then manager, George Little, a white saloon keeper and failed politician. The champion also appointed another white hanger-on, Sig Hart, to assist Little.

Of course, it had never been easy to be a black professional athlete in the USA. In 1885, one of the first professional black baseball teams had been forced to call itself the Cuban Giants in order to be able to play in towns where black participants would not be welcome. It was just about all right to be an exotic Cuban at a time when black athletes could not find work. Many attempts were made to form black baseball leagues between 1887 and 1919. Almost all of them failed.

This is the climate in which Johnson had to live, and, because he refused to conform to the image of a 'good nigger', the demand for a white heavyweight to beat him intensified once he had humiliated Victor McLaglen in his first bout as champion. In 1909, the young hopefuls were still being extracted by managers from factories and farms, the Army and the Navy and anywhere else offering the prospect of a 6ft, 14½-stone, preferably naive prospect willing to be tutored in the fistic arts and not too clever at reckoning his share of the purse money. So at first, his challenges were mostly established white fighters.

This was true of the second of Johnson's opponents, a real glutton for punishment who helped promote the fight himself. His real name was Joseph Francis Aloysius O'Hagen, but he fought for seventeen years and through 181 bouts as Philadelphia Jack O'Brien. Unlike Victor McLaglen, who had been little more than an enthusiastic novice, Johnson's second adversary was a professional to his fingertips. In 1901 he had visited Great Britain, where he won eighteen fights in a year, hardly breaking into a sweat. During this tour he was rather taken with being introduced by one English master of ceremonies as 'Philadelphia' Jack O'Brien, and he retained that nomenclature for the rest of his career. He was a resourceful, streetwise character and a skilled boxer, with a good left jab and a florid turn of phrase, both of which made him popular with reporters. Once, when asked what he thought of the great and much-avoided black fighter Sam Langford, O'Brien replied seriously, 'When he appeared on the scene of combat you knew you were cooked.'

In 1906, O'Brien became one of the few professional boxers to appear in newspapers other than on the sports or crime pages. He achieved a brief notoriety on a stopover in New York City when, because of his avocation, he was refused admission to a succession of good hotels. With his huge shoulders and a nose spread magnificently over his face it would have been difficult to mistake O'Brien for a librarian, and boxers were *personae non gratae* in respectable company. The *New York American* commented drily on the matter in an editorial, which with some hyperbole referred to the champion as 'the most eminent professor of the squared circle in the United States', and went on to sneer, 'yet when, with his valet and business manager and the rest of the staff necessary to the comfort and dignity of a champion heavyweight, he drove from hotel to hotel on Fifth Avenue, he was politely, but firmly, asked to seek some other spot, or, in the language of his associates in his own profession, "to skidoo"'.

By the time Johnson won the heavyweight title, O'Brien's career was coming to an end. He had plenty to look back on. He had won the world light-heavyweight title by knocking out Bob Fitzsimmons. The title fight had been in the nature of a grudge match, as in an earlier no-decision bout, Fitzsimmons was convinced, only the intervention of the police had saved his opponent from a knockout. 'I had it on him when I boxed him in Philadelphia until he yelped for help from the police and the bluecoats came to his assistance,' claimed the Cornish fighter sourly.

O'Brien paid little attention to his light-heavyweight title, preferring to look for good-money bouts among the big fighters. He had even fought twice for the heavyweight championship, in Los Angeles in 1906 and 1907, drawing with and then losing to Tommy Burns, a heavyweight as diminutive, shrewd and cunning as the experienced O'Brien himself.

Those bouts with Burns displayed O'Brien's sense of realism in spades. The first fight, refereed by retired champion James J. Jeffries, started with mutual tantrums when O'Brien objected to a curious trusslike belt being worn by Burns to protect, he claimed, an old injury. O'Brien objected hotly, declaring that the belt was just another example of Burns's gamesmanship and was an added source of protection for the champion. The challenger then tried to tear the belt from Burns's waist. In turn Burns tried to hoist down O'Brien's shorts. The dignified James J. Jeffries, who had been looking on in amazement, stepped forward and ordered Burns back to his dressing room to get rid of the support.

The actual fight was an anticlimax. It ended in a tame and apparently overrehearsed draw. The next day, a sheepish Jeffries, fed up with the whole tawdry affair, disclosed that he had been approached beforehand by both contestants to announce the verdict of a draw if the action had seemed at all close. Later, O'Brien, who had a tendency for garrulity, admitted, 'The promoter, (Bill) McCarey, had figured it out that, if we fought a spirited draw, he could bill the return match during fiesta week and make a small fortune by charging top prices.' To call the ensuing bout spirited would be an exaggeration, but the controversy gave the encounter far more publicity than the lack of action in the ring had merited. A return match was set up for six months later.

The second fight caused a sensation before it had even started. Burns walked to the centre of the ring and shouted self-righteously to the crowd, 'Gentlemen, I declare that all bets that have been made up to now are off! I agreed to lose to O'Brien but now we are both in the ring I want to tell you that I am here to win!'

There was such a sensation that when the startled O'Brien tried to speak he was howled down. The fight went the full twenty rounds' distance and was not much better than their first arid encounter had been. The reporter for the *Milwaukee Free Press* covering the fight wrote: 'The affair grew monotonous. It was either a clinch with Burns . . . or else O'Brien circled the ring with Burns standing in the center looking at him and the crowd hooting. In the last round Burns stood quite still several times and begged O'Brien to come and fight him.' Burns emerged a clear winner to retain his title. No weights were announced before the bout, but it was believed that both men scaled below the 12½ stone light-heavyweight limit. This meant that technically the Canadian was now also the world champion at the class immediately below heavyweight, but he never bothered to claim the championship.

Afterwards, an embittered O'Brien put his side of the sordid story to anyone who could be bothered to listen to him. Apparently he had run into Burns in a cigar store soon after their first bout. According to the challenger, Burns had tried to persuade him to take a dive in the eleventh round of their next bout. Virtuously, O'Brien had refused the offer. Ever adaptable, Burns had then offered to lie down himself if he was paid enough.

The second offer was of much more significance, as O'Brien pointed out self-righteously. 'This interested me, purely from a business point of view, of course. I could see that there was plenty to be made as heavyweight champion, so I agreed to pay Burns $3,500 to lose. He agreed, knowing that I would ease up in training.' O'Brien paused, almost at a loss for words at the enormity of

Burns's chicanery. 'He then ratted when we got into the ring,' he concluded, obviously shocked by the extent to which depravity could exist in the human soul.

However, approaching the Johnson bout, O'Brien had reason to believe that he was on a lucky streak. In New York in March 1909, as a warm-up for his bout with Johnson, O'Brien went in with the fearsome Stanley Ketchel, one of the greatest middleweights of all time, in what was billed as a ten-round, no-decision contest, in which a contestant could only lose if he were knocked out. For nine rounds of their contest O'Brien jabbed Ketchel silly. Then, towards the end of the final round, the swinging Ketchel finally caught up with his tormentor. Describing the sensation after he had been struck, O'Brien said: 'It just seemed as if all the lights went out.' As he fell, his head struck the edge of the resin box, which his second, Kid McCoy, had inadvertently left in the ring. 'It did not help my condition any,' said O'Brien with atypical understatement.

However, as the referee's count reached eight, with O'Brien draped helplessly over the ropes like a heap of washing tossed over a line, the bell went to end the bout. Most reporters present agreed that O'Brien had done enough in the early rounds to get their unofficial decisions, and Ketchel was left ruing the fact that he had not caught up with his elusive opponent two or three seconds earlier.

On the other hand, O'Brien, now approaching the veteran stage, decided that he was on a roll. To many, after fourteen years in the ring, he might have appeared a 'shot' fighter, but he still had enough of a reputation to draw in the crowds, given the right opponent. He was also extremely short of money. The only way for a big man to earn a decent purse in 1909 was to go in with Jack Johnson.

O'Brien decided to ignore the disparity in size and give it a go. 'Following the Ketchel bout, I returned to Philadelphia, where I did a little promoting, bringing heavyweight champion Jack Johnson in for a six-rounder,' he said.

It was not quite as simple as O'Brien made it sound. Johnson had no objection to going in with a much lighter man and one who notoriously had no great punch, and the fact that at 30, and after many hard fights, his prospective opponent was coming to the end of his career did no harm either. Even so, the champion was aware of his bargaining power. He knew that he had the whip hand in any project concerning his title.

First he insisted on the bout being a no-decision contest, knowing that even at his best O'Brien would never have had a chance of knocking him out. Then Johnson demanded a guarantee of $5,000, an exorbitant sum for six three-minute rounds with no likelihood of the title changing hands. O'Brien bit the bullet and agreed. At this point Johnson really started to turn the screw. Knowing that O'Brien had gone on record as disliking blacks in general and the champion in particular, he insisted on O'Brien making the long journey to a sleazy saloon in the black district of Pittsburgh to sign the contracts. O'Brien swallowed his pride, submitted to being patronised by the champion, and dourly made the two-way trip.

The challenger then went into training for the bout; supremely confident, Johnson did not put himself out to the same extent.

O'Brien was aided in his preparation by one of Philadelphia's more eccentric sporting patrons. Anthony Joseph Drexel Biddle was a banking millionaire who loved boxing and boxers. He was noted for causing chaos among those members of the noble art who were foolish enough to let him near them. 'He was in Jack O'Brien's corner with me once,' reminisced manager Billy McCarney wonderingly. 'He kept getting his foot stuck in the water bucket.'

Biddle was a throwback, in boxing terms, to the eccentric, not to say mad, aristocratic patrons of the old prize-ring, and Philadelphia Jack O'Brien was his White Hope. For his part, the fighter, who mistrusted managers, was perfectly content to let the influential and well-connected millionaire have some limited input into his career, as long as it cost him nothing. O'Brien even went along with his backer's church movement, Athletic Christianity, and suffered himself to be taken along to children's Sunday School meetings and displayed as an example of one of Biddle's holy warriors.

There were other boxers in the millionaire's extended family. It was his custom to invite local and visiting pugilists for a meal at his mansion and, once they had arrived, force them to spar several rounds with him in a specially constructed ring. Most of his guests went through the motions philosophically, but one White Hope, the towering Al Kaufmann, failed to catch the spirit of the affair. By accident or design he hit the useless Biddle with a substantial punch, putting the other man out of action for the rest of the day and forcing the cancellation of the proposed meal.

No one disputed the banker's dedication to boxing. On one occasion Biddle had persuaded former world heavyweight champion Bob Fitzsimmons to spar with his 10-year-old son. Fitzsimmons mistimed a jab and knocked the boy out. Anthony Joseph Drexel Biddle Junior recovered consciousness in time to hear his father, in all seriousness, congratulating Fitzsimmons on the efficacy of the blow.

As he did with everything, Biddle put his whole heart into O'Brien's preparation. He even fought a public four-round exhibition with his protégé to display his commitment. This gave the millionaire an idea. He suggested that next he should spar with the champion in order to see how fit Jack Johnson was. Jack O'Brien agreed to the proposal with alacrity. It was not disclosed whether he thought the plan a good one, or whether he just relished the thought of getting rid of his hearty patron for a few days.

In any event, Biddle turned up at the gymnasium in Merchantville, New Jersey where Johnson was going through the motions of training, and offered to be the champion's sparring partner. His pride suffered a blow when he was told that the champion was out driving with his wife. Biddle was forced to await Johnson's return sitting on a bench with other would-be sparring partners. In a confused attempt to conceal his identity the banker introduced himself as Tom O'Biddle, an Irish heavyweight. Johnson, who was not deceived, could hardly believe his ears, but there were newspapermen present among the usual hangers-on, so he shrugged his reluctant agreement, thinking that he was in the presence of yet another white basket case.

His view was reinforced when, at the first bell, Biddle uttered an ear-splitting yell and rushed at his opponent as if leading a bayonet charge. Lazily, the champion held him off at the end of a long, extended left hand, saying soothingly, according to some ringsiders, 'Hey, Colonel boy! What's your point? Don't go getting yourself all stirred up.' As Biddle's daughter Cordelia later wrote resignedly in her memoirs, *My Philadelphia Father*, her father was always stirred up. The millionaire banker was not accustomed to being spoken to in this manner, and anyway his dander was up. He threw a mighty right swing, catching Johnson on the ear and upsetting the champion considerably. Johnson aroused himself from his lethargy sufficiently to charge back at Biddle, unleashing a volley of punches. Prudently, the Philadelphian covered up in a corner for the remainder of the round. By the time the bell sounded Johnson had recovered his self-possession sufficiently to let Biddle live, and leave the ring in one piece.

The affair made the national headlines, with one newspaper commenting disapprovingly that the least Johnson could have done for the prestige of the Marine Corps was to allow Biddle, a reserve officer in the corps, to have floored him. The matter was taken as just another display of the champion's ostentatious lack of respect.

It was never recorded what advice his backer gave O'Brien about Johnson's condition when he returned to Philadelphia, but on the night of the fight newspapers commented adversely on the spare tyre that the champion was carrying about his midriff. The hall was packed, enabling O'Brien to comment approvingly, 'A full house turned out and I cleared over nine thousand dollars for my end.'

It was the end of the good news for the challenger. He was much lighter than Johnson and had never been much of a puncher even at his best. O'Brien boxed cautiously while Johnson was content to pad about the ring, exchanging badinage with ringsiders and occasionally cuffing his opponent about the head. Afterwards, as would be expected, there was some discrepancy among the contestants as to the route the bout had followed. Johnson's version took the form of a laconic, 'the result of the fight, although no decision was given, clearly showed that O'Brien would have to be eliminated as a contender.' O'Brien's summary was a more hopeful, 'I spotted Johnson forty pounds and had no trouble outpointing him.' The consensus among spectators and newspaper reporters alike was that, had there been a decision announced, Johnson would have won it out of sight, a view summarised by a Philadelphia newspaper, which reported, 'O'Brien got some very hard bumps and was pretty badly hurt at times, and there is no doubt that the Negro had the better of the contest.' In the record books the May 1909 bout is delineated as a six-round, no-decision contest.

It was almost the end of the road for Philadelphia Jack O'Brien, but he had one more good pay-day ahead of him. It lay in a return match with Stanley Ketchel, who was also being groomed for a title shot with Johnson. If Ketchel could defeat O'Brien decisively, it would strengthen his chances of a match with the heavyweight champion by the end of the year.

For his part, O'Brien was still trying to convince himself that he had done well enough against Jack Johnson to continue fighting at the top level. To make matters even better, A.J.D. Biddle seemed to have lost interest in him for the time being. 'Satisfied I had found myself, and was right again, doing my own managerial work, I signed for a return go with Ketchel,' O'Brien said, revelling in his independence, free from the interference of millionaire bankers.

The return bout took place in Philadelphia in June of the same year. O'Brien was guaranteed $5,000 as his share of the purse. The fight was a sell-out, thousands arriving to see if Ketchel could catch up with his opponent this time. 'I wore Irish green tights with a red, white and blue belt,' said O'Brien, describing the entrance of the gladiators. 'Ketchel wore flaming red tights and a smirk.'

It was all over in three rounds. Ketchel gave O'Brien a beating from the first bell. As O'Brien later admitted, when the referee, Jack McGuigan, stopped the fight, 'I had taken the same type of trimming from Ketchel that I handed out when I knocked out Bob Fitzsimmons four years previously to win a title.' He added to his friend Harry Pegg, 'Just remember, kid, pugilistic flowers bloom and they fade – that's life!'

Over the next four years O'Brien fought only eight more times, taking part in seven no-decision contests and being knocked out in five rounds by Sam Langford. Philadelphia Jack also became a great favourite among boxing writers looking for colour pieces. One of them, the great A.J. Liebling, once asked O'Brien what he really thought of Ketchel. It was the old fighter's considered opinion that his erstwhile opponent had been nothing but 'a bum distinguished only by the tumultuous but ill-directed ferocity of his assault'.

Anthony J. Drexel Biddle made only one more attempt to contact the old light heavyweight. He threw a large society dinner for his friends, and invited a number of old retired fighters to the event. It was the banker's intention to get the boxers to recapitulate some of their great bouts for the entertainment of his society friends. O'Brien was asked to spar with the formidable Joe Choynski, whom he had outpointed many years before, in 1902. Both fighters rebelled at being asked to provide a free Roman holiday for the assembled guests. They put up a display of such deliberate ineptitude that Biddle brought their reluctant bout to a halt and instead fought a much more spirited contest with his long-suffering son, Anthony Junior.

With O'Brien disposed of, Jack Johnson fought two more no-decision contests before the end of 1909. The best that could be said of his two opponents was that they were warm and upright, for most of the time anyway. In Pittsburgh, over six rounds he boxed Tony Ross, the ring name for Italian-born American Antonio Rossilano. Ross was a rugged fighter, weighing around 15 stone, but at a height of only 5ft 9in he always found difficulty getting close to taller, smarter boxers, of whom there were plenty around in the first decade of the century. Starting out in 1905, at the age of 20, by the time Ross came up against Jack Johnson he had engaged in twenty-three contests. He had won ten of them, lost six, drawn two and taken part in five no-decision bouts. The only names of any consequence on his record were former heavyweight champion Marvin Hart, who had defeated him on a foul in thirteen rounds, and Sam Langford, who had crushed him in five rounds.

However, Ross was a proud man and no quitter. A few years later, in a grudge match with Fireman Jim Flynn, Ross felt that he had been the victim of a home-town unofficial newspaper decision.

Indignantly he challenged the other man to continue their dispute with bare fists outside the arena. The equally fiery and, despite his ring name, equally Italian Flynn agreed and the two men went outside to finish off their business.

This was not the kind of background, nor was Ross the type of fighter, to give Jack Johnson sleepless nights. However, the champion was a major drawing card and 6,000 people turned up to see Johnson break Ross's nose in the first round, floor him for a long count and then toy with him contemptuously for the rest of the no-decision contest. The *Milwaukee Free Press* of 1 July 1909 remarked upon the champion's superiority throughout the bout: 'There was never a moment when the coloured man was in danger, but there were moments when he seemed a trifle surprised by the Italian's speed.'

It was Ross's brief moment of fame. He remained in boxing for another seven years, amassing a total of sixty-nine bouts and meeting at various times such White Hopes as Al Kaufmann, Frank Moran, Al Palzer, Gunboat Smith and Tom Kennedy. The day after the Kaufmann bout the *Tacoma Daily News* reported tersely, 'Jack Johnson was at ringside and laughed at the boxers.' Ross also engaged in periodic disputes with elements of the constabulary in the cities on his itinerary. In Louisville in 1912, the Italian American had to pull out of proposed contests with Al Palzer and Carl Morris because he was reported as being in hospital recovering from a clubbing administered by local police officers after the fighter had become involved in a saloon brawl.

Ross never came near a championship challenge again. Towards the end of his career he achieved a certain notoriety when, during a sparring session with the British lightweight champion Johnny Summers, the heavyweight Ross hit his sparring partner harder than Summers regarded necessary. Instantly, the 10-stone man replied with a sharp right counter, knocking the 15-stone Ross down and out.

By September 1909, Johnson had reached San Francisco, where he was matched in a ten-round no-decision contest against the local favourite, Al Kaufmann, 'the San Francisco Dutchman'. Kaufmann, who had ignored the script and knocked out boxing dilettante Drexel Biddle in their sparring session, worked as a blacksmith between fights. He was 22 at the time and could claim with some justification to have been the first of the genuine White Hopes. He was not an unknown substitute like McLaglen, nor cannon fodder as Ross had been. Kaufmann was regarded by many as a genuine prospect, and the first of Johnson's challengers since the black man had won the title to have a genuine chance in the ring with him. The champion acknowledged as much himself: 'About this time the giant fighter Al Kaufmann appeared on the horizon, and in him were placed the hopes of those so eager to have a white man again wear the championship belt.'

Kaufmann was over 6ft in height and weighed around 14 stone. He had turned professional in 1904, and caused something of a sensation by knocking out each of his first five opponents in the first round. Among his victims had been Jack 'Twin' Sullivan, so-called because his twin brother Mike was also a highly regarded professional. It is true that Jack was little more than a middleweight, but he was still a pretty useful one and in the first decade of the twentieth century less was made of weight differences between contestants.

There was no doubt that Kaufmann was the possessor of a respectable punch, but it was considerably enhanced by his judicious use of hand-wrappings. In those days there were few regulations as to what fighters should wear to protect their fists inside the gloves. The San Francisco man's favoured kind of wrapping was a type of heavy black mechanics' tape that was normally used for repairing machinery. Before one of Kaufmann's bouts, veteran heavyweight Tom Sharkey looked on in amazement as strand after strand of tape was wound into place around Kaufmann's fists by his handlers. Finally, the scandalised old fighter could restrain himself no longer. 'This guy's no fighter,' he blurted out contemptuously, 'he's an electrician!'

Kaufmann attracted considerable attention on the West Coast with his series of quick wins, and his handlers promptly put him in with another good, if much smaller, man, the ubiquitous Jack O'Brien. Unfortunately for the San Francisco boxer, O'Brien was much too clever for him. To make matters worse, O'Brien, who was commonly held to have no punch, actually knocked Kaufmann out in the seventeenth round.

The big fellow came back. In the four years between his loss to O'Brien and his bout with Jack Johnson, he had fourteen more fights, completing one ten-round, no-decision contest with Tony Ross and winning all the others, eleven by knockout. He was then matched with Jack Johnson, being regarded as the best available of local heavyweights and likely to draw a crowd.

There were many who thought that Kaufmann was in with a chance, but the fistic cognoscenti regarded the big fellow as strictly a dog, likely to be completely dominated by the champion. O'Brien and Ross had been outclassed by Johnson, they argued, while Kaufmann had been defeated inside the distance by the first and taken the full ten-round route by the second.

Kaufmann was reluctant to take on Johnson, and talked self-righteously of drawing the colour line. He said that his parents did not like the idea of his taking on a black fighter. In one interview he claimed that he would much rather box the white former Olympic heavyweight champion Sam Berger. Kaufmann also criticised Johnson for the manner of his display against Tony Ross.

In the event the San Francisco fighter hardly laid a glove on the untrained and patently out-of-condition Johnson. By the eighth round Kaufmann was out on his feet. For the last three rounds the champion literally held the big man up, refusing to let him go down. At the final bell, Johnson half-carried the exhausted Kaufmann back to his corner and gently deposited him on his stool.

The *San Francisco Call*, which had touted Kaufmann as a probable winner before the bout, had no doubt about the victor. Its headlines the morning after the fight screamed:

> Kaufmann Like a Babe in the Grip of Johnson
> The Black Champion Plays with the Blacksmith
> Johnson Declares Opponent Is Game.

Kaufmann went on fighting for another five or six years, mostly in no-decision bouts. After the Jack Johnson experience his confidence was ruined. He was knocked out by fellow White Hopes Fireman Jim Flynn and Luther McCarty and won only two more fights. A year after his attempt to dethrone the champion, Kaufmann was magnanimously employed by Johnson as a sparring partner.

4

THE HOBO

In 1909, Jack Johnson was having no trouble outclassing his opponents in the ring, but he needed a credible and charismatic opponent to start making real money from his championship title. While he waited for a young hopeful to be allowed out of the gymnasium on his own by his manager, he was approached by an unlikely challenger, but one who actually seemed capable of bringing suckers in through the turnstiles.

So precious were prospective White Hopes that managers were not above stealing them from one another. In fact, most managers were not above any nefarious act. One of the first fighters to be treated like a parcel in transit was the doughty middleweight Stanley Ketchel. Joe Coffman stole Ketchel from any or all of half a dozen barflies who had considered themselves to be custodians of the middleweight's future. Willus Britt stole Ketchel from Coffman, and Wilson Mizner was about to steal Ketchel from Britt, only the latter died first. This must have disappointed Mizner, who had a larcenous soul and would almost certainly rather have procured Ketchel by chicanery than just inheriting him.

It must be admitted that Ketchel was worth the bother. A hard, handsome, relentless, big-punching fighter of Polish/American descent, he is still rated by some experts as one of the best middleweights of all time. Born Stanislaus Kiecal in 1886 in Grand Rapids, Michigan, when he was only 12 he discovered the body of his murdered father in a hayloft. Only a short time afterwards Ketchel's mother was also murdered. The boy ran away from what was left of his home and headed west, hoping to become a cowboy. He rode the rods, panhandled, stole, did odd jobs and lived and fought in hobo shanty towns. He grew up fast and as a teenager ended up in the mining town of Butte, Montana. Here he visited a drinking joint called the Copper Queen, got into a dispute with the bouncer, beat him up and was given the dispossessed man's job by the owner.

One night, a local lightweight boxer drinking in the joint was impressed by the manner in which Ketchel knocked out a trouble-maker. He took the willing youth to a local gymnasium and instructed Ketchel in the basic points of boxing. Once the bewildered youngster could get his head around the fact that there could be rules for fighting, he took to the noble art with alacrity.

He had a chance to display his new-found skills when a showman called Texas John Halliday visited Butte, bringing with him his fighter, Jack Tracey. Halliday offered ten dollars to anyone who could go four rounds with his man. Ketchel was one of the first to respond.

Before an enthusiastic crowd of miners he knocked Tracey flat. This disappointed Halliday greatly. It was his habit to stand behind curtains on the dimly lit stage with a small sandbag in his hand; whenever one of Tracey's opponents hove into view, Halliday would shade the odds in favour of his man by bringing the sandbag down viciously on the head of the challenger, leaving Tracey to claim yet another knockout victory. However, on this occasion, Tracey did not even complete the full circuit to bring Ketchel within reach of the flailing bag of sand. He ran into one of the first punches the local man threw and lost all interest in the proceedings.

Later, one of Ketchel's publicity men tried to embellish the story by claiming that his man had actually swung Tracey round when they reached the curtain, so that the booth fighter took the impact of Halliday's sandbag instead. It is unlikely. At this stage of his burgeoning career Ketchel required little assistance.

His showing against Tracey was enough to make Ketchel embrace professional fighting with alacrity. He became very popular at halls all over Montana and gave his career a tremendous boost by going the distance in a four-round, no-decision contest with Tommy Ryan, the middleweight champion of the world, who was on a whistle-stop tour of the sticks to cash in on his title.

Ketchel's sterling performance against the champion was the cause of a heated public dispute between Ryan and his manager Jack Curley. Ryan pointed out between gritted teeth that the object of such tours was for audiences to see him toying lazily with local no-hopers, not trying to cope with unleashed wildcats. Curley responded that he had not expected to come across such a two-fisted terror so far from any centre of civilisation.

Ketchel took the hint. If he wanted to progress in the ring, he would have to base himself in one of the bigger cities. He decided to try his luck in Sacramento. By now he could have afforded to buy a train ticket, but old habits die hard and he dodged the railroad guards and risked his life by riding the rods to the West Coast.

His reputation preceded him, and he found a gaggle of would-be managers jostling for the privilege of signing him up. Ketchel had already had a manager or two, but out of sight, out of mind. As Doc Kearns, later one of the great boxing managers and a man who was just setting out in the game himself at the time, said, 'It was an era in which a fighter could have half a dozen managers in the course of a year. He hit town, dug himself up a manager who kept him eating until he fought, then took off for new precincts.'

In Ketchel's case, the lucky man was a San Francisco photographer called O'Connor. O'Connor latched on to Ketchel, gave him the ring name of the 'Fighting Hobo' and promptly matched the 21-year-old against Joe Thomas, generally regarded as the best middleweight since the retirement of Tommy Ryan. Ketchel and Thomas fought a blistering draw at Colma, a fight town south of San Francisco, one of the few which allowed bouts to go a distance of forty-five rounds. Ketchel at once demanded a rematch and asked for the loser's end of the purse to be advanced to him, so that he could bet it on himself to knock Thomas out.

His confidence was justified. Billy Roche, who refereed the contest, said of the return match in the *New York Times*, 'Never in my forty-five years' ring experience did I see so fiercely fought and so cyclonic a contest as that which ended with Ketchel knocking out Thomas in the thirty-second round.'

By now the only boxer with a claim to equal Ketchel's to the vacant world middleweight title was Jack 'Twin' Sullivan. When Ketchel challenged him, Jack said that the Fighting Hobo would have to beat his brother Mike first. This breach of fistic etiquette annoyed Ketchel, who told a reporter waspishly that the twin's action reminded him of that of a Civil War patriot who had sent all his relations to the front line to be killed while he stayed at home and prayed for victory.

When they met, Ketchel showed his displeasure by knocking Mike out in the first round. He then defeated Jack Sullivan and claimed the world championship. This aroused the ire of another claimant, Billy Papke, and he and Ketchel fought four times, each bout bloodier than the one before. Ketchel won the first contest, lost the second, then took the third and fourth. The loss was due mainly to the fact that when at the start of the bout Ketchel trustingly extended his glove for the customary handshake, Papke hauled off and hit the Fighting Hobo with a left and a following right, practically closing Ketchel's eyes. Dazed, Ketchel fought on to the twelfth round, when the referee, former heavyweight champion James J. Jeffries, stopped the fight. When they met for their third and fourth encounters, Ketchel was ready for Papke. There were no pre-match handshakes.

Ketchel's transparent ability to learn from his mistakes and the fact that he was now undisputed middleweight champion, attracted the attention of Willus Britt. Willus was the brother and manager of Jimmy Britt, a formidable lightweight of the time. Jimmy was supposed to be tough, but he was a milksop compared with his brother. On one occasion, when Jimmy was taking a beating in the ring and had been floored, Willus, from the safety of the ringside, hurled abuse at his brother for not fighting back, quivering with self-righteousness and screaming, 'Get up, you unnatural son of a bitch! Have you no regard for my feelings?' It was Britt who was supposed to have devised the so-called Californian Native Son decision, whereby any Californian boxing on home soil automatically got the decision if he was still alive at the end of the contest.

Britt's major flaw as a manager was that he was extremely superstitious. Before making any major decision he took out a battered pack of playing cards and dealt them according to a self-taught course of fortune-telling. He had to see how the cards would fall before committing himself to any course of action. He would never reveal the system behind his routine, so not even his closest associates ever knew what the cards were telling the manager, or whether he was ignoring their message if it meant that he might lose a buck or two.

O'Connor was so paranoid, with some justification as it turned out, about having Ketchel stolen from him that he would lock his charge in his hotel room at night. This was an almost ridiculously simple challenge for an operator of Britt's class. He absconded with the middleweight one evening by the simple measure of tiptoeing up the hotel's fire escape and bringing the credulous fighter down with him. Some reports had it that the fighter was clad only in a dressing gown as he fled into the night with his persuasive new handler.

One of the incentives that the fast-talking Britt had used to seduce Ketchel away from O'Connor and justify the 40 per cent of the fighter's purse that he demanded was the promise that he would arrange a series of New York fights for him. He was as good as his word. However, he also decided that Ketchel needed a change of image. Britt was too fastidious to want to be the manager of a hobo fighter. He decided to go upmarket. At first he thought of passing off his hopeful as a virginal college student fighting his way to an education, but taking into account the young boxer's amiably battered face and limited vocabulary, he decided to drop that idea.

Instead, on the train in he made the amenable Ketchel change into a facsimile of a cowboy's garb, including spurs and a ten-gallon hat. Thus attired, the docile but embarrassed champion was taken from newspaper to newspaper and introduced from the ring at a dozen different clubs and smokers.

The resultant publicity worked. In March 1909, Ketchel was matched with light-heavyweight champion Philadelphia Jack

O'Brien, and they had their celebrated ten-round, no-decision bout, with the final bell saving O'Brien when the count had reached eight.

His effort against the heavier O'Brien made Ketchel a major attraction, which was just what Britt had been hoping for. There was comparatively little money to be made among the lighter weights. The big dollars lay with the big men. It was something Britt had been mulling over ever since the quest for a White Hope had started. But Britt had his own plans. While other managers were finding giants and trying to turn them into fighters, Britt had found himself a fighter and would turn him into a small giant. Carefully he revealed his plan to the fascinated fighter. Ketchel would put on a few pounds and challenge Jack Johnson for the heavyweight title.

Ketchel, who was in fighting mainly because he liked hurting people but was never averse to making more money, was quick to see the merits in his manager's plan. There was, however, one major flaw, which he pointed out with some trepidation. There was no way in a thousand years that he would be able to beat the huge and multitalented Johnson.

Patiently Britt agreed with his protégé, although he was a little hurt that Ketchel should think that he had not covered that contingency. Of course, they would have to bring Johnson into the reckoning and persuade him to go easy with the middleweight. It should not be too difficult. In his previous fights in 1909, with McLaglen, O'Brien, Ross and Kaufmann, the champion had shown a marked disinclination to go into training. Against a feared and experienced adversary like Ketchel he would have to give up his roistering and get into condition, something he loathed.

On the other hand, if he could be persuaded that the wraps were on and that the fierce Ketchel would present no threat, then Johnson could continue with his hedonistic way of life, turn up for the title defence and go lazily through the motions, much as he had done against McLaglen and the others.

All that remained was to persuade Johnson, and Britt was a past master at the art. Years later, in a newspaper article George Little,

Johnson's manager, described the behind-the-scenes negotiations leading up to the contest. Willus Britt got in touch with the champion and pointed out that an ever-increasing aspect of a fighter's purse was the motion-picture rights. If Johnson and Ketchel were to spar amicably for the duration of the bout, he pointed out correctly, the resultant film of the twenty-round bout would fill theatres all over the world and bring in a lot of money for both fighters. Johnson needed little persuasion to go along with the scam.

Britt and Ketchel encountered trouble as soon as the middleweight champion started training. On the one hand, Ketchel wanted to get into shape, but he also had to put on as much weight as possible in order to look like a credible challenger. This meant hanging around the training camp eating and drinking, although Ketchel still continued with his pre-fight practice of spending hours soaking his hands in a bucket of salt brine in order to harden his fists.

Just before he went in with Johnson, Ketchel had a tune-up in a return fight with Philadelphia Jack O'Brien. This time Ketchel won on a third-round knockout, although years later the loser claimed that he had been paid to lie down in order to increase the publicity for the Johnson–Ketchel fight.

Ketchel's attempt to pad himself up and gain height in an attempt to look like a genuine heavyweight contender caused some hilarity among the fight fraternity at the weigh-in for the title bout. Jack O'Brien, now recovered from his two defeats at Ketchel's hands, was heard to jeer from a safe distance, 'Look at Ketchel, high-heel boots, padded shoulders, high-brim hat.' The weights on the weighing machine were doctored by the promoter to show that Johnson weighed 13½ stone while Ketchel was declared to be 12½ stone.

Johnson had his own problems in the run-up to the fight. He stayed with Belle Schreiber at a San Francisco hotel. The spurned Hattie McClay, Johnson's former mistress, booked into the same hotel. She took to lying in wait for Johnson and Schreiber and then leaping out to hurl drunken abuse at the pair. Once, in order to avoid the termagant, Johnson declared in his autobiography, he had to descend from his hotel room by a rope. There were even reports that finally, in order to keep the peace, the champion was sleeping with both women on alternate nights.

There was a great hope among members of the white establishment that Johnson would be defeated this time. The champion, who would not step off the sidewalk to let a white man pass, was building up his own store of folklore. Blacks felt that even if some of the stories were not true, they should have been. A favourite in the currency of gossip was that on one occasion in the Deep South the world champion had been stopped for speeding by a bullying local police chief. The officer had fined Jack Johnson fifty dollars on the spot. The black champion had handed over a hundred-dollar bill and revved up his engine. 'Ain't you waiting for your change?' demanded the police chief. 'Nope,' answered Johnson, waving a hand dismissively and speeding off in a cloud of dust. 'I aim to be coming back this way in an hour!'

Ketchel should have had no chance against a man 3 stone heavier and much taller, yet the fight was a sell-out, so great was the public desire to see a white fighter defeat the champion. Followers of boxing figured that the dynamic middleweight at least had a puncher's chance against any opponent. James Butler, a leading British boxing journalist, publicised the views of Duke Mullins, an Australian who had once helped train Jack Johnson. Mullins believed that Ketchel could pull off a surprise. 'He's just a human buzz-saw,' the impressed Mullins told the journalist.

The causes of what happened in the Johnson–Ketchel fight have been the subject of conjecture for over ninety years. The actual bout is easy to summarise. For eleven rounds at Colma, California, it was one of the most boring big fights for years, even by Johnson's recent standards. The champion played with his smaller opponent, while Ketchel showed no signs of his normally aggressive style. To emphasise the choreographed aspect of the fight, early on Johnson inadvertently hit Ketchel a little too hard. The challenger swayed dazedly and would have gone down if Johnson had not held him up. 'Where are you going, Stanley,' chided the champion. 'You and me ain't finished yet.'

Then, in the twelfth round, the previously comatose Ketchel suddenly hauled off and knocked the heavyweight champion down. The blow caused a sensation, not least with Johnson who had been placidly abiding by the script. Taking his time, the now-enraged black fighter got up and, as Ketchel came forward again, he hit the middleweight vindictively with a tremendous right hand, knocking the smaller man out. A San Francisco newspaper described this final round: 'Ketchel, suddenly rushing in, sent his right to the jaw. It struck the champion on the jaw and the big Negro fell upon his back and seemed to have injured himself. Ketchel rushed right at him, but the tricky champion was waiting for him. He swung a hard right to the jaw and quick as a flash shot a left to the body. As Ketchel fell backward Johnson sent in another right to the face and the white man went to the canvas as if shot, where he lay prone with blood gushing from his mouth.'

The point at issue was whether Willus Britt was in on the act, or whether the foolhardy lunge had been Ketchel's unprompted brainchild. It is difficult to imagine any dastardly deed being planned without Britt being an eager participant, yet Ketchel's record was littered with examples of independent addle-headed thinking and inept execution.

In a newspaper interview conducted in his dressing room immediately after the fight, Ketchel, who had left several of his teeth embedded in his opponent's glove, stressed his opinion that the difference in size had been the main contributory factor in his loss. He stated his intention of remedying that matter and then, demanding a return fight, he said, 'Tell Johnson the point is thirty pounds. When I make it I'm coming back and it will be a different story.'

At this point Wilson Mizner started to play a prominent part in the Ketchel story. He was one of the most unusual participants in the whole White Hope saga. Brawler, gambler, con man, wit and future Broadway playwright, the 6ft-2in, 15-stone Mizner followed his star with a vengeance. As a man who believed in advancement by stealth if not downright chicanery, his motto was

'Never try to get rich in the daytime.' Two of his uncles were generals and another was a governor, while his father had been a diplomat. The family had been dismayed when their 17-year-old scion had run away from home to become first a second to an unsuccessful fighter called Kid Savage and then a barker for a travelling medicine show.

Doc Kearns, then a mere youth but already a connoisseur of duplicity, first encountered him in the mining towns of the Klondike. At the time Mizner was a weigher in a saloon. He operated the scales upon which prospectors deposited their gold dust in exchange for gambling money. The sharp-eyed Kearns noticed that beneath the scales was an uncommonly fine carpet for a spit-and-sawdust saloon, and that it had a particularly thick nap. Settling down to enjoy the situation, Kearns watched appreciatively as, every so often, Mizner would 'accidentally' jog the scales, sending a faint shower of gold dust to the ground, where it was obscured in the nap of the carpet.

Determining to learn from a master, Kearns secured a part-time post as a messenger boy for the cheery and expansive Mizner. One of his duties was to retrieve the gold dust from the carpet after the saloon had closed each night. Mizner recognised in the youth a kindred spirit and took Kearns under his wing, counselling him sagely, 'If you make a mistake, make it in favour of the house.'

It was Mizner who introduced Kearns to the handling of fighters. At the time, among other activities Mizner managed a team of boxers and a fighting bear, putting on tournaments for the miners. To begin with, Kearns had fighting ambitions himself, but he gave them up when his ingenuity was not matched by his physical strength. He did, however, secure the admiration of Mizner when the manager discovered that Kearns was increasing his hitting power by clutching two iron bars in his fists inside the gloves. Unfortunately, unless Kearns could connect within the first couple of rounds, the bars made his arms so weary that his fists would start to drop, exposing his jaw to the other fighter's swings.

Mizner was more than just a motormouth. He had fought exhibition bouts with some of the leading heavyweights touring the mining camps, securing the sobriquet of the gentleman sparring partner. He was also perfectly content to back up his witty insults with action. He had appeared at least twice in New York courtrooms for starting bar brawls. A gem of information that he was perfectly prepared to pass on to others was, 'Always hit a man with a bottle – a ketchup bottle preferred, for when it breaks he thinks he's bleeding to death.'

A typically vainglorious story often told by Mizner, although no one ever corroborated it, was that on one occasion, in a San Francisco waterside saloon, he and the fighter Mysterious Billy Smith became involved in a punch-up with half a dozen longshoremen. There were several theories as to how Smith came by his nickname. The most likely is that when newspaper reports began to reach New York of the exploits of the California fighter, journalists speculated as to the background of the hitherto unknown boxer, hence his title. Doc Kearns, as usual, was more prosaic. 'If you fought Smith, it was always a mystery what he would do to you next – rub his laces across your eyes, butt you or hit you in the balls!'

In the saloon brawl, according to Mizner, at first all went well and their opponents went down like skittles. Then Mizner came up against one brawny dock worker who seemed impervious to his best punches. No matter how hard Mizner hit him the other man remained obdurately on his feet. Mizner was just beginning to wonder whether it might be the better part of valour to turn and run when Billy Smith glanced up briefly from the man he was pummelling to shout, 'Leave him, Wilson. I knocked that one out five minutes ago!' It transpired that Mizner's hapless adversary had become wedged on his feet between two pieces of furniture.

In his happy-go-lucky fashion, Mizner made and lost several fortunes in the goldfields. As his admirer Kearns said, 'He seldom had much for long, but when he had it he was a high roller.' In the end the rough justice of frontier life got too much for him, especially after he had been tarred and feathered by the riled citizenry of one town and carried out of it on a fence rail before being deposited in the mud.

Disillusioned, Mizner returned to the clubs and saloons of New York in which he always felt most at home. It was here that he first met Stanley Ketchel. Willus Britt had just taken over as the manager of the middleweight and had brought him to the East Coast in an effort to secure the match with Jack Johnson.

Britt realised that while there was little that he did not know about the criminal fraternity of California, here in New York he would be a mere babe in a concrete wood. He needed urgently a mentor who would steer him to the right sort of evil contacts in the Atlantic Seaboard underworld of prizefighting and show him the right people to fix. Almost everyone he asked told him that there was only one jovial and unprincipled denizen of the Great White Way capable of meeting the manager's lawless needs, and that was Wilson Mizner. Mizner knew both whom to cajole and whom to bribe.

He also had an eye for talent. When Jimmy Britt, Willus's fighting brother, declared that he was homesick in New York and wanted to return to the West Coast, Mizner promptly solved the problem by hiring a child singer called Groucho Marx, later to achieve Hollywood fame with his manic brothers, to soothe the lightweight with frequent renditions of popular songs.

Accordingly, Britt took Mizner on board as a minor consultant. Trusting no one, throughout their relationship he maintained a close and suspicious watch on his new colleague, remembering how he himself had purloined the middleweight from O'Connor. Mizner tolerated Britt's lack of trust because he had struck up a close affinity with Ketchel, a roisterer after his own heart. As he later wrote of the fighter, 'I think of him as a laugh, a pair of shoulders, and a great heart.'

Their partnership got off to an unsteady start when at their first encounter in a hotel room Mizner threw his hat onto the bed, arousing the superstitious Ketchel's wrath. After that they got on well. Mizner would join Ketchel on his regular jaunts to brothels and would match him drink for drink in the saloons. When Ketchel got too fighting drunk, Mizner could sometimes calm the boxer by reciting Kipling's poem 'If' to him.

At the time Mizner was in the process of recovering from an almighty bender, even by his own opulent standards. He had recently been divorced from the aptly named 'forty million dollar widow', Mrs Charles T. Yerkes, and Mizner had spent his settlement from the lady in considerable haste in case she changed her mind and took legal steps to retrieve the money. Among his other transgressions, the temporary Mrs Mizner had objected to the fact that her husband had turned a whole wing of her magnificent Fifth Avenue mansion into a training camp for fighters. Now her estranged spouse was broke again and in need of a meal ticket. Enter Stanley Ketchel.

In the end, whatever the ruse Mizner may have had in mind to steal Ketchel away from his manager, it proved unnecessary. Soon after the Jack Johnson fight, Willus Britt died, it was said, of a heart attack brought on by Ketchel's double-cross against Johnson, which had come so close to succeeding. It was certainly true that for weeks after the bout Britt had kept Ketchel's two missing teeth in his waistcoat pocket and was in the habit of displaying them lugubriously in saloons, lamenting the fortune he had lost when his fighter had walked into Johnson's haymaker.

In 1910, Wilson Mizner took over as Ketchel's manager, although to most denizens of the fistic world he was always regarded more as a glorified hanger-on than a guide. Still, it made a change from his most recent occupation of self-employed confidence trickster. Not that he lacked ability in that direction. The novelist Djuna Barnes said with awe that Mizner was so attuned to trickery that from a busy street he could hear a ten-dollar bill falling onto a thick carpet ten storeys up.

He soon wondered whether he had made a mistake by entering the fight game. Ketchel had always been a reluctant trainer, preferring to spend his time disposing of the money he was earning from his purses. Britt had been tough enough and nasty enough to insist that the fighter get into condition before his bouts, but Mizner was too similar in temperament to Ketchel to have the same influence. He was only 33, to Ketchel's 24. He began to suspect that he was being too lenient when on the first day of one training session Ketchel reeled happily into the camp accompanied by four willing young ladies.

Boxing in New York was still in a state of contradiction, being both illegal and tremendously popular. Anyone engaging in a prizefight stood in danger of being arrested and fined $500 or sentenced to a year's imprisonment. To get around the law and cater to public demand, 'athletic clubs' sprang up all over the city. Ostensibly private institutions, membership was available in every saloon for the price of a couple of dollars, which entitled the new 'member' to attend one so-called exhibition at the club. Even so, the clubs could still be raided if the local police had not been bribed adequately enough. Nevertheless, boxing flourished and eager young men were to be found in training all over the city.

Being in attendance at a Stanley Ketchel training camp, however, should have carried with it a health warning. When the tough one-time featherweight champion Abe Attell was asked how he had come by his newly broken nose, he lamented, 'Ketchel did it with a brick. He was throwing it at a sparring partner and I walked into the line of fire.' On another occasion the temperamental fighter fired a shot out through the door of his bedroom when roused too early for a training run. The bullet from his Colt .44 went through the leg of his backer and friend Pete (the Goat) Stone, a nightclub owner.

On yet another occasion, before an exhibition fight, Ketchel went missing. Desperately, Mizner searched the local brothels and saloons. Eventually he found his fighter drunk in bed with two young ladies. When asked afterwards what he had done at the sight, Mizner had shrugged. 'What could I do?' he asked. 'I told him to move over!'

Mizner was never much of an example to his fighter. Emil Friedlander, who had a room next to the playboy's apartment at 142 West Forty-Fourth Street, complained bitterly of his neighbour's habit of serenading visiting wealthy widows at all hours with soulful ballads. Friedlander also objected to Mizner's self-proclaimed 'Campfire Boys commuting to the Orient', the manager's colourful description of his frequently held and well-attended opium-smoking parties.

Most of Ketchel's minor opponents on the road were not nearly good enough for him, which sometimes led to lapses in concentration on the part of the fighter. Once, when a friend visited the middleweight in his changing room before a fight, he found Ketchel in his fighting gear but concentrating on learning the words of a song from a sheet of paper in his hand. It transpired that local dignitaries were giving him a testimonial dinner after the bout and Ketchel had promised to sing a comic song called 'O'Brien Had No Place to Go'. Even as Ketchel was jogging down the aisle to the ring through the screaming crowd his lips could still be observed moving as he sang the song to himself.

Mizner sometimes displayed an equally perfunctory approach. The manager put elegance before everything. When he seconded Ketchel against Jim Smith, the former gunslinger turned sports writer Bat Masterson, writing in the *New York Morning Telegraph*, reported, 'Wilson Mizner was on deck, of course, bossing the fight in the champion's corner. He was dressed as though for a party instead of a fight and did not soil his immaculate attire by swinging a towel or dashing water with a sponge.'

The happy-go-lucky Mizner was perfectly prepared to let his friends and drinking companions share in his management chores. One of his saloon-bar associates was the sports writer for the *New York Morning World*, 'Hype' Igoe. Igoe had received his nickname because he was so thin that he reminded his friends of a hypodermic syringe. On one occasion, Igoe was deputed by Ketchel and Mizner to handle the fighter's incidental training expenses. Feeling that he was being overcharged, Igoe refused to pay a bill. A court order was taken out against him and the obdurate writer was forced to spend a day or two in the Ludlow Street jail. When he emerged from his brief incarceration, Igoe was met by Mizner and a crowd of well-lubricated cronies, all dressed in convicts' striped suits, waiting to take him to a 'coming-out' party at Healy's restaurant.

Managing Ketchel might have done wonders for Mizner's social life but it was not providing the express train to wealth that the new manager had hoped for. In fact, the depressing fact dawned on the handler that despite his youth Ketchel was probably already a shot fighter. Years of hard fighting and high living had already taken their toll on the champion, and he had little left but his reputation. Wurra Wurra McLaughlin, the splendidly named sports editor of the *New York World*, was one of the first to bring this to the attention of his readers when he wrote that Ketchel had ruined himself by 'hitting the hop', or excess drinking.

There was only one hope left, another lucrative pay-day with Jack Johnson in a return match for the heavyweight title before Ketchel retired. To get that bout, two things were needed: Ketchel had to defeat a few well-rated fighters and he had to beef up to genuine heavyweight proportions.

The problem with the first stipulation was that Mizner could not be sure that, on his current form, Ketchel could defeat the top-ranked heavyweights. Accordingly, Mizner decided to help things along. He matched Ketchel with the great black fighter Sam Langford. Langford was regarded as second only to Johnson in ability, and was avoided by most white fighters and their managers. When he did fight white men, Langford was often under wraps, knowing that he would only get paid if he let the other man go the distance.

It was an important piece of matchmaking. *Boxing* summed up its significance: 'A victory for either man will give the winner a clear claim which Jack Johnson will find it difficult to ignore.'

Early in 1910, Langford and Ketchel fought a six-round, no-decision bout in Philadelphia. The black fighter was generally regarded as having 'carried' Ketchel throughout the fight. Beforehand, the promoter, Sunny Jim Coffroth, called both fighters in and explained to them that if they agreed to fake an exciting six-rounder, he would then build on the public interest aroused by rematching them in a genuine forty-five-round bout for the middleweight title and a purse of $30,000.

Both men agreed to the proposition, but Ketchel, paranoid after having failed in his own attempt to double-cross Jack Johnson, was afraid that the black fighter might cheat him. Accordingly he hired men to follow Langford to ensure that he was going easy on his training as promised.

Mizner later told his lawyer that the fight had been choreographed like an old-time melodrama, with first one boxer apparently in trouble and then the other almost going down before making a miraculous recovery. As Langford was fond of saying, 'Never bet on anything that talks.' Ketchel and Langford shared $13,000 for their fight, $9,000 – the larger share, of course – going to the white fighter, but that was before Ketchel and Mizner had to start making disbursements to various interested parties. Ketchel needed as much as he could get: his latest bill for a hectic two-week stay at the Bartholdi Hotel in New York had amounted to $593.00.

Three weeks after the Langford fight, Mizner was called upon to use all his managerial wisdom when Ketchel fought heavyweight Porky Flynn in Boston. There was a dreadful storm that evening and Ketchel got it into his head that the bad weather presaged the imminent end of the world. If this was the case, he reasoned, what did it matter who won the fight that night? Wilson Mizner managed to persuade the fighter that settling some of their gambling debts would be a matter of considerable urgency should Armageddon be postponed for a couple of days. Ketchel saw the point and knocked Flynn out in the third round. Magnanimously he then brought his opponent round by throwing a bucket of water over him.

Next Ketchel fought Willie Lewis in New York. Increasingly concerned by the fragile state of his charge, Mizner took care of Lewis, who agreed not to strive for a knockout. The night before the fight, fellow manager Dan Morgan noticed Dan McKetrick, Lewis's manager, lighting several candles in a church before dropping twenty-five cents into the offertory box. This gave the wily Morgan the idea that Lewis would be trying for a knockout after all, and he placed his bets accordingly. He was right. From the first bell Lewis swarmed all over Ketchel, forcing his opponent to fight back desperately. Revealing a flash of his old form, Ketchel managed to knock Lewis out in the second round. Morgan told his biographer John McCallum in his book *Dumb Dan* that afterwards, when McKetrick bemoaned their failure to capture the championship, Morgan had commented that obviously Lewis's manager had not put enough in the offertory box. 'You tried to get the world's middleweight title for only two bits!' he pointed out reprovingly.

Things were looking grim for Mizner and Ketchel. They had received a great deal of bad publicity over the Langford affair, and there were even stories circulating that an up-and-coming young middleweight called Frank Klaus had also been paid to go easy with Ketchel in a no-decision bout around this time. As if this was not enough, Ketchel had been diagnosed with syphilis and was believed to be addicted to opium.

In 1910, gambling, especially on sports, was flourishing in the USA. Where there were wagers there was always the possibility of corruption. The results of more and more major sporting events were suspected of being 'fixed' by gamblers. In 1908, the team physician of the New York Giants baseball team was expelled from the sport for offering an umpire $2,500 to favour the Giants in his decisions. In the same year, New York outlawed betting on horse racing after a number of scandals concerning horses being 'pulled' by their jockeys so that they would not win. There were many rumours of fighters being encouraged to box to orders.

It was the misfortune of Mizner and Ketchel at this time to come up against the dangerous young gambler and fixer Arnold Rothstein, who was just beginning to make a mark as an illegal bookmaker with his expressed philosophy of 'If a man is dumb, someone is going to get the best of him, so why not you?' Rothstein wanted Ketchel to take a dive in a fight, still to be arranged, as part of a betting coup. Mizner and his fighter were already spending more money than they could afford on paying opponents to lie down, so they could hardly now entertain the reverse procedure. Virtuously they rejected Rothstein's overtures. This annoyed the gambler, and it was rumoured that he had put a price on Ketchel's uneasy head.

Wilson Mizner decided that it was time to regroup. For some time he and his fighter had held court at the Woodlawn Inn on the outskirts of New York, where it was always open house and where free booze flowed for reporters, writers and show-business personalities. A change of image was patently required. Mizner announced to the newspapers that from now on Ketchel's only objective would be to ready himself for another bid to take Jack Johnson's title. So determined was Ketchel to fight as a heavyweight, Mizner went on, that he had already put on extra muscle and could no longer make the middleweight limit and consequently would give up his claim to the title and become a fully fledged heavyweight.

Before buckling down to training, Mizner and Ketchel went to Reno, to see Jack Johnson make his latest defence of his title, against former heavyweight champion James J.Jeffries. It was apparent to both Mizner and Ketchel that Jeffries had no chance against the champion. As Mizner later told the story to several newspapers and many hangers-on, Ketchel suddenly decided that it would be unthinkable for Jeffries to let whites down by being humiliated in the ring. He approached Mizner with a plan. Ketchel was due to be announced to the crowd from the ring before the fight. He told the horrified Mizner that as he shook hands with Jeffries in front of the assembled thousands, he would suddenly unleash a right-hand punch to the former champion's jaw, knocking him unconscious and thus rendering him unfit to fight, so cancelling the bout.

Mizner was able to point out a slight flaw in his fighter's reasoning. They had both bet all the money they could spare on Johnson to win. If the fight should be cancelled, bets would be called off. Fortunately, after much persuasion, Ketchel was able to see the point of this argument and reluctantly abandoned his project. Anyway, he had been recruited as one of the timekeepers for the contest, so it would be a pity to bring the bout to a premature conclusion when he was going to have such an excellent free view of it.

After Johnson had won easily, Mizner and Ketchel left, scattering challenges to the champion from all directions. They travelled back to San Francisco in the company of writer Jack London. They got very drunk and at one point the three of them stole a hansom cab and hurriedly drove off in it, with Ketchel throwing money to the irate pursuers.

It was easy enough for Mizner to get newspaper space by now. Reporters were always willing to devote columns to a man who could coin such maxims as 'The gent who wakes and finds himself a success hasn't been asleep' and 'Be nice to people on your way up because you'll meet them on your way down.'

To show that he was taking his boxing seriously, Ketchel even left New York and set up a training camp on a farm near Conway in Missouri. The ranch belonged to the self-styled Colonel R.P. Dickerson, a former private in the Spanish–American war, a wealthy and influential local landowner and sports enthusiast.

Wilson Mizner temporarily left Ketchel to his own devices at the camp. Mizner's first successful play, *The Deep Purple*, was running in Chicago and for the moment monopolising the manager's attention.

Ketchel and Mizner had become involved in so many scams and con tricks that the fighter became nervous and travelled about armed. Sports writer and honorary assistant manager Hype Igoe, who often accompanied the former middleweight, said, 'I never knew him sit down to a meal in any big town without first laying his big blue six-shooter across his lap.'

Ketchel's meals on the farm were served in a cook's small house by a woman called Goldie Smith. Almost automatically, Ketchel hit on her to such an extent that he aroused the jealousy of a farmhand called Walter Dipley, Smith's boyfriend. On the morning of 15 October 1910, as Ketchel sat eating his breakfast, Dipley crept up behind the fighter and shot him with a .22-calibre rifle. The bullet lodged in Ketchel's left lung. As his victim slumped to the ground, Dipley picked up the boxer's revolver, hit him on the head with it and fled, taking with him a ring from the dying man's finger and the contents of his wallet.

Ketchel was rushed to a hospital in Springfield, where he died. Dipley was hunted down and arrested high in the Ozark Mountains. He and Goldie Smith were both tried for collusion to murder. Dipley was found guilty and sentenced to life imprisonment. The same verdict was also brought against Goldie Smith, but it was later reversed and she was released.

The great sports writer Damon Runyon wrote solemnly of Ketchel's pre-eminent place in the hearts of many boxing fans. 'It has been my observation that the memory of Ketchel prejudiced the judgement of everyone who has ever been associated with him. They can never see any other fighter.'

The news of Ketchel's death was brought to Wilson Mizner as he sat playing poker for high stakes at the Millionaires' Club. Selfish, flamboyant, untrustworthy but with a great gift for a phrase, Mizner murmured, 'Start counting to ten; he'll get up!'

5

A HOT DAY IN RENO

As many would-be managers were beginning to discover to their cost by the beginning of 1910, it took time and money to develop a White Hope. Great raw-boned giants with the bloom of youth on their cheeks and an avaricious glint in their eyes were beginning to emerge from the factories and farms in response to newspaper stories about the fortune that awaited a successful white heavyweight. As soon as they appeared they were being snatched into cluttered big-city gyms by wrinkled and ever-optimistic handlers looking for meal tickets.

For most of the clumsy tyros there lay months of expensive training and tutoring ahead before they could be launched in the ring against punch-drunk trial horses, but, when they did meet these hand-picked opponents, too often the Hopes were flattened by the hopeless ones. Credible challengers would eventually emerge, the managers were sure of that, but it would take another couple of years before any of them were ready to face Jack Johnson.

In the meantime the public was clamouring for a white man to defeat Jack Johnson. Promoters were circling like sharks, waiting for the opportunity to match a White Hope against the champion. One of the first to announce his intentions was the Australian Hugh D. McIntosh, who had put on the Johnson–Burns championship fight. Weeping crocodile tears of remorse at having given a black man the opportunity to win the title, in April 1909 McIntosh arrived in New York and told a reporter from the *Milwaukee Evening Wisconsin*, 'Now that a negro is the champion, because of the fight which I promoted in Australia last fall, I shall do all that lies in my power to reverse the situation . . . If possible I will bring the present champion into conflict with a white man who may wrest the honours from him.'

There was only one possibility on the horizon. That was the retired, undefeated former champion James J. Jeffries. A solitary man, he had given up trying to cash in on his former fame. For a time he had toured as Davy Crockett in a stage production of *The Man from the West*. The intended dramatic climax had been for Jeffries, clad in fringed buckskin, to use all his strength to hold a broken door shut against the attacks of the real wolves being used in the production. At the same time the former champion had to make sure that he was not obscuring from the gaze of the audience the slender form of his 6-stone leading lady. Neither the wolves nor the anorexic actress had satisfied many audiences, so in a revised version the former champion would take his curtain-calls, hurry into the wings and reappear in fighting costume to go three rounds with a sparring partner. Sometimes he would even spar between the acts. Even this did not catch on. William Brady, his producer, complained, 'Although Jeff was a fairly good actor, the public would not go to see him.'

With some relief Jeffries had given up the stage and had been living quietly until the requests for him to make a comeback. Jeffries did not want to fight again. He was happy with his alfalfa farm and saloon and, at more than 4 stone overweight, knew that it would take months of agonising training to get back into condition again – that is, if at the age of 34 he could ever regain his old fitness and agility.

The pressure from the public for Jeffries to fight Johnson was tremendous. In April 1909, the *Chicago Tribune* even printed a photograph of a young girl pointing tremulously at the camera, with the caption: 'Please, Mr Jeffries, are you going to fight Mr Johnson?'

Slowly Jeffries began to consider the prospect of a comeback. He went on a diet and began stepping up his exercise. Finally he decided that if the doctors cleared him and told him that he could get back into shape, he would consider fighting Johnson.

First he approached his old manager, William Brady, who had guided him to the heavyweight title back in 1899. To his dismay, Brady rejected him out of hand. The reason that the veteran gave was that he was too busy producing another Broadway play. However, during his partnership with Jeffries he had put on as many as eight Broadway shows a year without letting it affect his managerial duties.

In fact, the producer would not entertain resuming his association for two reasons. He had grown disillusioned with the prize ring, especially in New York, because of the amount of corruption which had crept into the sport. 'Night after night,' he complained in his autobiography *Fighting Man*, 'fake fights were pulled off all over the city.'

Another reason for Brady's refusal was his fear that Jeffries would get badly hurt by Johnson if the two should meet. When Jeffries said that he was determined to go through with the fight, Brady told him, 'If you do, you'll regret it as long as you live, for Johnson will surely beat you.' Brady said that following this Jeffries never spoke to him again.

As a result Jeffries called upon an old friend, Sam Berger, to handle his affairs. Berger, a studious, reflective sort, had won the heavyweight gold medal at the 1904 St Louis Olympics, the first time that boxing had been introduced at a modern Olympiad. In Athens in 1896, it had been rejected by the organisers as 'ungentlemanly, dangerous and practised by the dregs of society'. Only Americans had entered in 1904. Berger, a member of the San Francisco Olympic Club, turned professional after winning his Olympic championship but did not have a glittering career. The highlight of his paid record was a six-round, no-decision bout with Philadelphia Jack O'Brien.

By the time he was approached by Jeffries in 1909, Berger had abandoned the ring in favour of a successful business career, which was to culminate in the ownership of a large San Francisco clothing store. However, he was prepared to put all this on hold to handle negotiations for Jeffries and act as one of his sparring partners in the initial stages of the old champion's comeback.

Next, Jeffries sailed for Carlsberg in Germany, to be examined by doctors at this weight-reducing haven and begin his self-imposed regime. He stayed there for three months and lost 2 stone in weight. He also encountered King Edward VII of Great Britain, who was taking the waters. The monarch was interested in boxing to the extent that when Tommy Burns had been evading the challenges of Jack Johnson he had scornfully referred to the champion as 'a Yankee bluffer', forgetting that Burns was a Canadian. The king and the prizefighter met in the streets of Carlsberg, where Edward hailed the huge American with a hearty, 'Hello there, Jim Jeffries! Going to fight the black fellow, eh? Jolly good!'

The British magazine *Boxing* noted with approval the efforts of the former champion to regain fighting fitness and seemed to be in no doubt as to the eventual success of his comeback. 'James Jackson Jeffries, ex-boilermaker, retired champion heavyweight and now wealthy farmer, has come out of the quietude to regain for the white section of Americans the world's premier honours, and is taking the baths at Carlsberg.'

Towards the end of the year, Jeffries sailed back for the United States and announced that he was prepared to challenge Johnson for the latter's crown. In the meantime, Sam Berger had been engaging in a series of secret meetings with George Little and Sig Hart, Jack Johnson's co-managers, hammering out the details of the fight. They announced to promoters that those wishing to bid for the contest should submit sealed bids, to be opened on 1 December 1909. In order to avoid time-wasters, and as a sign of solvency, the fighters announced that each bid should be accompanied by a cheque for $5,000.

This led to a frantic competition to put on the bout. Soon Tex Rickard emerged as one of the promoters jostling to stage the tournament. A hard-hearted, crafty but fair man, who was renowned for always paying his debts, Rickard had worked as a lawman, saloon-keeper, gambler and general entrepreneur. In order to bring visitors to his saloon at Goldfield, Nevada, he had already promoted a fight for the world lightweight championship between Joe Gans and Battling Nelson. To add a touch of drama to the occasion, Rickard had put the entire $30,000 purse in gold eagles in the window of a local bank.

Ever restless, Rickard had moved on to another Nevada frontier mining town, Rawhide. Here, in order to publicise his gambling saloon, he had persuaded the best-selling novelist Elinor Glynn to visit the town. In order to impress the author and encourage her to write about Rawhide, Rickard had simulated a gambling session, an attempt to put out a fire and even a gunfight with blank ammunition and the plentiful use of ketchup on the 'dead' miner. Glynn believed everything she had seen and returned East to write of Rickard and his cronies in the *New York American*, describing them as 'brave fellows fighting nature to obtain from her legitimate wealth'.

Although in 1908 he subsequently lost all his money in a fire which had destroyed his saloon in Rawhide, Rickard did not allow this to depress him for long. His reputation for probity was such that he could always raise money.

In this instance he borrowed it from a millionaire business associate, Thomas F. Cole. Armed with his friend's cash Rickard then went to work. Several days before the closing date for bids, he went to Pittsburgh, where Jack Johnson was appearing in vaudeville.

First the Texan visited Etta Duryea at the boarding house she was sharing with the fighter. The champion usually introduced her as his wife, but in fact they were not married until 1911. Getting straight to the point, Rickard asked her what she desired most in the world. Etta Duryea replied that she would like a fur coat. Rickard promised her one if she would use her influence to persuade Johnson to accept the bid for the fight he was about to submit.

Next Rickard visited Jack Johnson backstage at the theatre. Etta had made it clear that the high-spending champion was short of money. From his wallet Rickard produced $2,500 in high-denomination notes and pressed them upon the champion. In response Johnson told him that he had heard that the highest of the credible bids that were about to be made would be $100,000.

That was all that Rickard wanted to know. He suspected that with his generous ways he had already half-won the champion over. In order to maintain his advantage, he travelled to New York in the same train as Johnson and Etta for the opening of the bids. Stopping only to buy Etta her fur coat, Rickard then took the ferry across the Hudson River to Meyer's Hotel in Hoboken, where the bids were to be scrutinised.

At once Rickard embarked upon a frenzy of negotiating behind the scenes. He found Jeffries and his new manager Sam Berger cold and unwelcoming, but Berger did condescend to hint that the fight had been as good as wrapped up in advance by a friend of his, actor and playwright Jack Gleason, representing the Californian promoter Sunny Jim Coffroth.

Rickard hunted down Gleason and told him that he had secured the allegiance of Johnson. If Gleason would betray Coffroth and could persuade Jeffries, through Berger, to look favourably on the Texan's bid, Rickard would give Gleason half the profits ensuing from the mooted tournament. Rickard was never afraid to spend a dollar in order to make two.

Gleason knew when he was on to a good thing and agreed without hesitation, although he warned Rickard that Berger would also have to be taken care of financially. Rickard hurried back to the hotel room, which was crowded with would-be promoters of the bout, while many more had submitted their bids through the post and by messenger.

One by one the bids were opened in the crowded, smoke-filled room. Jack Johnson was present but Jeffries did not arrive, leaving Berger to represent his interests. In the event, some of the major players submitted disappointingly small offers. The great Hugh D. McIntosh tendered only $75,000 for the bout to be held at Rushcutters Bay in Sydney, while the august members of London's National Sporting Club came up with a paltry $50,000.

On the other hand, there were several wildcats bandying about enormous sums. A St Louis promoter proposed an astronomical $150,000, while a New Orleans syndicate was prepared to go to $110,000. These, however, were regarded as bids of dubious provenance, with the promoters unlikely to be able to come up with the full sum when the chips were down.

All the established favourites among the promoters, as Johnson had divulged in Pittsburgh, offered sums of $100,000 or a little under. Then Rickard's bid was opened. It was for $101,000, plus a percentage of film and vaudeville rights. That was not all. In addition to the obligatory cheque for $5,000, his envelope also contained fifteen $1,000 bills. Promoters present said that Johnson's eyes widened at the sight of the banknotes tumbling invitingly onto the table before him.

It was all over bar the shouting. Johnson accepted his new patron's offer with alacrity; Berger was scarcely less forthcoming. Tex Rickard had secured the rights to stage what was soon being called the 'Fight of the Century'.

In the meantime, promoter James J.Coffroth had been waiting in another hotel for news of his bid for the bout. Years later he told a reporter of the experience. 'I waited and waited,' he recounted ruefully. 'Gleason was to have telephoned me the outcome of the deal. There was no telephoning. I tried to contact Gleason. He wasn't to be found. Finally it dawned on me that perhaps Jack Gleason had made what he figured was a more advantageous deal for himself. That turned out to be the case . . . I was out in the cold!'

At first Rickard planned to stage the championship in San Francisco, the leading fight town on the West Coast. However, he had reckoned without the spite of Sunny Jim Coffroth, who was far from cordial as a result of losing in the bidding to stage the bout. Coffroth used all his local influence to get the bout cancelled. In this he was aided, sometimes but not always unwittingly, by a parcel of inept and often corrupt local politicians.

Even the hard-boiled Rickard was amazed by the degree of public larceny on display in California. Consignments of wood intended for the construction of a new stadium were stolen in broad daylight while bribed policemen looked the other way. City councillors demanded handouts or wads of free tickets. Delegations from women's organisations crowded into the Governor's office, pleading that the forthcoming fight be cancelled on the grounds of its potential brutality.

The most damaging canard, however, and one that Rickard suspected owed its origins to Coffroth, was that the fight would not be worth seeing, as its result had been determined in advance. Johnson, it was rumoured, had agreed for a consideration to lie down to Jeffries, knowing that if he won the white boxer would then retire again, leaving Johnson free to mop up the remaining white contenders and regain his title with ease.

Before long, the Governor of California, James N. Gillett, was as fed up with the disputes surrounding the bout as Rickard was. There was an ever-increasing antipathy to the thought of a black versus white contest and all the trouble that it might cause. In the end Gillett vetoed the bout, saying in exasperation, 'We've had enough of prize fights and prize fight promoters. They've been breaking the law long enough and we'll have no more of it!' Rickard was almost as relieved, although he declared having already spent a quarter of a million dollars in trying to bring the championship to California.

Several cities offered to take the place of San Francisco, and Rickard settled on Reno in Nevada, mainly because of its good railway connections. He set up his headquarters in a substantial house in the city, from which tickets were sold and information about the fight was issued. Tom Corbett, brother of the former heavyweight champion James J. Corbett, established his betting parlour in the same building. It was to be almost the last throw of gambling in the city. Up until 1910 it had been legal in the area, but by the end of the year a citizens' group known as the Progressives managed to get it banned.

The fight seemed to be off when James J. Jeffries suddenly refused to box in Nevada. Patiently Rickard investigated the situation and discovered that the former champion had reneged on a $25,000 gambling debt he had incurred while playing the tables at Reno five years earlier, thinking that he would never have to return to the city.

Rickard took the setback in his stride. He approached the casino involved and negotiated a repayment of fifty cents in the dollar on the debt, to be taken from Jeffries's earnings from the fight. As the former champion eventually emerged with the sum of $192,000 as his share of the takings, he cannot be said to have done too badly from the deal. Nevertheless, when the startled Jeffries was greeted upon his arrival by a huge crowd at the railway station in Reno, he fled. Later he justified his action by claiming that he was scared of crowds, but it is more likely that he feared one or two armed and disgruntled creditors might be lurking among the mob.

Almost at once, Rickard started fanning the flames of publicity, an area in which he excelled. From the start he had decided to emulate promoter Hugh D. McIntosh at Rushcutters Bay and referee the championship contest himself. However, he told reporters that he had drawn up a shortlist for the post, which included the President of the United States, former champion John L. Sullivan, and the creator of Sherlock Holmes, British author Arthur Conan Doyle. The conservative and low-key President Taft refused to be drawn into the matter, but Sullivan and Doyle, both more gullible, were immensely flattered.

Behind the scenes Rickard managed to dissuade the disappointed ex-champion, but the author seriously considered the matter, especially after he had received a letter from the editor of the *New York Morning Telegraph*, which said, 'It would indeed rejoice the hearts of men in this country if you were at the ringside when the great Negro fighter meets the white man Jeffries for the world's championship . . .' After much thought, the 50-year-old Doyle, the author of several classics of the prize ring, including *Rodney Stone*, declined to be considered, saying, 'My friends pictured me as winding up a revolver at one ear and a razor at the other.'

By this time, both contestants had started serious training. Jeffries's camp was sited at Moana Springs, two miles south of Reno, selected because it had the latest in electric wiring, while Johnson trained at Rick's Resort. Jeffries arrived from California on 23 June in a specially chartered Pullman car. He was being assisted by a gallery of former stars of the ring who were anxious to see the black fighter beaten.

His chief trainer was the tetchy former heavyweight champion James J. Corbett, who had twice lost to Jeffries. Long before that, when he was just starting out, Jeffries had served as Corbett's sparring partner, but had proved so clumsy that he had been relegated to the task of helping rub Corbett down after his sparring sessions. Proudly, the new senior trainer told reporters that the past was of no account. 'I volunteered my services to Jeff to help him in his heroic one-man crusade.'

Also in the entourage was Joe Choynski, the greatest heavyweight of his era never to win the title, a victor over Johnson when the black fighter was just starting out. He had also fought a draw with Jeffries; so he could be forgiven for feeling a little resentful at being little more than a glorified sparring partner when the two principals in the fight were sharing more than $200,000, and this attitude carried over into his work about the camp.

Choynski had always had a shrewd eye for a dollar. The dropout son of a Yale-educated newspaper editor, he had been the first fighter to refuse to fight for the customary 80–20 per cent split for winner and loser. To be on the safe side, he always asked for a 50–50 division. He was a fine fighter; Jeffries and Johnson both conceded that he was the hardest hitter they had encountered. Corbett had beaten Choynski but also had a healthy respect for him, even if he did refer to him now and again as 'a little runt'.

Making up the rest of Jeffries's training team were the pompous William Muldoon, Civil War veteran and former heavyweight wrestling champion of the world; a notable black fighter called Bob Armstrong; and another one-time wrestling champion, Martin 'Farmer' Burns.

With Jeffries in a highly nervous state and surrounded by such a collection of luminaries, it was only to be expected that there would be disputes. Jeffries was always sullen before a fight and his enormous weight-reduction programme had shredded his nerves.

The first conflict occurred when Jeffries would not obey Corbett's order to rise at five o'clock in the morning to start his road work. The fighter had refused, snarling, 'Don't tell me what to do; I've got to do the fighting.' And as time passed, Jeffries was pushed almost to breaking point by William Muldoon's constant reminders – 'Remember, Jim, you must win for the white race.' To make matters worse, in a public sparring session with the 42-year-old Choynski, Jeffries could hardly land a punch on his elusive opponent. The *Baltimore Express* said, 'the aged Choyniski [*sic*], lean and fit and hard as nails, appeared in white tights as the first victim. Choyniski has been working long enough to show some real speed and wind and he went after the big bear with a succession of left hooks and chops at the head . . .'

After this opening debacle Jeffries had to be talked out of abandoning the whole project. Corbett persuaded him to stay by promising that the former champion would not be asked to do so much sparring. This attracted the opprobrium of many of the former fighters visiting the camp. Indeed, the straight-talking Stanley Ketchel was banned from the site for commenting loudly on Jeffries's lack of serious ring work.

The middleweight was not the only one to be denied access to the training camp. Even the great John L. Sullivan was turned away by his former conqueror, Corbett, who had taken exception to a remark in Sullivan's ghosted column in the *New York Times* in which he referred to his belief that Jeffries could only win if the fix was in. Corbett and Sullivan had a heated argument at the door of the cottage Jeffries occupied on the site, before the older man turned and stalked off in a huff. Tex Rickard and Muldoon had to work quickly to effect a reconciliation between the two old champions the next day. Even so, the *San Francisco Chronicle* got wind of the situation and celebrated it with a banner headline: 'Corbett in Hot Words, Bars Sullivan from Jeffries' Camp'. Corbett, disgusted by all the controversy and by Jeffries's stubborn refusal to spar more, told a friend dismally, 'He's worrying. This isn't the Jeff I used to know.'

All sorts of people were turning up at the camp flourishing press credentials and representing themselves as fight experts. The novelist Jack London, back on a temporary winning streak after the publication of his celebrated boxing short story *A Piece of Steak* in the *Saturday Evening Post*, arrived fresh from being mostly on the losing side in a couple of saloon brawls in Reno. He had been doing Rickard's job for him by vigorously beating the drum in the *New York Herald* for the 'Fight of the Century', declaiming, 'And so I say again to all you men who love the game, have the price and are within striking distance, come. It is the fight of fights, the crowning fight of the whole ring, and perhaps the last great fight that will ever be held.'

Ignoring Johnson's roster of victories over white opponents, many refused to believe that the black fighter was capable of defeating such a paragon as Jeffries. In the *Chicago Tribune*, Alfred Henry Lewis was curtly and cruelly dismissive of the whole race: 'As essentially African, Johnson feels no deeper than the moment, sees no farther than his nose, and is incapable of anticipation. That same cheerful indifference to coming events has marked others of his race even while they were standing in the very shadow of the gallows.'

At the training camp, missing all the obvious signs, London reported that Jeffries was 'kittenish and frisky in a huge way, full of "joshes" and bubbling with grim laughter'. Best-selling novelist Rex Beach, basking in the success of his Alaskan gold-rush novel *The Spoilers*, was at hand to make the confusing statement, anatomically speaking, that he considered Jeffries unbeatable because his rib cage was so pronounced that no fighter could penetrate it to strike at the white fighter's vital organs.

However, Jeffries's entourage were soon quarrelling fiercely and openly among themselves and with anyone who dared to criticise their training methods. When former middleweight champion Billy Papke foolishly told Farmer Burns that Jeffries was not looking good, the dispute developed into an open slanging match. Papke did not back off, although it might have been better for the middleweight if he had. Instead he took a couple of swings at the 47-year-old Burns. The old grappler smashed the other man to the ground in a wrestling hold and made him concede defeat in front of more than 400 spectators at the training session.

Next a dispute flared up between the old opponents James J. Corbett and Joe Choynski. Whether they were in disagreement as to the training regime being imposed by Corbett or whether they were just reliving their old scraps is not clear, but the increasingly sullen and reclusive Jeffries had to be called from the shelter of his cottage to make the adversaries simmer down and shake hands. A press photograph of the event was published, with the inscription, 'Jeffries the Peacemaker'.

In a forlorn attempt to lighten the situation two entertainers were recruited in the shapes of minstrel Eddie Leonard and comedian Walter Kelly. The two rather bewildered men settled in the camp, but there was no discernible improvement in the overall morale.

The patient Rickard was having a few problems with Johnson as well. The champion, who had arrived on 26 June, had taken to driving at high speeds outside his training camp in his yellow roadster. When cautioned by the police for dangerous driving, he had proved obstreperous. The promoter was called in to persuade Johnson to lock his car away until after the fight. Then the champion sacked manager George Little after losing a poker hand to him, claiming, probably with justification, that he had been cheated. Eventually, Little was grudgingly restored to the fold, only to fall out with the champion once more when Etta Duryea told Johnson that the manager had made advances towards her and had even presented her with a diamond ring. This time the manager and fighter parted permanently, and Sig Hart took on the mantle of sole handler, although everyone knew that Johnson was very much his own man and always had been.

When Hugh D. McIntosh arrived at Rick's Resort, he thought that the champion looked oddly lethargic in his preparations against his main sparring partner, former challenger Al Kaufmann. The tall white fighter had fought only two unconvincing no-decision bouts with Philadelphia Jack O'Brien since losing to Johnson in San Francisco the year before, and was glad of the work, even if Johnson did patronise him mercilessly.

When the Australian voiced his fears, Johnson confided in him that he was only taking things easy in order to lengthen the betting odds against him. He advised his Australian promoter to back him with as much as he could afford. Reassured, McIntosh backed the champion for almost $20,000 at odds of ten to seven against.

Up until the last moment the vast majority of the white public could not envisage defeat. Among many similar forecasts, one contemporary magazine, *Current Literature*, departed from its customary review of books to mention the forthcoming fight and to express the view that Jeffries was bound to win as the brain of a white man was far superior to that of a black. The *Omaha Daily News* was one of hundreds of publications to concur, stressing the importance of the bout and predicting that Jeffries would defeat Johnson '. . . and restore to the Caucasians the crown of elemental greatness as measured by strength of brow, power of heart and lung, and withal, that cunning of keenness that denotes mental as well as physical superiority'.

Jeffries, always a solitary, dour man, withdrew further into himself. He took to going off alone, ostensibly on fishing trips. A reporter from the *New York World* came across the ex-champion standing amid the rushing waters of a river in spate, talking morosely to himself. Displaying unexpected consideration and tact, the journalist tiptoed away.

Despite the evidence of their eyes, many reporters tipped Jeffries to win. This was reflected in the bookmakers' odds. The contest attracted worldwide attention. Special trains to Reno were chartered from most major cities in the USA. About fifty Pullman cars stood in the station, serving as overflow sleeping accommodation for the packed hotels. Those who could not get to Reno flocked to their local telegraph offices to hear blow-by-blow accounts transmitted from the ringside. In Chicago, spectators paid to watch electronic figures on a large screen act out the movements in the ring being relayed by the telegraph operators. The wealthy railway magnate Cornelius Vanderbilt had a telegraph line erected from Reno to his Rhode Island home, allowing his guests to follow the progress of the fight.

In London, the *Daily Telegraph* report of the fight, on 5 July, stated, 'As early as nine o'clock crowds began gathering in front of newspaper offices in Fleet Street, anxious for news of the fight. An hour later the numbers in one part alone had reached nearly a thousand, and by eleven o'clock three times as many had assembled, spreading across the street, almost from side to side.'

It was much more than a title fight. Many believed that the honour of the white race was at stake. Police authorities in a number of cities cancelled all leave for their officers. Armed deputies patrolled Reno to keep order between the races. Wilson Mizner, who had accompanied Stanley Ketchel to the fight, noted ominously, 'A vast multitude of Negroes had come to see this fight and it was freely predicted that if Johnson won, all these Negroes would not get safely home.'

On the night before the fight, according to the testimony of his wife, Jeffries spent hours standing shivering in his nightgown at their open bedroom window, saying nothing and staring sightlessly out into the dark. Soon after the fight was over Mrs Jeffries told the

New York Times that her husband had had to be dissuaded from withdrawing. The only cloud on Johnson's horizon on the day of the bout was an attempt by a process server to thrust upon him a writ from the estranged George Little.

The usual crowd of 'sports' seen at all major contests had arrived for the event. The *New York Morning Telegraph* of 3 July reported on some of the colourful characters present. They included the Two-By-Six Kid, Oregon Jeff and Bull Con Jack. All of them were going through hard times. The reporter commented, 'Men that to my absolute knowledge could not ask the captain what time the ship left if tickets around the world were a dime a smash seem to have arrived on the scene a little the worse for wear.'

At noon, the gates of the yellow-pine ampitheatre were opened, with fifty off-duty law-enforcement officers frisking spectators for concealed weapons in case an attempt should be made on Johnson's life. As its members flocked in, the largely white crowd sang such hit songs of the day as 'All Coons Look Alike to Me', and one specially written for the contest, the oddly named 'Jim-a-da-Jeff':

> Who give-a da Jack Jonce one-a little-a-tap?
> Who make-a him take a big long nap?
> Who wipe-a da Africa off-a da map?
> It's da Jim-a-da-Jeff . . .

The fight took place on a sweltering 4 July, Independence Day and thus a public holiday. At 1.30 in the afternoon both boxers entered the ring. Johnson was wearing a long dressing gown and was sheltered from the broiling sun by an acolyte carrying an umbrella. Jeffries was hustled into the ring accompanied by seven seconds. He wore an old suit over his fighting shorts and had a flat cap on his head to shield his eyes from the sun.

Rickard entered the ring knowing that the promotion was a financial success if not a sell-out. Admission had been paid by 15,760 spectators, and there were almost 700 in on complimentary tickets. The unsold seats were filled when an estimated mob of 1,500 people gatecrashed over the fence. Seats in special boxes cost fifty dollars each, ringside seats went for forty dollars, while standing room in a distant enclosure cost ten dollars. The title bout was the only fight on the bill. Exaggerated accounts circulated of the amounts the two participants were to be paid. In the end, Johnson received $145,600, while Jeffries was paid $192,066.

From the opening bell, Jeffries never had a chance. He was cut to ribbons by the jeering, ever-smiling champion. Jeffries, like Burns before him, went forward bravely, but he was meeting a well-conditioned Johnson at the top of his form. For the first twelve rounds, Johnson handled his opponent like a baby, pushing him back in the clinches and cutting his face with sharp hooks and jabs.

In the fifth round Johnson started chatting to the spectators at ringside, a sure sign that he knew that he had nothing to beat. From the first round Corbett had been shouting obscenities at the black fighter in a vain effort to distract him. Johnson merely smiled. On one occasion he bundled the hapless and dazed Jeffries to the ropes above the white-faced Corbett. 'Where do you want me to put him, Mr Corbett?' he enquired with a gold-toothed smile. Corbett swore again. Johnson ripped a right into Jeffries's body that made the ex-champion groan. 'How about that one, Jim?' Johnson asked, gazing down enquiringly at Corbett. He returned his attention to the helpless Jeffries. 'Come on, now, Mr Jeff, let's see what you've got,' he invited, whipping his blood-soaked glove into the other man's face.

When the bell went for the start of the fifteenth round Jeffries had to be helped out of his stool by his depressed seconds. He staggered towards the waiting Johnson, who knocked him to the canvas with a right hand. Jeffries slid under the ropes but groggily pulled himself back to his feet. Johnson floored him again. Jeffries got up at the count of nine. The crowd was howling for Rickard to stop the fight in order to protect the white fighter from the humiliation of a knockout. The referee hesitated. Johnson grinned and moved in. Jeffries swayed, his hands at his sides, eyes blank and head lolling helplessly. A right hand exploded on his mouth and the white man went down for the third time.

He got up again but it was all over. Rickard stopped the bout, led the rubber-legged Jeffries back to his corner and returned to hoist the champion's hand in a sign of victory. Johnson, probably tongue-in-cheek, offered to give his gloves as souvenirs to Jeffries and Corbett, but was hustled away out of danger by Sig Hart.

In his syndicated newspaper column Rex Beach summed up the views of the white spectators at the bout: 'Today we saw a tragedy. A tremendous, crushing anticlimax has happened and we are dazed.' The headline of the *San Francisco Chronicle* of 5 July summed it all up: 'Johnson Wins Easily in Fifteenth Round'. Graceless as ever, Jack London commented sourly that faster, better fights could be seen every day of the year in many of the smaller clubs in the land. In his ghosted column John L. Sullivan called it a poor, one-sided fight but conceded that Johnson had fought fairly. The *Los Angeles Times* warned its few black readers grimly, 'Do not point your nose too high. Do not swell your chest too much. Do not boast too loudly.'

Nevertheless, when news of the result got out there were the long-feared race riots. On 6 July the *New York Times* announced:

Deaths from Fight Riots
In these cities fatalities resulted from fights
Occasioned by the Johnson victory at Reno:

New York City	1
Uvalda, Ga	3
Little Rock, Ark.	2
Houston, Texas	1
Omaha, Neb.	1
Mounds, Ill.	1
Tyler, Texas	1
Total	10

There were other disturbances in Ohio, California and Pennsylvania. Many black people were assaulted and eventually it was estimated that some fourteen had been lynched, shot or knifed as a direct result of the big fight. In Pittsburgh, blacks ejected whites from streetcars. In Norfolk, Virginia, sailors from the naval base battled with blacks in the streets, and marines had to be called out to restore order. Future trumpet great Louis Armstrong recalled that as a 10-year-old boy he had to flee through the streets of New Orleans in order to escape a white mob which had just heard the result of the title fight.

Congress itself sought to prevent audiences witnessing the humiliation of a white fighter at the hands of a black by hastily passing a bill forbidding films of the fight to be transported from one state to another. A half-hearted attempt to get round this stipulation by placing chairs and a film projector on the United States side of the border and a gigantic screen on the Canadian side came to nothing.

The victory made Johnson rich, at least temporarily, but it finished him in the USA. He confined himself to repeating what everyone already knew, that he was the best heavyweight boxer in the world, and made no attempt to become a spokesman for his race, although black journalists and civic leaders urged him to take on this responsibility. Nevertheless, his confrontational, flamboyant personality made him a marked man. He was regarded by the white establishment, especially after the post-Reno riots, as a threat to good order throughout the land.

Overt efforts were made to bring him to heel. The following year Representative Seaborn Roddenberry of Georgia introduced a constitutional amendment to ban interracial marriages. In the immediate aftermath of the Jeffries fight at least two southern white ministers advocated from the pulpit that Jack Johnson should be lynched.

The day after the fight, James J. Jeffries was interviewed by reporters as he boarded a train with his wife Frieda to return to the farm. 'I guess it's all my own fault,' he said. 'I was getting along nicely and peacefully on my alfalfa farm, but when they started calling for me, and mentioning me as the white man's hope, I guess my pride got the better of my good judgment.' In reply to a question from one of the writers he shook his great bruised and battered head. 'I don't think I could have beaten Jack Johnson at my best. I don't think I could have beaten him in a thousand years,' he said.

The newspapers describing the fight were universally condemnatory, even in faraway Great Britain. The *Daily Telegraph*

86

snapped, 'The days of the ring are over. Whatever glories it once possessed have vanished. The Reno encounter was deplorable, not only because it was disgusting but because it aggravates the coloured problem.' The London *Daily News* sniffed, 'The only hopeful light about the affair is the growth of the American resolve that this shall be the last.' Even the stately *Times* delivered its own rather muddle-headed reproof: 'If the old-fashioned, straight-forward fighting had prevailed at Reno, Jeffries would never have been knocked out.'

One significant side effect of the Reno bout was the withdrawal of James W. Coffroth as a major player in the White Hopes stakes. The promoter of the Ketchel–Johnson title fight and many other championship contests was virtually legislated out of the fight game in 1910 when the State of California, alarmed by the direction the sport was taking, banned prizefighting. Deprived of his power base, Sunny Jim abandoned promotion, apart from one brief return in the First World War. Instead he redirected his considerable energies to the profitable organisation of horse racing.

6

'HIS CHIN BEGINS AT HIS KNEES!'

In the first decade of the twentieth century, sport was becoming an increasingly important adjunct to daily life in Great Britain. Its profile was raised even higher when the 1908 Olympics were held in London. The Games formed part of the Franco-British Trade Exhibition and were held at the newly constructed White City stadium, capable of housing 70,000 spectators.

From the start the Games were wreathed in controversy. The British newspapers, offended by the self-confidence displayed by some of the visitors, launched a virulent anti-American campaign. The Americans sought to prevent Tom Longboat, a Native American representing Canada, from running in the distance events, claiming that he was a professional. The Swedish wrestlers walked out of the Greco-Roman wrestling. In the final of the shot-put the English representative, James Barratt, had to withdraw when an American rival dropped the shot on his ankle. The American tug-of-war team withdrew from their match against the City of Liverpool Police, representing Britain, because the policemen were wearing boots.

The most hotly disputed event was the final of the 400 metres. Officials claimed that the three American finalists had impeded the British entry, Lieutenant Wyndham Halswelle. The judges therefore broke the tape before the leading American could breast it, and insisted that the race be rerun. The Americans refused to compete again, so Halswelle ran the final on his own.

The officials were in the news again in the marathon. This started from the royal lawn at Windsor Castle, so that Queen Mary could witness it. Subsequent marathons were run over the distance from Windsor Castle to the White City stadium, 26 miles, 385 yards. A shepherd from Capri, Dorando Pietri, entered the stadium ahead of the other runners, but collapsed from exhaustion before he could reach the finish. Officials helped him over the line but the shepherd was disqualified for not completing the course unaided.

The gold medallist at the London Olympics who attracted the most attention among the fight fraternity was the boxing heavyweight champion, an East End police constable called Albert Oldman. Managers offered him blandishments and contracts. The canny Oldman refused both. Instead he parlayed his fighting reputation into a job as a sergeant in the Ceylon police force, where he remained for years in untroubled tropical bliss. Some wondered at the policeman's apparent lack of fistic ambition, until it was pointed out by realists that Oldman's path to Olympic gold had consisted of knocking out his initial opponent in the opening round, securing byes due to withdrawals through injuries in the next two heats, and then in the final knocking out his second, extremely exhausted adversary almost with the first punch he threw.

By 1908, the year in which Jack Johnson first visited the country in his pursuit of Tommy Burns, boxing was becoming a popular sport in Great Britain. The stately National Sporting Club catered for aristocratic and wealthy patrons of the sport, while at the other end of the scale there existed a variety of dubious and occasionally riotous small halls. What was lacking was a visionary promoter who could make fighting with gloves appealing to the middle classes.

The London halls ranged from the Bermondsey School of Arms, with room for only several hundred spectators, to Wonderland, off the Whitechapel Road, capable of housing ten times that number. Some music halls utilised their spare capacity by running boxing tournaments in the afternoon, while scattered about were boxing booths in which local champions took on all comers at weekends and on public holidays. In the smaller halls, preliminary fighters did not get paid by the promoters, but relied on putting up crowd-pleasing fights and earning 'nobbings' as they went round with their hats afterwards.

The National Sporting Club had opened its doors in 1891 and was widely regarded as the headquarters of British boxing. It was an autocratic, parsimonious institution, with the referee officiating from outside the ring and no cheering allowed during the rounds. It seated a thousand members and their guests, most clad in evening dress. Its season ran from October to June, when tournaments were held on Monday nights. Patrons would usually dine in the club first and be summoned to the auditorium by an electric bell for the first bouts at 8.45 in the evening. It instituted the system of Lonsdale Belts to be presented to British champions, but also undertook the self-imposed ordinance of declaring that only fights taking place in the club would be considered as being official championship fights.

In the more plebeian halls, prices of admission ranged from three pence at the Canning Town booth, where the fearsome black fighter Peter Felix repelled up to a dozen brawny challenges a day, to the newly established Ring on the east side of Blackfriars Road. Here there were three separate bills a week. Ringside seats cost three shillings but cab drivers were allowed in for half-price after nine-thirty at night.

Most of the arenas, even the more salubrious ones, could be dangerous places. Fights between betting gangs prowling the halls were common, and an unpopular decision from a referee could easily cause a riot, with glass bottles being hurled down from the gallery at the heads of spectators at the ringside. Sometimes an enterprising pickpocket would turn off the gas lighting at the meter, while his associate 'dips' hurried through the gloom, extracting wallets from the pockets of bewildered marks.

One of the worst and most highly determined examples of organised crime at a boxing tournament took place at an open-air arena at the Memorial Ground in Canning Town on 31 July 1909. American Jimmy Britt was fighting the British Johnny Summers in their third encounter. The previous two bouts had been spectacular and their rubber match had attracted a huge crowd. Britt had just been knocked out in the ninth round, when a wave of over a hundred thugs rushed into the arena from behind, knocking spectators to the ground and robbing them in an orchestrated frenzy of mayhem. Sports writer James Butler, who was present, wrote, 'It was daylight robbery on a gigantic, wholesale scale.

Watch-chains were snapped, race glasses cut from straps with razors, wallets lifted unceremoniously, even spectacles snatched from their owners' noses!'

It was estimated that the thieves got away with several thousand pounds that afternoon. The thugs even chased patrons out of the arena as far as the local railway station, knocking them down and robbing them in the street. When matters had cooled down a little and Summers and Britt, the participants in the main event, went to the office to get their purses, they discovered that the entire takings had been stolen as well. Each boxer received only a fraction of his promised purse.

Nevertheless, thousands of fans followed boxing from a safe distance and encouraged the developing search for a national White Hope. However, the sport's patrons prided themselves, on very little available evidence, on being men without prejudice, as exemplified by a paragraph in the first edition of the magazine *Boxing*, which pontificated, 'We in this country do not care much if the champion be white or black, so long as he is "a good fellow" and conducts himself as a boxer should.'

The first White Hope to appear on British soil was a most unlikely character. His name was William Ian 'Iron' Hague, a former fairground boxer from Mexborough in Yorkshire. He had been given his nickname as a schoolchild because he never cried when he was given the strap or cane. He was also famed locally for his willingness to smash his fist into a brick wall for a halfpenny.

A gargantuan eater, heavy drinker and chain-smoker, the stocky Hague could hardly have been called a natural boxer, but he was brave and the possessor of a heavy right swing. After a brief spell down the pits Hague began to supplement his income by challenging booth fighters for a few shillings at travelling fairs. It was hard work but not as difficult as chipping away in the dark with a pick in 8in of headroom in cold, dark, damp tunnels.

Hague ran away from home at the age of 16 to become a travelling boxing-booth fighter. He fought up to a dozen times a day, scrapping at night by the light of paraffin lamps, with fresh sawdust occasionally strewn on the ground to conceal the blood. Hague was paid twelve shillings a week if he won consistently, while the challengers would get five shillings if they lasted the distance of three rounds. When there were no challengers from the crowd, Hague would go in with the booth odd-job man, called Ginger, who would challenge the booth heavyweight from the crowd in a faked 'gee' fight. Fight fans who were in the know would sometimes slip Ginger half a crown to turn the bout into a genuine one, forcing Hague to punch back with all his force.

Soon the big-punching Mexborough heavyweight got noticed, and a local businessman called Billy Biggs offered to become his patron if Hague would allow a well-known local welterweight called Tommy Stokes to spar with him and give his opinion of the big man's potential. Hague emerged with credit from the sparring session, being given the accolade of a coming lad.

There was no doubt as to Hague's willingness and power of punch, but thus far he had not been fully tested by the drunken novices challenging him at the fairgrounds. In order to judge Hague's stamina and courage, a bare-fist fight to the finish, to be held in a field, was arranged with a district colliery champion. Again Hague emerged with flying colours. He was given one pound for his trouble and launched upon his professional career.

At first, the 18-year-old, 14-stone Iron Hague fought almost entirely in the North of England. The powerful youth did well, and after one victory against a miner he was declared the pitman's champion. Next he was given his biggest challenge to date by being matched in Doncaster against Albert Rogers for the Heavyweight Championship of Yorkshire. When the promoter Billy Bridgewater was asked by what right he was bestowing this title on the winner, he cannily invited his questioners to dispute with the winner his right to be called the best big man in the county. There were no takers.

The bout was held in 1905, with 4-oz gloves, over twenty rounds, for a purse of £30 and a side-stake of £25. Side-stakes were usually provided by the backers of a fighter, who would divide the winnings with their man. Sometimes, before a fight, a hat would be passed among the spectators in order to provide the agreed side-stake. Before the contest started it was agreed with referee Tom Gamble that he would officiate with the side-stakes in his pocket. Before the last round started, he would tot up the scores and, depending upon the action in the last round, he would walk straight over and give the money to the victor as he raised the fighter's glove.

This was a necessary precaution. It was a custom of the time that, when a fight ended, a decision would not be valid unless the side-stakes had been handed to the winner. If the referee was still adding up his score, the gangs of betting boys would exploit this caveat by jumping into the ring, if they thought that their man had lost, and forming a threatening line to prevent the official walking across and paying up.

The fight with Rogers took place before a large crowd in the Doncaster Drill Hall. Hague had even been given the luxury of a personal trainer before the bout, but had started as he meant to go on by completely disregarding the finesse of the boxing art. When his handler tried to persuade the heavyweight to use his left hand, Hague had merely grunted that he had a perfectly good right and would rely on that. In fact, it was all that he needed against Rogers. He knocked his opponent down with it in the sixth round, prompting Rogers's seconds to throw in the towel.

As a result of his early successes, over the next four years Hague was gradually matched with better-class opponents, although he was still fortunate to be paid much more than ten shillings a bout. His most notable victim during this period was the black American middleweight Frank Craig, whom he defeated in Sheffield in four rounds. Known as the Coffee Cooler, Craig had once been challenged in a restaurant to a street fight by a 15-stone local bully. When the other man would not go away, Craig excused himself to his companion, saying that he would be back before the cup of coffee on the table had cooled. True to his word he had taken the other fighter outside, chilled him with one punch and returned to resume his coffee and conversation.

Craig had been touring the northern music halls with a demonstration of buck-and-wing dancing and an exhibition of the latest terpsichorean craze, the cakewalk. The dancing was followed by a challenge to any man in the audience to last three rounds with him. Shortly before his bout with Hague in 1908, the black fighter had achieved a certain notoriety after being involved in a riot in Sunderland. In his challenge match at a local theatre, Craig knocked out the steelworks champion with the first punch he threw. This incensed the stricken man's workmates in the audience and they stormed the stage to deal with Craig, forcing the manager to drop the heavy safety curtain.

Craig locked himself in his dressing room, while the angry crowd waited for him outside. Unfortunately, a black acrobat on the bill, who bore a superficial resemblance to the middleweight, emerged from the stage door first and was badly beaten.

Between fights, Hague usually returned to the tough world of the touring booths. After his victory over Craig, the British heavyweight was regarded as a coming man and was signed up by Jim Watson's prestigious booth to travel round the different northern fairs. Hague was such a major draw that Watson only hired one other fighter to accompany the heavyweight. This was the bantamweight Joe Goodwin, a veteran of over 300 fights.

It was intended that on their travels Goodwin would meet challenges from everyone under 11 stone, while Hague would take on the huskier members of the crowd. The massive sum of £5 was offered to anyone lasting three rounds with either booth man. As a pound a week was an acceptable wage at this time, the booth offering was large indeed and drew many would-be survivors.

On one occasion, at Northampton, a burly heavyweight of a miner refused to meet Hague, insisting on meeting the 9-stone Goodwin instead. Many of the collier's workmates were with him, so to refuse the challenge would have risked the tent being torn down. Reluctantly Goodwin gave away more than 4 stone and went in with the big man. Hague and Watson, the booth proprietor, did their best to assist their diminutive colleague. They talked the miner into allowing both fighters to wear lethal 4-oz gloves, instead of the usual 'pillows', in the hope that Goodwin would land a few hard blows early on, before the miner's superior strength told.

Admission prices were doubled, but the tent was still packed. As another way of aiding Goodwin, Watson acted as timekeeper while the burly Hague stood over him, scowling menacingly at any of the miner's friends seeking to glimpse the amount of time being shown on the watch. They both knew that Goodwin's only chance was to defeat the miner in the first few rounds.

Goodwin's initial barrage disconcerted the collier and drove him back. Hague and Watson saw to it that the three-minute round lasted more than five minutes, only ringing the bell when Goodwin showed signs of slowing up. The miner had shipped so much punishment during the extended first round that he came out discouraged and exhausted for the second session. Goodwin immediately whipped over a right to the jaw, knocking the collier senseless. After so much action the crowd went home, happily carrying their semi-conscious champion with them.

Soon afterwards, as a result of his success over Craig, Iron Hague was invited by the National Sporting Club to enter a competition it was holding for novice heavyweights. Hague knocked out all his opponents to win the tournament. In 1909 he was invited by the impressed NSC to fight for the British championship at the National Sporting Club. His opponent was the champion, Gunner Moir, a squat, heavily tattooed man with a good right hand. Jim Moir had last defended his championship two years earlier with a first-round knockout in 169 seconds against Tiger Smith, and he was expected to dispose of his overweight opponent with similar ease.

Hague scored a surprise when he connected early on with his right swing and knocked out the Gunner in the first round. The time was 167 seconds, two seconds less than it had taken Moir to beat Smith. For this Hague received his largest purse to date, £350.

Hague was entering the big time at an opportune moment. Britain was basking in pre-war prosperity, and sporting events were being well attended. Association football, once centred mainly in the north, became a national sport after Tottenham Hotspur defeated Sheffield United 3–1 in the 1901 Cup Final and redeemed the honour of southern clubs; cricket also attracted many spectators.

The new champion returned to Mexborough in triumph and was met by a large crowd. Hague celebrated by throwing handfuls of coins out of his cab window to children in the street as he was driven home. Six weeks later he had the most important bout of his career and one that cemented his position as a temporary White Hope. In the previous year, when Jack Johnson had visited great Britain en route to Rushcutters Bay in Australia, he had promised the committee of the National Sporting Club that, if he beat Tommy Burns there for the title, he would return to London and defend it against Sam Langford at the club.

Once he had won the championship, Johnson refused to honour his commitment to the club. This might have had something to do with the circumstances of his first visit to the NSC, when he was ordered to wait in the hall while his white manager Sam Fitzpatrick was invited into the inner sanctum to discuss terms for the bout.

Hague was brought in as a substitute to fight the great Langford. While he and Moir had been preparing for their British title fight, both boxers had been asked by Arthur 'Peggy' Bettinson, manager of the club, if they were prepared to fight the black boxer. Displaying a strong sense of self-preservation, Moir had replied immediately, 'No, sir!' Equally true to form, Hague had enquired vaguely who Langford was. When it was explained to him that the man regarded as second in the world among the heavyweights only to Jack Johnson stood but 5ft 6in tall and weighed less than 12 stone, the Mexborough man replied, 'Fight him? I'll knock his head off!'

True to form, the chain-smoking, hard-drinking and lazy Hague did no training for the fight, as he was still celebrating winning the British title. Although he was now a champion he still appeared on the booths, enjoying the boozy relaxed atmosphere of the fairgrounds. Bettinson, who was to referee the bout, visited Hague a few weeks beforehand to find the Englishman taking an afternoon siesta, his customary cigarette drooping from his lips. When Bettinson asked him why he was not training for Langford, Hague scoffed, 'He doesn't weigh twelve stone, does he? Whatever chance has a man of that weight got with me?'

Former world heavyweight champion, British-born Bob Fitzsimmons, who was on a variety tour of Great Britain, also visited Hague's training quarters at Mexborough's Montague Arms Hotel, but he was so disgusted by the heavyweight's lethargy that he spent most of his time with his back to the ring chatting to his old mentor, 78-year-old former bare-knuckle champion Jem Mace. Almost thirty years before, at his touring booth in faraway New Zealand, it was Mace who had urged Fitzsimmons, then a young blacksmith in Timaru, to turn professional.

For his part, Langford had just as poor an opinion of his opponent as Hague had of him. After the black fighter had sparred a three-round exhibition contest with strongman Thomas Inch at the National Sporting Club, Inch tried to warn Langford and his manager Joe Woodman of the power of Hague's punch. Both men laughed at him, regarding Langford as being far superior in class to the English heavyweight. Woodman was so confident that he bet Langford's entire purse on his man to win.

Hague's manager, on the other hand, did make one effort to gain an advantage for his man. He contacted Frank Craig, whom Hague had beaten several months earlier, and paid him to enlist as one of Langford's sparring partners, to send back messages on the American's progress in training. But Langford and his manager Woodman were too shrewd to believe that a man with Craig's pride would sign on as a mere sparring partner; they guessed the real reason for his appearance at their training camp. Accordingly, at their first three-round sparring session Langford gave Craig such a sustained beating that the other man promptly packed his bag and left.

To everyone's surprise, when the real fight started, on 24 May 1909 at the National Sporting Club, the Yorkshireman briefly got lucky when, in the third round, he landed a heavy swing on Langford's head, sending his opponent crashing to the floor. Only Jack Johnson had ever floored Langford before. When the black fighter got up, Hague bullied him to the ropes and flailed away desperately, but none of his wild blows landed. Langford, who was receiving £2,500, the largest purse of his entire career, recovered his equilibrium and soon made short work of his opponent.

Hague went right-hand crazy, while Langford concentrated on ducking and countering with stiff lefts to the body. In the fourth round Langford pressed forward, jabbed three times to the face, then landed a right to the point of the jaw, which knocked Hague unconscious, giving Langford a quick victory. One of Hague's seconds made a vain attempt to revive the fighter in time by dashing a bucket of water over his prostrate form from the apron of the ring. When Bettinson tried to intervene, Langford waved him back, saying quietly, 'He will not stir, sir.' Bob Fitzsimmons, who was sitting in the audience in full evening dress, was distinctly unimpressed by the British fighter's performance.

Commenting on Langford's grogginess when he rose from the knockdown, *Boxing* lamented, 'Only the fact that Hague was dead out of condition saved him. Iron puffed and blew and could not keep on to his man.'

Nevertheless, Hague's brief moment of glory in the third round was enough to qualify him as a temporary White Hope. There was a tremendous sensation when it was announced that Hague was to be groomed for a contest with Jack Johnson. A man who could floor Langford, it was reckoned, might be able to floor any opponent.

An American syndicate offered to back Hague and take him to the USA. Scornfully the British champion spurned the opportunity, preferring to remain in the proximity of his favourite alehouse. *Boxing* commented sadly on the heavyweight's dereliction of duty: 'All Hague's travelling, hotel and other expenses [were] to be paid,' it reported, 'and, in addition, an allowance of £5 a week was to be made to him for pocket money. Every conceivable facility was to be afforded him to get as fit as possible and to acquire the finest possible training experience.'

Hague's new backer, F.J. Law, owner of the Montague Arms Hotel in Mexborough, tried to persuade his heavyweight to go to the USA as the latest European White Hope, but the insular and unambitious Hague would have none of it. Instead, he went to Plymouth and fought a swinging, aggressive and slightly crazy Irishman, Petty Officer Matthew 'Nutty' Curran. Curran was apt to go off the rails in his enjoyment of a fight, and as a result had been disqualified on a number of occasions. This time Curran connected legitimately with lethal effect quite early on in the fight and Hague had to be supported out of the ring.

Because the bout had not taken place at the National Sporting Club, Hague was deemed by that superior body not to have lost his title. Indeed, the committee now invited him to defend his crown against Bill Chase, a Notting Hill butcher. Chase was a novice who, like Hague before him, had won a competition at the NSC. Chase knocked Hague down early on, but the Mexborough man still had his punch, and he got up to knock the butcher out. This caused one animal-loving member at the ringside to murmur, 'Won't the bullocks be pleased!'

Hague had half a dozen more fights. He lost to Jewey Smith, but again retained his title when the NSC refused to recognise Smith; he then outpointed Smith in a return contest. Next, in 1911, Hague was invited to defend his title at the NSC against Britain's up-and-coming White Hope, Bombardier Billy Wells. Their fight was for the first Lonsdale Belt to be awarded in the heavyweight class. Hague's Yorkshire connections begged their man to take the fight seriously. A victory over Wells would mean the heavyweight securing for himself some very lucrative matches in England against the ever-increasing number of visiting Americans.

In one of the most curious pairings in the history of the sport, he was inducted into the training regime of the aesthetic Welshman Freddy Welsh. An ardent physical culturist and devout vegetarian, Welsh was the British lightweight champion who a few years later would win the world championship at his weight. A strict, harsh, humourless man subject to fits of depression, he harried Hague from morning till night at his training camp.

What was worse, he made the corpulent heavyweight eat just one main meal a day, and a vegetarian one at that. After a morning of running, ball-punching and physical exercises, Hague was allowed to devour a single nourishing plate of potatoes, beans and macaroni cheese, garnished with two poached eggs. To drink, the beer-swilling Mexborough man was given the choice of water or milk. Hague protested long and loud, to no avail, but the chastened and mutinous heavyweight was dispatched to London by his trainer in, by the heavyweight's standards, peak condition.

Early in the fight Hague connected with his overarm right. For a moment Wells tottered, but he recovered to jab his way out of trouble. Gradually he got on top of the game Yorkshireman, flooring Hague four times and ending the bout with a mighty right-hand punch in the sixth round.

Bereft of his title, it was the end of the road for Hague as a White Hope. He fought on, beating a few no-hopers but losing to the good men he encountered in the ring. Immediately after the Wells bout, he met Scot Jim Robb in his home town. He was still showing the effects of Freddy Welsh's strict training regime, causing the *Mexborough and Swinton Times* reporter to comment approvingly of their man, 'He turned out better than I think I have ever seen him and he had a healthy colour.'

Robb never landed a punch or even made a lead. Hague hit him once on the chin. The local reporter wrote, 'Robb tumbled down in an inglorious heap, grovelled on his stomach amongst the resin, was counted out, dragged to his corner, and left the ring explaining to his own seeming satisfaction what had happened.'

A month later, Hague fought another White Hope, the Cumbrian Tom Cowler, who would go on to make quite a stir in the USA. They fought for a side-stake of £25, and Hague was knocked out in eight rounds.

The search for a viable and young English White Hope continued. All over the country promoters wishing to draw the crowds would advertise a White Hope tournament and invite a few inept clumsy giants to swipe away at each other. And there was no shortage of would-be hopefuls. Much was made at the time of the plight of a certain Corporal Lightfoot of the Royal Scots Guards, one of the many huge soldiers who had taken up boxing. He had displayed some skills in the Army as a heavyweight boxer, and managers were eager to buy him out. His regiment refused to let him go, citing the regulation applying to service footballers, who, because of the depredations wreaked upon forces football by the incursions of professional managers, were forbidden from resigning in order to join one of the burgeoning football league clubs.

With Hague out of the reckoning, the time for the emergence of another national White Hope was ripe, and in 1910 it looked as if one had arrived in the person of Bombardier Billy Wells. A well-built, handsome, wavy-haired young man of 22, Wells had achieved considerable success as a heavyweight in Army competitions in India, where he had been serving in the Royal Artillery, culminating in three wins in contests at Poona to take the All-India championship.

Army boxing continued to flourish. In 1908, Colonel Sir Malcolm Fox, Inspector of Gymnasia, led the way by encouraging the Brigade of Guards to hire professionals to teach its men to box according to Queensberry rules, in order to develop aggression in recruits and aid skills in bayonet fighting. Other units had followed this example, and in India young Gunner Wells was coached by the professional Jim Maloney, who had once been a well-respected lightweight.

Maloney had his own training camp, which was sponsored by the military. He had been quick to spot the young heavyweight's potential and had urged Wells to buy himself out and profit from the craze for White Hopes sweeping across Great Britain. Wells was a cautious man but he could see the sense of the experienced fighter's advice. He paid the necessary £21 release fee and returned to England, arranging for Maloney to follow him and become his manager.

Wells had been demobilised with the rank of bombardier, equivalent to corporal, an appellation which he used throughout his ring career, even when he became a sergeant major upon his recall to the colours during the First World War. Soon after he had landed back in Great Britain, Wells went to the offices of the trade magazine, *Boxing*, and asked for advice. The editor, John Murray, arranged for the ex-bombardier to have a private trial with the highly rated and very experienced Gunner Moir. For two rounds Wells boxed beautifully, but in the third the Gunner caught up with him and put him down with a hard body punch. Still, the All-Indian champion had shown up well enough to be offered a job as Moir's sparring partner.

Although he had held the British heavyweight title, Moir was never regarded as a White Hope. He had been defeated in ten rounds in a world-title challenge against Tommy Burns. During this bout, among other sharp practices the crafty Burns had trapped Moir's glove under his arm while he was hitting the Englishman, while also managing to give the impression to referee Eugene Corri that it was Moir who was doing the holding. Afterwards Moir commented on the incident with shocked dignity in his instructional book *The Complete Boxer*: 'I permitted myself, foolishly, to become sufficiently exasperated to draw Mr Corri's attention to the actual state of affairs, with the result that I had my face cut open in two places.'

Wells acquitted himself well in the role of sparring partner to Moir and embarked upon a career as a professional boxer. He started by knocking out Gunner Murray in the first round, attracting the interest of a celebrated referee, Eugene Corri. Corri idly mentioned to a reporter that the young ex-soldier might even one day develop into a fitting opponent for Jack Johnson. The newspaper splashed the story across its sports pages and Wells was famous before he had even emerged from the novice stage. His next fight was against Corporal Brown of the Coldstream Guards in the arena off the Whitechapel Road known as Wonderland. It was there before a large and expectant crowd that the young heavyweight displayed two of the traits that were to prevent his ever scaling the fistic heights – nerves and a soft heart. W. Barrington Dalby, who was in the crowd that night, described in his book *Come In, Barry!* how Wells was literally shaking with fright before the bout. The fighter's seconds did their best to calm their man, but one of them turned to a ringside spectator and muttered in disgust, 'He's no good – too long in the bleeding belly!'

In the first round Wells caught his opponent with a good punch but seemed disinclined to press home his advantage. Taking heart, Brown bundled into his opponent, scoring with some heavy blows. In the second round Brown gained in confidence and started hitting the cautious Wells almost at will. The former champion of all India was booed back to his corner when the bell ended the round. During the interval Wells's chief second did his best to stir his charge, hissing at him the immortal phrase, 'Get out there and get wicked!'

The vehemence of his second and the disapproval of the crowd seemed to transform Wells. At the start of the third round he danced across the ring on his toes, stunned Brown with three superb left jabs and then caught his opponent on the chin with a sweeping right. Brown tottered forward, collapsed and was unconscious for twenty minutes.

After this, for a time Wells could do no wrong. He had received only eighteen shillings for one of his first professional bouts, but he was soon doing much better than that. Crowds flocked to his fights and the handsome young heavyweight with the spectacular straight left became a public idol. The seal was placed on his success when the Australian promoter Hugh D. McIntosh landed in Great Britain and began promoting tournaments in London, living up to his promise of taking boxing away from the fleapits of the East End and the cloistered aristocracy of the National Sporting Club, and making it a sport for the respectable and well-heeled middle class.

In order to do this McIntosh needed a drawing card, preferably a heavyweight White Hope. Again Eugene Corri came to Wells's aid, judiciously recommending the young heavyweight to the Australian promoter. 'I told him that Wells was his man, good-looking, a real clean boxer, and becoming more popular every day as the boxing world was getting to know him.' McIntosh signed up Wells at £100 a contest, and put him in with a series of apelike British heavyweights, emphasising the 'beauty and the beast' aspects of the matches. With one exception, Wells did him proud, scoring a series of knockouts and making even the most cynical fight fan wonder whether at last England might be producing a world-class heavyweight.

Then Wells blotted his copybook. He was matched with the ponderous veteran Gunner Moir. Only a year before, Wells had earned a few shillings sparring with the former champion. A packed house turned out to see the bout, as rumours were spreading that the anticipated walkover against the Gunner was a mere preamble to Wells being matched for the world championship against Jack Johnson.

For three rounds Wells gave Moir a boxing lesson. His glorious left hand was seldom out of his shorter opponent's face. Twice his right hand tumbled Moir to the floor. The crowd cheered and marvelled at the display of a thoroughbred. Towards the end of the third round, Wells smashed Moir to the canvas once more. Groggily the Gunner stood up. Wells measured him lazily with a long left before moving in to apply the closure with his cocked right. As if acting instinctively, the dazed Moir swayed inside Wells's extended left arm and hit the tall man hard in the stomach. The young heavyweight gasped, doubled up and fell to the floor, where he remained while the referee counted him out.

'I felt sure that I had the Gunner beaten to the world by the end of the first round . . .' wrote Wells ruefully in his book *Modern Boxing*. 'He got home one rib drive, however, right at the start, and then proceeded to use his strength in the clinches.'

Dedicated fight fans seemed embarrassed rather than annoyed by Wells's loss. It was claimed that Wells had been handicapped earlier in the fight by his apprehensive manager Jim Maloney shouting, 'Stand back, Bill!', whenever his heavyweight had Moir in trouble.

The Bombardier was too popular and his connections were too good to allow him to be summarily discarded. Less than two months later he was given a chance to redeem himself by being matched against the capable American journeyman Porky Flynn.

Wells rose to the occasion by outpointing the American in a rousing contest dominated by the Englishman's left hand. In the end Flynn, for all his experience, was reduced to scuttling backwards behind a barrier of arms crossed over his head.

Immediately afterwards, referee Eugene Corri and Peggy Bettinson, manager of the National Sporting Club, took Wells to the Fulham gymnasium of professional strongman and boxing enthusiast Thomas Inch, known as the Scarborough Hercules. They asked the physical culturist to take the heavyweight under his wing and develop his physique and strength. Inch put Wells on to a successful regime of lifting light weights, increasing his stamina and punching power.

The wealthy and successful bodybuilding instructor had become a force in the British quest for a White Hope. He announced as much in the weekly *Boxing*. 'Mr Thomas Inch, the famous physical culture expert, is prepared to undertake the full cost of training, etc., any likely applicant. Mr Inch will do all he can for any really good big man who comes forward, being anxious that England should not miss the chance of a prospective world's champion . . .'

Under the tutelage of Inch, Wells was then matched against Iron Hague at the National Sporting Club for the Yorkshireman's British heavyweight title. Wells knocked his opponent out in the sixth round. Afterwards a rueful Hague said that the well-conditioned Wells had hit him harder than Sam Langford had.

That was enough. Wells's backers were not going to risk their prospect getting unravelled again by matching him against some hard-punching second-rater who might connect, as Moir had done, with a lucky punch. The time was ripe to make some serious money in a really big fight. It was announced that Wells would box Jack Johnson in London for the world heavyweight title. To many it did not seem such an unlikely concept. After the Hague fight, the editor of *Boxing* stated, 'Given the necessary strength and stamina and a little more experience of possible dangers Wells should stand a good chance.'

Another subject for the headlines of that year was the arrival in Great Britain of Jack Johnson, heavyweight champion of the world and fugitive from American justice. He had been forced to flee from the USA after being accused of violating the Mann Act by transporting a prostitute across state lines. In effect, all that Johnson had done was travel with his mistress of the time, Belle Schreiber, but this had been enough for the authorities to arrest the champion and then release him on bail. Johnson had skipped the country and was about to embark upon a tour of the music halls, which would take in London, Marseilles, Lyons, Paris, Brussels, Berlin, Bucharest, Budapest and St Petersburg. His twenty-minute act consisted of some bag-punching, a training exhibition, a perfunctory display of dancing and accompanying himself on the bass viol while he sang 'Baby's Sock is a Bluebag Now'.

Journalist Norman Clarke visited Johnson in his dressing room at the Golders Green Hippodrome during this tour and commented on the numerous wardrobe trunks piled in his room, each filled to overflowing with patent leather boots, silk shirts and other expensive items of clothing. Clarke was particularly impressed with Johnson's partner, on and off stage, the white Lucille Cameron. He recalled in his autobiography *All in the Game*, 'Both in figure and face I have rarely seen such a beautiful creature; she had the head and features of a Greek goddess, and when they danced together, as they did in the show, Jack certainly in no way marred the picture.'

The Times gave a cautious and condescending welcome to the black champion. 'He sported rather more gold teeth than are worn by gentlemen in the shires, and enough diamonds to resemble a starry night, but he was on the whole a far more pleasant person to meet in a room than any of the white champions of complicated nationality whom America exports from time to time to these unwilling shores.'

The match was promoted by a shrewd Lancashire financier called Jimmy White. Never afraid to splash out, when White had once failed to find a taxi to take him to an appointment, he had flagged down a London bus, paid its passengers to disembark and then given the driver £5 to take him straight to his destination.

The championship match was scheduled over twenty rounds. Posters were exhibited all over London, advertising the forthcoming bill at the Empress Hall, Earls Court. First, Sid Burns of Great Britain would fight Georges Carpentier of France in a final eliminator for the European welterweight title. This would be followed at ten o'clock sharp by a bout for the World Heavyweight Championship, between Jack Johnson, champion of the world, and Bombardier Billy Wells, champion of England. Seat prices ranged from five guineas at ringside to ten shillings and sixpence. Bombardier Billy Wells could be seen training on Thursdays and Saturdays at 5 p.m.

It was the fight of the century for British fans. Tickets were snapped up almost as soon as they were printed. Then disaster struck. It was announced that strong objections had been lodged against such an interracial bout and that there was a strong demand for the championship contest to be called off.

The demand was being led by the Revd Dr F.B. Meyer, recently appointed as Secretary of the Free Church Council and eagerly looking for a way of publicising himself and his office. He was also looking for a cause through which to rally the different Free Churches under his leadership. Opposition to a boxing match, particularly one with racial connotations, would ally the denominations and provide his council with a crusade. In a skilfully conducted publicity campaign in the newspapers, Meyer reminded the public of the race riots that had occurred after Jack Johnson's victory over Jeffries in Reno, and played up the inherent brutality of boxing, which, he pointed out, still had only semi-legal status in many parts of the world.

People began to take sides in the controversy almost at once. Some participants, and these included more than a few muscular Christians among the clergy, defended the manly art of self-defence. Others were equally fervent in their belief that it was a barbaric exercise carried out, largely unsupervised, in squalid conditions.

Ammunition was given to the anti-boxing squad when no less an authority than Lord Lonsdale, doyen of the National Sporting Club, entered the lists and announced that the Johnson–Wells bout should be cancelled at once, because matching the white man against the black was tantamount to a 2-year-old being forced to fight a 3-year-old. However, critics of the noble patron pointed out coolly that he was probably only jealous because Jack Johnson had spurned the NSC and its niggardly terms.

Public meetings began to be called in London and other large cities to denounce the proposed match. The 'colour question' was increasingly mentioned. The Secretary of the Baptist Union wrote sternly, 'There can be no greater disservice to the Negro race than to encourage it to see glory in physical force and in beating the white man.' A letter to *The Times* gave the testimony of a peer, who stated that an earlier victory of Johnson over a white boxer had caused unrest against colonial rule in Fiji. A contrary opinion was expressed at a meeting of supporters of the tournament, when it was gloomily predicted that banning boxing would almost inevitably lead to an increase in the use of swords and revolvers.

A summons was issued and the principals in the affair suddenly found themselves hauled before the bench at the Bow Street Magistrates' Court, answering a writ issued by the Director of Public Prosecutions.

The defendants were accused of threatening to commit a breach of the peace. The Solicitor-General, Sir John Simon, prosecuted, assisted by Travers Humphries and Richard Muir. Promoter Jimmy White was defended by Eustace Fulton while Wells and the other defendants were represented by Henry Curtis Brown. Jack Johnson, iconoclastic to the end, handled his own defence. His arrival at the court was greeted with cheers from a large crowd waiting outside in the street.

While the defendants were assembling, the Revd F.B. Meyer was busy. He announced to the press that he proposed to accompany the Bishop of London to Balmoral, where the Home Secretary, Winston Churchill, was staying as a guest of King George V. There he would present Churchill with a petition condemning the proposed twenty-round Earls Court fight, signed by the Archbishop of York and many of the land's great and good who were opposed to the bout.

Churchill was too old a hand to be caught in a confrontation with zealots. Hastily he sent Meyer a telegram: 'Matter is receiving close attention. Shall be very glad to receive memorial by post but do not consider it necessary to ask you and the Bishop of London to undertake such a pilgrimage.'

Discussing the forthcoming case, *The Times* commented disapprovingly on the implications should the fight be allowed to continue: 'The effect of an encounter between champions of different colour may not have any meaning for patrons of the 'science' who assemble at Earl's Court, but it will nevertheless be felt in corners of the earth of which they may never have heard.'

When the hearing started, Johnson handled himself very well in the witness box. Shrewdly he cross-examined one of the police witnesses. The officer tried to impress the court by quoting from the rules of boxing. Johnson flashed his lazy grin. 'Officer, you're

109

reading from a record under the ledge of that desk,' he chided. He then asked the superintendent how he knew that the proposed fight would cause a breach of the peace. When the man prevaricated, the champion pressed home his advantage. 'Have you ever seen a boxing match?' he pounced. The officer admitted that he had not. 'You have no idea what they are?' persisted the defendant. The superintendent agreed that he had not. Johnson turned with an air of triumph to the magistrate. 'The witness may go,' he said airily. 'I'm through.'

Before the case could reach its climax the freeholders of Earls Court served an interlocutory injunction to prevent their property being used for the tournament. It was granted, effectively ending the matter. The case against Jack Johnson and his co-defendants was adjourned *sine die*.

As usual the champion had the last word. When the magistrate asked him if he had anything to say, Johnson replied with dignity, 'Speaking for himself, Johnny Johnson wishes to say that he will not box with Mr Wells in the British Isles or anywhere else where the British Government have control.'

The Times, which had earlier been quite welcoming, now turned on the champion, noting sternly that in the USA Johnson was regarded as a 'flash nigger' and that he was 'a type not to be encouraged by those who have to keep ten millions of black men in subjection to the dominant race'.

Disappointed by the cancellation of his proposed bout with Jack Johnson, Wells consolidated his position by knocking out the South African heavyweight Fred Storbeck at the National Sporting Club. During the contest, Storbeck offended Wells by swearing at him. This reaction betrays perhaps unexpected sensitivity in a former ranker, but the English heavyweight almost literally made the South African eat his words by repeatedly ramming a straight left like a telegraph pole into Storbeck's mouth for the remainder of the fight.

There was some talk of a Major Arnold Wilson, the then major promoter, staging a bout in London between Wells and the fast-rising American Luther McCarty for a version of the World Heavyweight Championship, cutting out Jack Johnson altogether.

The fair-minded Wells would have none of it. Johnson was the champion and everyone knew it.

However, there was no doubt that some really promising young heavyweights were coming along in the States. The best way to prepare for a genuine tilt at the title would be for Wells to cross the Atlantic and defeat some of their home-grown White Hopes. Unfortunately, by this time it was widely known that Wells was always susceptible to a heavy punch. A future opponent, the American Frank Moran, said of the British heavyweight disparagingly, 'His chin begins at his knees!'

7

THE HOPES AND HOPEFULS
ASSEMBLE

In the USA, the Johnson–Jeffries fight in 1910, with all its attendant publicity and ramifications, gave boxing an enormous boost. Public interest was fanned even further by Johnson's defiantly arrogant public attitude, and what to the white establishment was his annoying habit of regarding himself as the equal of any other man, no matter what his colour.

To a populace more accustomed to the anodyne stance outside the ring of less aggressive black fighters like the amiable Sam Langford, this was hard to bear. Langford, it was generally agreed, 'knew his place'. Before one of his fights, promoter Hugh D. McIntosh had tried to persuade him to attend a banquet in order to publicise the tournament. According to sports writer Trevor Wignall, who was present, the fighter declined at once. 'I wouldn't feel good with all them white gentlemen,' he averred.

The flamboyant Jack Johnson was succeeding in annoying a considerable proportion of the white population. He was often arrested for dangerous driving, and flaunted an increasing number of white women in his life. After his defeat of James J. Jeffries there was a growing public demand for another white challenger to be found.

There were plenty of hopeful backers looking to find one. All over the country promoters and managers were scuffling to dig up a big white youth who could both take a punch and deliver one. Boxing promised high rewards for fighters sufficiently charismatic or vicious to draw the crowds, especially if they weighed 15 stone or more.

Some of the searchers were big-time managers; others had nothing but glib tongues and hope in their hearts as they searched the highways and byways for the White Hope who would make their fortunes. At the lower end of the scale were impresarios like one-legged Otto Floto, who put on fights in Cripple Creek, Colorado. On Saturday nights Floto would drag fighting drunks out of saloons and propel them to the Butte Opera House, where he would thrust them into a ring and charge a dollar for admission.

Other promoters were more ambitious in their quests for White Hopes. Between them they travelled thousands of miles by train on their bizarre pilgrimages, stopping at every small hall where there might be the possibility of finding a promising big, young white heavyweight. On the West Coast, James J. Coffroth, a lawyer, had matters pretty well sewn up for a time, even if he had lost out to Tex Rickard in the competition to promote the Johnson–Jeffries bout. He was a shrewd, ruthless, cold man, always making alliances and then falling out with his partners. For a time he had promoted fights in San Francisco, but incurred the displeasure of the authorities for a number of reasons. As a result the promoter moved just outside the city limits and built an arena in rural San Mateo County, where he made a lot of money promoting world-title fights in the first decade of the twentieth century.

During the same period in the USA, boxing was legal only in the states of Nevada and California. This was emphasised by the fact that between 1901 and 1915 every heavyweight-title bout promoted in North America was held west of the Mississippi, many of them by Coffroth and his associates.

The Californian had some claim to being boxing's first individual promoter. As a young man he had attended several tournaments in New York, usually put on by shady syndicates. Disgusted by the squalor and inefficiency of these events, the young man had decided to run properly organised promotions with just one man – himself – at the helm.

For all his faults the venal Coffroth realised that in order to succeed as a manager and promoter he had to keep his fighters happy. He had a fixed scale of payment for his main-eventers. He assigned 60 per cent of the gross receipts from his promotions to be divided between the two boxers. In the case of popular headliners this was sometimes increased to 70 per cent. It was left to the participants to decide how they would share their allocation. Sometimes the split would be 75–25, but now and again, in the case of grudge fights, it might be 90–10.

Coffroth boasted that the sun always shone on his West Coast promotions, thus gaining the sobriquet of 'Sunny Jim'. He was also a well-read man and no milksop. At one stage in his career he fell foul of the law, allegedly by attacking the manager of Battling Nelson with a pair of scissors after a dispute while counting the gate receipts for a lightweight-title fight between Nelson and Coffroth's man, Joe Gans.

One of his main rivals in the search for a White Hope, Jack Curley, had made a dubious grubstake from co-promoting the second Gotch–Hackenschmidt wrestling match in Chicago. This was so widely suspected of being fixed that the city police chief stepped into the ring before the contest could start and announced that all bets were off. The resultant scandal caused wrestling to be banned in Illinois for years, and Curley was now looking to promote top-class boxing matches, hopefully featuring his own heavyweight, if he could find or manufacture one.

Curley was a born showman and salesman, promoting anything likely to show a profit and also a number of events that had no chance of a financial return at all. A glib, persuasive one-time newspaper man and unsuccessful heavyweight boxer, he had managed the affairs of the elderly and constantly bickering former bare-knuckle fighters John L. Sullivan and Jake Kilrain as they toured giving exhibitions with tent shows. Over the next few decades he was to promote everything, from flea circuses to political meetings, wrestling shows, operas and boxing championships.

There were dozens of others of greater or lesser importance. Only Rickard, restless and iconoclastic as ever, had departed the scene for the time being. After his controversial Reno promotion, he had left for South America, to become a cattle-rancher in Paraguay, and was not to return for five years.

The only traits that most of the would-be managers and promoters had in common, now that the cold but straight Rickard was no longer around, were a complete lack of probity and a reckless willingness to rob anyone ragged. Rickard had been a Texas border marshal and as a professional gambler had faced down some of the toughest miners in the Yukon. He always claimed that the average boxing manager and promoter made the professional gunfighters he had encountered look like pussy cats.

Jack Blackburn, a top black lightweight of the era, summed up the attitude of his fellow fighters of all colours when he said that whenever he fought, although he took a size 8½ shoe, he always wore size 10s, so that he could keep his purse in them – which he insisted on being paid in advance in silver dollars and twenty-dollar gold pieces – 'otherwise the promoter would have been gone when the fight was over'.

The major managers, like Jack Curley, Jimmy Johnston, Dan McKetrick and Dan Morgan, ran up enormous tabs for feeding, housing and training the huge labourers, lumberjacks and cowboys they were enticing into the gyms with their newspaper adverts for heavyweights of the right skin colour.

Many of the first White Hopes fell by the wayside. Others continued fighting, though merely as cannon fodder for the next wave of aspirants. Managers clinging gamely to the wreckage of their dreams tried to make up for the deficiencies of their white heavyweights by bestowing frightening names on them: George 'One Round' Davies, Tom 'Bearcat' McMahon, 'KO' Bill Brennan, 'Roaring' Al Reich, Joe Muller, the Fighting Gorilla, and so on.

The first White Hope to achieve any prominence from 1911 onwards was a Salpulpa heavyweight, Carl Morris, a railway fireman. When he had attained a certain amount of prominence, his press releases stated that the heavyweight had taken to the professional ring as a result of hearing the result of the Johnson–Jeffries bout at Reno on 4 July 1910. Morris, it was stated, had been coming into Salpulpa in the cabin of a freight train at the time. When he heard the outcome of the fight, he threw down his shovel and swore to enter the ring in order to avenge white honour by taking the title back from the black boxer.

The great Jack Johnson in his prime. *(Getty Images)*

FITZ'S VIEW OF CHAMPION JACK JOHNSON

Where it all began! Jack Johnson and Tommy Burns's heavyweight title bout at Rushcutters Bay, outside Sydney, Australia, on 26 December 1908. *(Antiquities of the Prize Ring)*

A Vancouver cartoonist disparages the efforts of an outclassed Victor McLaglen to come to terms with Johnson in their 1909 no-decision bout held in Canada. *(Daily Province, Vancouver)*

White Hopes Victor McLaglen and Tom Kennedy both went on to have lengthy Hollywood movie careers. Here McLaglen menaces the seated Kennedy in the 1945 film *Rough, Tough and Ready*. *(Author's collection)*

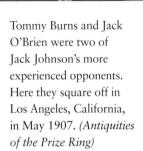

Tommy Burns and Jack O'Brien were two of Jack Johnson's more experienced opponents. Here they square off in Los Angeles, California, in May 1907. *(Antiquities of the Prize Ring)*

Stanley Ketchel prepares for his 1909 title bout against Jack Johnson by training with his black sparring partner, Bob Armstrong. *(Antiquities of the Prize Ring)*

AT WONDERLAND.

Friend of the boy who gave the punch (turning to young man in collar who has criticised aloud). "'IT 'IM BELOW THE BELT, DID 'E! WHERE DO YOU FINK 'IS BELT OUGHT TER BE! RAHND 'IS FURRID!"

This cartoon brings to life Wonderland in London's Whitechapel Road, one of the centres of British boxing in the first decade of the twentieth century. English White Hope Bombardier Billy Wells fought here on his way to the top. *(Punch/Author's collection)*

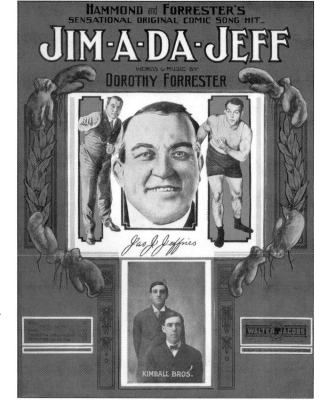

Sheet music for the song 'Jim-a-da-Jeff', lauding the former heavyweight champion James J. Jeffries and sung by the white section of the crowd before Jeffries's unsuccessful comeback attempt against Jack Johnson at Reno in 1910. *(The Lester S. Levy Collection of Sheet Music, Special Collections, The Sheridan Libraries of The Johns Hopkins University)*

The Search ^{for}_a White Champion

(Under the auspices of Mr. Hugh D. McIntosh).

KING'S HALL

(Reached by City & South London and Bakerloo Tubes, and all Trams and 'Buses crossing the Bridges.)

Thursday Evening, Sept. 15th,

COMMENCING AT 8.30 P.M. SHARP.

The first of an eliminating series to find a real British Champion.

Twenty 3-minute rounds between

Bomb. WELLS and Sgt. SUNSHINE

(Regarded as the best Heavy-weight in England.)   (To be in the ring at 10 p.m.)   (Royal Irish Fusiliers. Iron Hague's latest conqueror.)

Mr. Eugene Corri has kindly consented to referee.

A fifteen 3-minute rounds contest between

SID BURNS and P.O. ROCHE

(Aldgate. Considered a World's Champion.)   (To be in the ring at 9 p.m.)   (Winner of the Welter-weight Championship at King's Hall Tournament.)

A ten 3-minute rounds contest between

BILL RAYNER and WALLY PACK

(Islington.)   (Late Lynn A.C.)

A six 3-minute rounds contest between

YOUNG COHEN and HARRY RAY

(Aldgate.)   (Stepney.)

ALL CHAMPION BOUTS.

Reserved Seats, £1 1s. and 10s. 6d. On sale at Keith Prowse, District Messenger Offices, Alfred Hays, and all other Booking Agencies.

General Admission, 5s. and 2s. 6d.

Secretary, JAMES E. BRITT, Room 4, Walter House, Bedford Street, Strand, W.C.

A typical advert from *Boxing* magazine promoting the search for a White Hope to challenge Jack Johnson. *(Boxing/Author's collection)*

Jack Johnson and Al Kaufmann arriving for Johnson's title defence against James J. Jeffries at Reno in 1910. Kaufmann had once been an unsuccessful White Hope opponent of Johnson but this time he had been reduced to the status of sparring partner to the champion. *(Antiquities of the Prize Ring)*

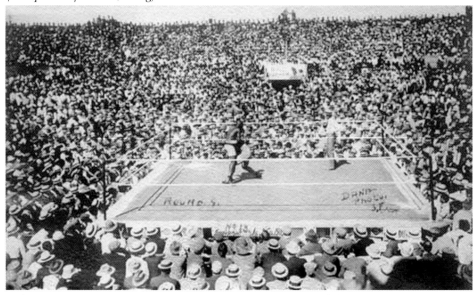

Jack Johnson outclasses James J. Jeffries at Reno. *(Antiquities of the Prize Ring)*

Above: Canadian White Hope Arthur Pelkey. He never won another bout after his opponent Luther McCarty collapsed and died during their contest in Calgary in 1913. *(Antiquities of the Prize Ring)*

Above, right: South African White Hope George 'The Boer' Rodel. His manager claimed erroneously that Rodel had been a hero of the Boer War. *(Antiquities of the Prize Ring)*

Racism was endemic in boxing during Jack Johnson's reign as champion. In this cartoon from a 1913 French magazine the black fighter is complaining that he has been called 'lily-livered'. *(Author's collection)*

A hero outside the ring as well as inside it, French White Hope Georges Carpentier (front) qualified as a pilot during the First World War. *(Author's collection)*

The end of an era. The gigantic Jess Willard, the last White Hope, takes the title from Jack Johnson at Havana, Cuba, in 1915. *(Getty Images)*

It is more likely that Morris, aided and abetted by his friend, a telegraph operator named Bill Stone, realised how much money could be made under the circumstances by a successful white fighter. At first, after turning professional, Morris operated in the Oklahoma region. Cumbersome and slow but the possessor of a mighty punch, the heavyweight won his first seven bouts on knockouts. Among his victims was an over-the-hill but still well-rated Marvin Hart, one-time claimant to the world heavyweight title. There were murmurs, however, that Morris's third-round knockout victory over Hart had been a little too easy, and that perhaps the new heavyweight's record was being padded a little in order to further his career. The *Milwaukee Free Press* even published Morris's rejoinder to such gossip: 'Carl Morris, the Oklahoma hope, is out with a hot denial that his victories have been frame-ups.'

Nevertheless, the civic fathers of Salpulpa took great pride in their rising fistic star. Before long the town's official letter-heading was changed from 'Salpulpa, queen of the great Oklahoma oil-and-gas belt' to a more prosaic 'Salpulpa, home of Carl Morris, Oklahoma's hope of the white race'. Mothers began naming their babies after the new local hero. Excursion trains, no longer stoked by Morris, were run from all over the state so that the heavyweight could be seen in training. To show their gratitude for the publicity he was engendering, the civic fathers launched a public subscription to provide the heavyweight prospect with a free house.

Before long, news of the hard-punching white giant percolated east. Big-city managers began to descend hungrily on Salpulpa, dangling all sorts of incentives before the dazzled eyes of the heavyweight. Bill Stone, the railway telegraphist who had persuaded Morris to turn professional, was bought out early in the deal. The *Milwaukee Free Press* of 30 January 1911 announced, 'Tulsa, Oklahoma. A deal was consummated here late Saturday night and a contract closed by which F.B. Ufer, a wealthy oil man and sportsman of this city, purchased W.F. Stone's contract with Carl Morris, the "hope of the white race", for a consideration of $25,000 . . . Ufer is worth half a million dollars. He is a big oil operator and proposes to make a world's heavyweight champion out of Morris at any cost. Tomorrow he will order equipment for a $5,000 dollar gymnasium with all the latest paraphernalia. He will employ Bob Armstrong, Joe Choynski and other well-known trainers to take charge of Morris.'

Ufer soon lost interest in his new charge and a series of managers began to play 'pass the parcel' with the former fireman. Jack Curley had him for a time, Tom Jones showed a fleeting interest, and towards the end of Morris's career Nate Lewis took over. In between there were plenty of others.

The problem was that Morris soon lost his allure for the money-grabbers. It all went wrong in his first fight in New York, on 15 September 1911. For his introductory bout in the big time, Carl Morris was put in cruelly over his head. He was matched with the veteran Fireman Jim Flynn in a ten-round, no-decision contest in a top-of-the-bill fight at Madison Square Garden. Between 1910 and 1917, the Frawley Law was in operation in New York. It allowed only so-called 'exhibition' bouts over ten rounds, with no decisions being rendered.

If Morris had done well in the eyes of ringside reporters, with a scalp like Flynn's on his belt he would have been fast-tracked into a championship match. But the naive Morris was nowhere near ready for an experienced and fearless, if limited, fighter like Flynn, who knew every trick in the game and had invented a few of his own.

Flynn, born Andrew Chiariglione, in Hoboken, had turned professional in 1901 and had already fought and lost to Jack Johnson, Tommy Burns and Sam Langford. On his way to the ring, where Flynn was waiting, Langford had poked his head round the door of the white man's dressing room. One of Flynn's seconds, a man called Russell, was chopping up a dozen oranges into segments. Langford asked him what was going on.

'The Fireman likes to suck on oranges between rounds,' replied the second brusquely.

Langford shook his head. 'He won't be needing all that fruit,' he said presciently, before heading for the ring, where he knocked Flynn out in the first round.

All the same Flynn was tough and experienced. At 5ft 9in he was short for a heavyweight, but had developed into a swinging, gutsy, dirty, very brave second-rate fighter, far too good for the novice Morris.

Morris's backer, the oilman Frank Ufer, was well aware of this and tried to bribe Flynn 'to go into the tank'. Flynn agreed, once he had bartered the price up to $7,500, to throw the fight. Unfortunately rumours of the impending transaction reached the ears of the fearless sports writer of the *New York Morning Telegraph*, Bat Masterson, a former frontier-town gunslinger of the Old West. In his column of 10 September 1911, Masterson caustically wrote, 'There have been a good many cooked-up affairs pulled off in the prize-ring, as everybody knows, but hardly one quite as daring or that smells so much like a polecat as the one between Flynn and Morris.' Masterson then bullied Fireman Jim into admitting his role in the fix-up and gave the confession the leading spot in his next column.

As a result the fight was conducted fairly, if bloodily. Flynn subjected Morris to a solid thrashing over the entire distance. For a while spectators marvelled at the White Hope's fortitude, but even the most hardened among them eventually became sickened at the slaughter. By the halfway stage the referee had been forced to change into a fresh shirt and the ringsiders, with no changes of wardrobe available, were soaked in Morris's blood. The New York statutes may have declared that no decision could be announced, but reporters covering the contest wrote that Morris had lost by a street and had his inadequacies highlighted in the process.

The next day the *New York Times* described Morris's condition in sickening detail. 'When the bout ended the right side of Morris's face was battered out of shape. His right eye was completely closed in the third round, and not even a bit of surgical work by one of his attendants, who lanced the swollen flesh beneath the eye, did anything to restore sight to the closed optic. His mouth was out of shape, too, and a huge bruise extended from his temple to his lower jaw. It is doubtful if any pugilist has been battered out of shape as he was in this bout.'

It was time for damage limitation. Morris's handlers kept him out of the ring for several months while they employed black star Joe Jeanette to coach their man in the gymnasium. Jeanette did what he could to iron out the more glaring deficiencies in the white man's style, but no one could transform the lumbering former fireman into a skilled exponent of boxing.

There still remained the punch. Morris was always capable of flooring novices and no-hopers, and for a time after the Flynn debacle the heavyweight was fed a diet of glass-jawed second- and third-raters. Before the end of the year he had rehabilitated himself to a certain extent by disposing inside the distance of such unknowns as Bill Bass, Denver Jack Geyer and Al Williams.

But every seasoned member of the fight game who had witnessed the thrashing Morris had received from Fireman Jim Flynn knew that Carl Morris would never scale the heights. Fellow prospects like skilled boxer Tom Kennedy and tough-jawed Jim Stewart were able to avoid or soak up his heavy punches and take him the no-decision distance easily.

After a time, Morris became disillusioned with the fight game and went back to Oklahoma. However, he soon realised that even being a trial horse was preferable to the back-breaking and ill-paid task of feeding the insatiable maw of a locomotive for ten hours a day. He returned east, found another manager and became a full-time fighter again. He still rattled off his quota of knockouts against lesser opponents, but he was now regarded as a good, tough man, not a promising contender.

Morris managed to reinvent himself several times. First he cashed in on his former glory by billing himself as the Original White Hope. Patrons would still pay to see someone who once had been touted as Jack Johnson's next opponent. A clergyman-turned-press agent called Ingraham was employed to sell the new Carl Morris to the public: 'Morris trains diligently, and at all times refrains from doing anything that would in the least impair his ability,' ran one unctuous release. 'He denies himself many things that appeal to his appetite lest they should endanger his chances of victory.' Then the former reverend concluded with a flourish, 'If the Apostle Paul could recommend the Roman Soldier as an example to the Christian, why may we not learn a lesson from this victor of many a hard-fought bout?'

But virtue was not a particularly saleable quality. Morris's goody-two-shoes persona did not last long. Instead his next manager in the string came up with the image that was to remain with Morris for the rest of his career. He was now billed as the world's dirtiest fighter. What is more, he lived up to it. The youngster who once had been comprehensively out-fouled by Fireman Jim Flynn became the more mature past master at such extra-curricular activities as gouging, hitting below the belt, kneeing, hitting on the break, butting and rabbit-punching to the nape of the neck. And that was in his more restrained exhibitions.

So effective was Morris at his new skills that he even secured the reluctant admiration of Wild Burt Kenny. Until the advent of the revamped Carl Morris, it had been Kenny who claimed to be the foul fighter of the century, noted for his triple lead – with the head, the elbow and the knee. He had been celebrated on a notorious one-man invasion of Ireland for being disqualified in two successive bouts for kicking his opponents after he had decked them.

After his latest makeover, Morris in mid-career made Kenny look like a sissy. In the ring he was said to resemble a mad grisly bear. If there was not a riot at the end of one of his bouts, with spectators throwing chairs and bottles at him, Morris felt that he had failed in life. Towards the end of his career, one newspaper suggested that, in consideration of his skill in stunning opponents with his head, the soon-to-be-ex-boxer might consider looking for a new post 'with the Butterick Company on Goat Island at Butte Monte'.

Carl Morris was still around a decade later as cannon fodder for the up-and-coming Jack Dempsey and other young heavyweights. At one time, the Salpulpa heavyweight had employed Dempsey as a seventy-cents-a-day sparring partner and had treated the younger fighter with such contempt and meanness that Dempsey developed a lifelong animosity towards the giant. At the tail end of Morris's career he was knocked out three times by the emerging Dempsey, once in the first minute of the first round. Dempsey admitted later that Morris had been the only opponent he had genuinely hated.

Morris's time as a prospect may have passed him by, but there were plenty lining up to take his place.

The first semi-official gathering of some of the White Hopes occurred on 11 May 1911 at the National Sporting Club in New York. Promoter Tom O'Rourke announced that, in order to produce a Caucasian heavyweight capable of challenging Jack Johnson, he was bringing together the cream of the white heavyweights in a knockout tournament. In the same month the influential sporting newspaper the *Police Gazette* commented approvingly on his efforts: 'Tom O'Rourke is the only promoter who is making a rational effort to develop new material in the professional heavyweight division with a view to bringing out a man capable of battling against Johnson and winning back the title of champion for the white race.'

O'Rourke was a charlatan and conman of sufficient calibre to maintain the reluctant admiration of such hard men as Coffroth and Curley. He broke into the game as manager and promoter of a number of black fighters in the lower weight divisions whom nobody else wanted to look after; in the ring parlance of the time, black boxers 'did not draw flies'. O'Rourke compensated for his altruism by taking 50 per cent of his fighters' purses and by forcing them to box to orders. Even as early as the turn of the century, when the phrase 'anything goes' could be said to have been the motto of professional boxing, O'Rourke was famed for his wheeling and dealing and was often accused of 'fixing' the results of the fighters he managed in order to engineer betting coups. The *Milwaukee Evening Wisconsin* of 8 February 1900 was so incensed by the manager's finagling that it accused O'Rourke of choreographing many of the bouts in which his fighters were involved:

The following is a list of some of the battles that have taken place within a year over which there have been charges of crookedness, wrong decisions or some kind of foul play.

In all of them Tom O'Rourke has been a prominent factor, either as manager of one of the principals or manager of the club. In several cases it has been clearly shown that the battles were 'fakes' expressly made for betting purposes . . .

Walcott vs. Lavigne	San Francisco, Oct 29, 1897
Sharkey vs. Corbett	Lennox Club, Nov 22, 1898
West vs. Bonner	Lennox Club, Jan 17, 1899
Walcott vs. Creedon	Lennox Club, April 25, 1899
etc. etc.	

All these bouts involved champions or near champions. It is a sign of O'Rourke's influence that he was able to attract such luminaries.

Despite his best efforts, Tom O'Rourke found that managing black fighters, even fistic geniuses like Joe Walcott and George Dixon, was not a passport to the sort of wealth he envisaged. The big money lay with the big white men, specifically the White Hopes. So he opened the New York National Sporting Club and organised a series of tournaments in the hope of discovering a suitable white heavyweight. The *Police Gazette* described one of these events: 'O'Rourke firmly believes that the only way to discover real white heavyweights is by holding a tourney open to all comers, the contestants to be matched by lots to meet in bouts of four rounds each, the elimination process finally bringing the two best men together . . .'

Presumably O'Rourke got around the restrictions of the Frawley Law by having cronies among the newspaper fraternity rendering unofficial decisions to decide which fighters went on to the subsequent rounds of his shows.

At first these White Hope tournaments attracted a reasonable number of entries. The contestants for one of O'Rourke's competitions were announced as being a 6ft-9in heavyweight from Jacksonville; a Texan backed by a wealthy banker from his home state; 20-stone Herman Tracey from Bradford, Illinois, who it was claimed (by the club's press agent) had killed an ox with a right-hand blow; Joe Rogers, a 19-stone wrestler; the amateur heavyweight boxing champion of Canada; and a

Philadelphia entrant with a considerable reputation as a slugger in his home city.

Unfortunately, the standard of boxing offered by these putative White Hopes was bad enough to discourage the promoter considerably, and he decided to concentrate on an Iowan amateur called Al Palzer, whom O'Rourke had seen in an unpaid bout in a small New York hall. This was generally known among the New York fighting cognoscenti, who treated the 11 May tournament with considerable suspicion.

Accordingly, the more capable and better managed of the White Hopes were steered well clear of the tournament by their handlers. For one thing, the purse money on offer was negligible. For another, no self-respecting manager was going to allow his charge to run the risk of walking into a sucker punch and thus losing all credibility so early in the game. A clinching argument was that O'Rourke, the promoter, was going to ask for a share in the winning behemoth as a reward for staging the day's proceedings. There was also a strong suspicion among the more cynical – that is, all the other managers – that the tournament was being staged mainly for the benefit of O'Rourke's own novice heavyweight, the hard-punching 20-year-old blond Iowan farm boy of German descent, Al Palzer, in order to get his tall 16-stoner an instant reputation.

At the age of 12 Palzer had run away from home in Winneshiek County, Iowa, and for the next eight years had worked at a variety of labouring jobs as he made his way across the country, even serving a short hitch in the US Navy, before being spotted by O'Rourke winning an amateur heavyweight competition in New York. He had been promptly signed to a five-year contract by the manager.

It was announced that twenty-three heavyweights had been carefully selected for the White Hope tournament. In reality it was open to anyone, even one optimistic middleweight who turned up with his boxing shoes wrapped in a newspaper. On the day, eleven wannabes arrived and were matched against one another in a series of four-round eliminating bouts taking place over the entire day and evening. As the big fellows came and went, so did the spectators, disgusted by the abysmal standards of the boxing on display.

Pint-sized and irascible Liverpool-born manager Jimmy Johnston, who had turned up in the hope of stealing somebody else's prospect, was so incensed by having to forgo his customary poker game in order to witness the display of mass ineptitude in the ring above him that he finally lost his temper. Tearing off his jacket, the pugnacious former bantamweight loudly offered to fight each and every one of the Hopes present in the hall. The diminutive Johnston, who was known in fight circles as the Boy Bandit, found no takers.

Among the sheepish entrants ignoring the feisty challenger was the dour Fred McLaglen, Victor's brother. Fighting out of Winnipeg as Fred McKay, he claimed the heavyweight championship of Eastern Canada, but it was largely suspected that he had bestowed the title on himself after some obscure logging-camp free-for-all.

In his first bout in the tournament, McKay came up against a journeyman called Sailor White. It was a sign of the Sailor's lack of ability that even Fred's sibling Victor McLaglen had managed to knock him out, although in an earlier meeting White had defeated McLaglen.

In the first round of his bout with White, McKay was almost spectacularly successful. Even hardened handlers and managers had emerged from the dressing rooms to watch McKay hand out a thrashing to the ex-sailor. In the second round, however, White landed a solitary crushing right-hand blow, knocking McKay unconscious. The potential backers, realising that the Englishman was not going to provide them with a free ride on the gravy train, vanished like the melting snows. One of them, manager 'Dumb' Dan Morgan, noted of the abandoned fighter: 'He had to carry his own bucket back to the dressing room when he came to.'

As had been generally expected, Al Palzer, the 'house' fighter belonging to Tom O'Rourke, emerged as the favourite to win the tournament. He had been training in secret for months, and before the tournament he had won two fights on knockouts and had fought a ten-round, no-decision bout with another prospect, Frank Moran.

In the first heat of the competition, Palzer outpointed an unknown called Joe Rogers. Most of the other entrants having either eliminated one another or been driven in shame from the club by the catcalls of the spectators, that left only Sailor White for Palzer to meet in the final.

White, still dazed by his unexpected victory over Fred McKay, knew better than to upset influential manager and promoter O'Rourke. Pacifically he allowed Palzer to cuff him around for four rounds. During the fight, Jack Johnson made an ostentatious entrance and sat at the ringside for a few minutes watching with unconcealed disgust as the two finalists went through the motions. When asked if he was learning anything from the two sweating White Hopes, the champion gave his wide, gold-toothed smile. 'I'm learning plenty,' he replied contentedly.

All these moves and countermoves were followed avidly by a boxing-mad public. The wily politician Theodore Roosevelt, who always had his finger on the general pulse, capitalised on this interest by disinterring a phrase from the old prize-ring when, in 1912, he announced his intention of seeking his party's nomination as candidate for the presidency. 'I have', he said proudly, 'thrown my hat into the ring!'

Back in the real ring, O'Rourke's tournament achieved its ambition in establishing the winner as an up-and-coming heavyweight, and when Palzer went on to knock out another White Hope, Tom Kennedy, and stopped trial horse Al Kaufmann in the fifth round, some followers of the ring actually began to concede that perhaps Palzer was the best young white heavyweight around. Shrewdly, at this stage O'Rourke would only let his protégé box in New York, where the Frawley Law decreed that fights should last no longer than ten rounds and that no points decision could be rendered at the end of a bout. This meant that unless Palzer should be knocked out, officially he could not lose.

The heavyweight, like most of his peers, was also picking up some loose change on the vaudeville circuit. The *Milwaukee Evening Wisconsin* of 2 April 1912 announced, 'Al Palzer, the New York heavyweight, who has challenged the present champion, Jack Johnson, will be seen at the Star next week as an added attraction with the Jardin de Paris Girls and Abe Leavitt, the "live-wire" comedian. Palzer will box six rounds with his sparring partners and local aspirants at every performance.'

His bandwagon gathered momentum in 1912, when the English heavyweight champion Bombardier Billy Wells visited the USA for several fights. With some trepidation, Tom O'Rourke accepted a contest with Wells on behalf of his charge. Palzer had been marking time, like most current heavyweights, by knocking out Sailor White, but had then been forced to take time off to have an operation on his damaged nose.

The bout with Palzer was intended to gain Wells an international reputation. Palzer was the heavier of the two by several stone but both men were comparative novices. Palzer was engaging in his eleventh professional bout, while Wells was having his tenth, although he had boxed as an amateur and in the Army.

Their Madison Square Garden contest, while it lasted, was spectacular. Wells started by outboxing the Iowan with his famous straight left. Towards the end of the round Wells dropped his opponent heavily, but Palzer regained his feet, shook his head and was fighting back at the bell. The second round was a repetition of the first, with Palzer plodding forward gamely while Wells boxed his head off. In the third and final round things changed. Palzer had worked out the Englishman's style, or had had it worked out for him by his cornermen. He ducked under Wells's left lead and hit the Bombardier hard in the stomach. Wells floundered miserably on the canvas, like a landed fish, and did not regain his feet in time.

The result did far more for Palzer than winning the dubious White Hope tournament had done. While Wells disconsolately returned to England after one more fight, Palzer was suddenly in great demand, his white heavyweight championship taking on a fresh international lustre.

Even so, it was not always easy for Palzer to draw the crowds. On one occasion, when he was matched with Charlie Miller, the sale of tickets was so disappointing that Jimmy Johnston, who was promoting the bout, decided to take extreme measures. The Secretary of State at the time was William Jennings Bryan, a charismatic public speaker. With his tongue in his cheek, Johnston sent a telegram to Bryan, offering him $300 to deliver from the ring a lecture on a subject of his choice before the Palzer–Miller bout.

Jennings, who recognised a fellow self-publicist when he saw one, treated the offer solemnly and declined with thanks. That was all that Johnston had been waiting for. He sent copies of both telegrams to all the local newspapers. The resultant publicity started the tickets moving freely again. All, as one of Johnston's competitors said with reluctant admiration, for the cost of a dollar telegram.

Unfortunately, Palzer let his opportunities slip. Increasingly homesick and disappointed by the percentages of the purses being passed on to him by O'Rourke, the heavyweight fell out with his manager. He went off in a huff and refused to train, turning down a number of offers for good-money bouts against meaningful opponents. In an interview with the *Police Gazette*, Palzer enumerated some of his grievances: 'I have only sixty dollars to my name, yet I've won many thousands of dollars in the boxing game . . . On the road I have been getting a few hundred dollars now and then, while O'Rourke has been keeping big money each week. He's tried to get me to drink wine and go out with the fly set . . . but I refused, as I never drink anything stronger than tea or coffee and I want to be fit all the time. I don't believe that O'Rourke is on the square with me and I'm going to break away from him. He made me sign some kind of contract once, but he never let me have a copy of it. He won't let me fight anybody unless he can get the lion's share of the coin, and I am tired of it all.'

The garrulous O'Rourke retorted in a scandalised fashion, accusing his White Hope of extreme disloyalty, claiming that the heavyweight was ungrateful and untruthful and pointing out that the boxer was attached to his manager by a cast-iron contract. The big man sulkily stayed out of the ring for more than four months before engaging in a minor six-round, no-decision contest with trial horse and former Jack Johnson opponent Tony Ross in Philadelphia.

Reluctantly, Palzer then allowed himself to be reconciled with his manager, and at last signed to defend his white heavyweight championship against another promising White Hope, the former cowboy Luther McCarty, but his heart was no longer in boxing.

Even though Jack Johnson was busy living the high life and touring with his lucrative vaudeville act, and had not entered the ring since his contest against Jeffries in 1910, the search for a White Hope continued to dominate the headlines.

James W. Coffroth, one of the leading promoters, admitted that only a white heavyweight challenger would draw the crowds against Jack Johnson. In an interview in the French publication *La Boxe* in 1911, he admitted that it would be impossible in the USA to match Johnson against one of his black challengers like Sam Langford or Joe Jeanette. 'It would be a great fight, the two negroes would not miss the opportunity to inflict the necessary and sufficient hiding that we would be entitled to expect from them. But the problem is that in America, they would not stand a chance of success. Why? For the only reason that the Blacks are hated in America. A fight that would put two of them face to face would not attract big crowds.'

So would-be white challengers rolled off the assembly lines almost with the regularity of Henry Ford's new Model Ts, although with less durability. Tom Kennedy was one of them. Because, unlike most boxers of the era, he had fought as an amateur, he was regarded as almost effeminate by some of his peers and given the quite erroneous title of the Millionaire Boxer. Managed by Dan McKetrick, a sports writer, he secured some creditable wins but lost a considerable amount of face when he was defeated by Bombardier Billy Wells in the latter's second fight on his visit to the USA.

Kennedy plodded on. He fought a particularly good ten-round, no-decision bout with a red-headed ex-sailor called Frank Moran. The two big men became close friends. When the globetrotting Moran was scheduled to sail to Europe for a series of contests, the former adversaries celebrated heartily together the night before, and a rather drunken Kennedy dutifully stumbled on board the liner to see his friend off. He fell asleep, and when he woke up the vessel was many miles out to sea. Not at all put out, Moran invited his fellow heavyweight to join him for an indefinite holiday. He promised the purser to pay the other man's fare retrospectively from his European purses, until Kennedy could line up his own fights overseas.

The sporting world was then surprised by the announcement that another White Hope had appeared on the scene. George Hackenschmidt, the Russian Lion, well into his thirties and the former heavyweight wrestling champion of the world, let it be known that he was going into training to re-emerge as a boxer in order to challenge Jack Johnson. An Estonian, Hackenschmidt was an enormously strong man, capable of pressing a weight of 20 stone over his head.

Journalists who witnessed his early training sessions wondered, however, if perhaps he was still concentrating too much on the development of strength at the expense of speed when the Russian carried a 5-hundredweight sack of cement on his shoulders, with a heavyweight sparring partner perched on top of the sack.

Nevertheless, the wrestler's attempt at transmogrification into a boxer secured plenty of publicity, until an Australian reporter revealed that Hackenschmidt had pulled exactly the same stunt a few years before, at another quiet time in his professional career.

It had happened on a tour of Australasia in 1907. Hackenschmidt had tried to launch a similar publicity campaign then, claiming that he was going into training for a boxing match with Philadelphia Jack O'Brien. Gunner Moir, the British heavyweight fighter, who was a member of the wrestler's troupe, claimed that he had given the Russian boxing lessons and that his pupil showed great promise.

Unfortunately, Sydney reporters with a keen eye for a story had persuaded the grand old man of Australian boxing, Larry Foley, to visit the gymnasium in which the wrestler was training and spar a few rounds with him. Foley was credited with introducing modern boxing methods to Australia.

Although he had been 60 years old at the time, Foley had had no trouble with the lumbering and inept Hackenschmidt. Leaving the ring, Foley had told the reporters curtly that any third-rate heavyweight boxer would dispose of the Russian Lion with ease. Hackenschmidt thereupon announced with dignity that he was taking Foley's advice and sticking to wrestling.

When the American newspapers realised that, five years later, the Russian was merely resurrecting his 1907 ploy in order to bring the crowds back to his vaudeville act, they dropped him abruptly from the register of White Hopes.

There were plenty of giants willing to take his place. Managers continued to find and boost new prospects. Six-feet-four-inches-tall Fred Fulton was rated for a time. Big and strong, he was championed enthusiastically by his manager Jack Reddy. The handler gave newspapers a list of his heavyweight's abilities, which, he claimed, eminently suited him for the title of the best of the White Hopes.

These characteristics included: 'He is as fast on his feet as a lightweight. He can outbox any heavyweight. He has a straight left that no heavyweight of the present time can block. If necessary he can dance around any heavyweight in the business for hours. He has a knockout punch in either hand. He has never had a black eye or bloody nose. He is of Scotch–Irish parentage. He has never chewed, smoked or drank. He is positively sure no man in the world can beat him.'

Fulton rattled off a string of victories, many of them by knockouts, defeating Al Kaufmann, Arthur Pelkey, Jim Flynn and Gunboat Smith, but a knockout loss to Al Palzer set him back. He lost two torrid bouts with the newly savage Carl Morris. In each one Morris displayed his full repertoire of dirty tricks. The quick-tempered Fulton replied in kind with such energy that on both occasions he managed to get himself disqualified first. After their first bout, the referee said that he could have ruled Morris out at least twenty times if only he had not ejected Fulton from the ring first.

Eventually, in 1917, after the White Hope campaign was over, Fulton lost face when he was outsmarted in a gymnasium spar by Australian middleweight Les Darcy. Darcy was going through a bad patch himself, having smuggled himself out of Australia during the First World War, contrary to regulations, to pursue his boxing career in the USA while many of his peers were fighting and dying.

Nevertheless, he was a fine boxer. A reporter from the *Globe*, who witnessed his gym humiliation of the huge Fulton, wrote, 'The result was a revelation. Despite his recent inactivity Darcy gave the slow-moving Minnesota White Hope a boxing lesson which was abruptly terminated by Fulton pulling off his gloves after two rounds.'

Some of the new White Hopes managed to attract backers of great prestige. When the Englishman from Helsingham in Cumberland, Tom Cowler, crossed the Atlantic, coincidentally just before the outbreak of the First World War in 1914, he managed to get a fight in Canada, where he was seen on a theatrical tour by no less an authority than James J. Corbett. The former world champion declared that the young man was a heavyweight of great promise. Corbett even gave the Englishman tips on his ring performances. 'The fellow has something these other alleged heavyweights didn't have,' the old heavyweight champion told the *Beloit Daily News* of 23 July 1915. 'He's got the best left jab I ever saw or felt and I have seen and felt, also dodged, quite a few.'

In Great Britain, Cowler had defeated some fair second-rate heavyweights like Iron Hague and Ben Taylor. He started off well enough in the USA, holding his own in no-decision contests against Gunboat Smith, Porky Flynn and Bill Brennan, but he lost to Battling Levinsky and was knocked out by Jack Dillon and, in the first round, by Fred Fulton. In 1916, less than two years after he had arrived in the States, Cowler announced his retirement. The *Washington Post* of 13 February 1916 said of the Cumbrian, 'His physicians have advised him to retire, as he is said to be in poor health and his condition such that further bouts might prove dangerous.'

Jim Corbett, his erstwhile mentor, concurred, publicly washing his hands of the Englishman. 'There's a lad who possessed all the physical make-up of a champion,' he said bitterly. 'I took a fancy to him because I admired his style and I liked the way he punched. He had everything that a good fighter should have. He was clever, he was fearless, but he couldn't think.'

132

Cowler continued to fight sporadically, but, as an Englishman active in New York while his fellow countrymen were engaged in a war, he encountered a great deal of hostility. This was evidenced in the *Des Moines Register* of 15 January 1917. Describing Cowler's fight with the former sailor Gunboat Smith in Rochester, the ringside reporter wrote of Smith's manager Jim Buckley's actions at the start of the fight, 'At the opening of the round Buckley stood up straight with his face pressed against the ropes and yelled to the Gunner as follows: "Fight him hard, Gunner! Remember that you were there when your country wanted you, right there on Uncle Sam's battleship. Remember that you didn't run away at the first sight of danger!'

The references to Smith's patriotism must have puzzled the Gunboat, a former heavyweight champion of the Pacific Fleet, because, by his own admission, he had spent most of his sea duty in the waters off China and Japan serving time in the brig for insubordination. However, the writer went on to report that Cowler, who lost in the tenth round, was obviously affected by Buckley's remarks: 'Cowler is tired of being asked why he isn't in the trenches.'

Cowler was reduced to the status of a mere 'opponent', fighting wherever he could earn a few dollars, crossing and recrossing the continent by train. A list of the cities in which he fought gives some idea of the peripatetic life led by the White Hopes. Between 1915 and 1919 Cowler visited, often more than once, New York, Boston, Rochester, Wheeling, Buffalo, Providence, St Louis, Minneapolis, Philadelphia, Jersey City, Oakland and Baltimore.

In 1919, after Johnson had lost his title, Cowler actually fought the fat and washed-up former champion in Mexico City. Johnson still had enough to knock the Englishman out, but Cowler was as game as a pebble. Shortly before the end, Johnson muttered to him, 'Why don't you give up, Tom?' to which the Cumbrian replied rather incoherently, 'I shall when you leave me alone!'

An unusual White Hope was the Canadian Sandy Ferguson. A big, brave and reckless man, Ferguson was born in New Brunswick in

1879 and started boxing when he was 19. He fought out of Boston and was undefeated in his first sixteen contests. He soon developed a reputation as a man who would fight anyone anywhere. Unlike most of his white contemporaries, Ferguson never drew the colour line and went in with most of the leading black fighters of his era.

From an early age Ferguson displayed a reckless streak which was to cause him considerable grief. In 1901, he secured a post as sparring partner to the gangling Cornish-born Bob Fitzsimmons, the former world heavyweight champion. Ferguson proved to be no respecter of persons, as the *Police Gazette* of 15 June reported with a straight face: 'Bob Fitzsimmons has lost his sparring partner, "Sandy" Ferguson, of whom great things were expected. While boxing the other night "Sandy" started to mix it up with Bob. The result was a smashed ear, a bloody nose and several other catastrophes for "Sandy", followed by his sad departure for his home in Boston.'

In the same year, still smarting from the adverse newspaper publicity, Ferguson embarked upon a ten-fight tour of Britain, where, in three fights, he lost to, beat and drew with a leading English heavyweight, Ben Taylor. He was overmatched, however, when he came in as a last-minute substitute for Bob Armstrong to box one of the leading black American heavyweights, Denver Ed Martin, at the National Sporting Club. Ferguson put up a very brave show before being beaten in the fifth round.

Ferguson's courageous display against the big black fighter was commented upon favourably when the Canadian returned home at the beginning of 1903. He was regarded as a good rough-and-tumble fighter who needed only to pay more attention to his training to be worthy of a title shot against James J. Jeffries. If ever there was a time for a white fighter to go carefully and avoid all the hard men while his contender status was strengthened, it was now.

Instead, feckless and broke, Ferguson agreed to meet the new rising black star Jack Johnson over ten rounds in Boston. Ferguson fought bravely but was outclassed by the black boxer. One newspaper account said that the white fighter was made to look a novice against the silky skills of the Galveston man.

For a white fighter to have gone in with Jack Johnson once could have been seen as an error, but the foolishly brave Ferguson then fought the future champion four more times over the next three years. In fact, Ferguson was a heavy drinker and had an expensive lifestyle, when he could afford one. Mixed-race matches were frowned upon in many quarters, but they drew large crowds, and even losing to a prominent black fighter like Johnson, Langford or Jeanette could earn a white boxer a good purse.

Ferguson soon drank away most of his money from the first Johnson bout, and the next month he turned up with boozy optimism at the black fighter's contest with Joe Butler at the Philadelphia Athletic Club. After Johnson had knocked Butler out in the third round, Ferguson reeled into the ring and challenged the victor to a return match. Johnson, who had not even broken into a sweat against Butler, looked at his challenger with the anticipation of a cat offered a saucer of cream, and agreed quickly, before the white man could change his mind.

They fought a six-round, no-decision bout in the same hall two months later. This time Ferguson did better, but all the newspaper verdicts went in his opponent's favour. Ferguson then boosted his record with an impressive first-round knockout against Bob Armstrong, a veteran black fighter. This victory may have given Ferguson delusions of grandeur, although it is more likely that he had drunk most of his ring earnings away again and was broke. He accepted an offer to fight Johnson over twenty rounds in Colma in December 1903. Johnson won handily over the distance, although Ferguson won plaudits for his phlegmatic endurance.

Ferguson, however, was already building up a reputation as an unreliable fighter. On 26 March 1904, the *Police Gazette* reported that the Boston-based fighter had stormed out of a proposed match in Gloucester, Massachusetts. 'The main attraction was to have been between Sandy Ferguson of Chelsea and Walter Johnson, of Philadelphia, but owing to some disagreement in the choice of a referee, Ferguson would not go on and left the club.'

Ferguson met Jack Johnson in another six-round, no-decision meeting, and then, a year later, on 18 July 1905, the two men had their most spectacular clash. It took place at the Pythian Rink in Chelsea, Massachusetts. By this time the Canadian heavyweight had built up quite a following with his spectacularly inept efforts to best Johnson, and a large crowd turned up to see what his opponent would do to him this time. Every seat was taken in the packed, sweltering hall, and at the back standees were crushed shoulder to shoulder in a swaying mass.

The first three rounds were probably the best Ferguson had ever fought. He stood toe to toe, slugging it out with Johnson, who was forced to abandon his normal defensive mode. The crude Canadian landed a number of crushing right hands on Johnson's shaven head, and even forced the black man back to the ropes on several occasions.

By the fourth round Ferguson's lack of fitness caught up with him, and Johnson began to surge forward as the crowd screamed to the white fighter not to give up his advantage. The contest was so exciting that brawls were breaking out all over the hall between supporters of the two heavyweights.

By the fifth round, Ferguson had shot his bolt and was beginning to foul Johnson in a desperate effort to stay in the match. In the sixth round he hurtled a left hook deliberately into his opponent's groin. Johnson screamed and fell writhing to the canvas. In an effort to fool the referee and get him to start the count, Ferguson leapt over the ropes and headed from the ring through the incensed crowd, trying vainly to give the impression of a victorious fighter abandoning the field of conflict in triumph.

The referee was not deceived. Sternly he called the white fighter back to the ring. When the wide-eyed innocent returned, protesting vehemently, the referee disqualified him. A riot broke out in the hall. Chairs were thrown and punches exchanged, while non-belligerents tried to push their way through to the exits. In the end the police had to be called in to restore order.

By this time Ferguson was probably giving more trouble to his managers than he was to his opponents. Between 1904 and 1912 he is recorded as having at least four different handlers. As soon as one gave up on the wilful fighter, another could soon be found to take on the heavyweight for a percentage of his purses. Among the venal but misguided ten-per-centers associated with Ferguson during this period were Alec McLean, Johnny Mack, Carl Harris and George Little.

The 1905 fight with Johnson sickened Ferguson of managers and the fight game for the time being. He was only 26 but he had had over fifty hard fights and was going nowhere. Temporarily he abandoned the ring. In 1906 he had only one fight and there were none in 1907. Still he was not ignored in the police reports of local and national newspapers. The *Milwaukee Free Press* of 4 April 1907 reported, 'John Alexander Ferguson, known in the ring as "Sandy" Ferguson, challenger of Johnson and Jeffries, has been sentenced to four months in jail in Boston for idleness and disorderly conduct. This is the second term "Sandy" is serving in jail.'

Between court appearances Ferguson made sporadic attempts to earn a legitimate living. Briefly he returned to Nova Scotia. On one occasion at least he secured the commendation of his skipper when, serving as a deckhand on a mackerel ship putting out of Gloucester, he was reported to be the only crew member who was not fighting drunk when returning from a bout of shore leave.

Ferguson also revisited prison after he had been found guilty of hitting his wife on the arm with a frying pan. And in 1908 he had two bouts. True to form he selected about the hardest opponents he could find, losing in twelve rounds each to Sam Langford and Joe Jeanette.

Then, in 1909, as the White Hope campaign got under way, Sandy Ferguson found himself in demand again. By the standards of most white heavyweights he had quite a creditable record. He had dodged no one and had fought the new world champion no fewer than five times. Responding to the rustling of dollar bills, Ferguson made a comeback. In his adopted home city of Boston he knocked out two young White Hopes, Jim Barry and Al Kubiak, and, still on his own turf, found Sam Langford in a charitable enough mood to let him go twelve soporific rounds for a drawn verdict.

Suddenly, to his surprise, Sandy Ferguson found himself being touted in the newspapers as, along with Jim Flynn, an experienced White Hope. It was too good to last. Ferguson was too unstable to stay and consolidate his position in the States. Instead he went off for a wild old time in Paris, which was welcoming American fighters.

The *Portland Daily Advertiser* of 6 May 1909 commented, 'Another American heavyweight pugilist is on his way to England and France. This time Sandy Ferguson, the big Boston slugger, whose twelve-round bout with Sam Langford in Boston last week was called a draw, is the one in search of fame and coin on the far side of the big pond.'

In Paris he beat and lost to Joe Jeanette, but he soon succumbed to the multifarious pleasures of the French capital and eschewed training completely. When he returned to the USA, Ferguson was wildly out of condition. This did not prevent him from accepting an offer to fight Jeanette yet again. They met at the Boston Armory Athletic Club. Their fight was a disgraceful one. The two men mauled and pushed and exchanged few clean blows. Jeanette launched the few attacks that did take place, while Ferguson hid behind a wall of crossed gloves. In the seventh round the white man's manager quit in disgust and stormed out of the arena. In the eleventh round, the *Milwaukee Evening Wisconsin* reported, 'Ferguson stalled the entire eleventh round, with the crowd yelling and hooting at his efforts to quit without deliberately lying down.' At the end of the twelve rounds, to the fury of the crowd, which had rejected the local man because of his lack of fighting spirit, Ferguson was declared the winner. The referee, Jack Sheehan, explained lamely that, while Jeanette had landed the most punches, Ferguson's blows had been stronger.

The news of Ferguson's 'victory', when it was announced in the newspapers, enhanced his reputation as a White Hope. There was talk of matching him yet again with Jack Johnson, should he repeat his win over Joe Jeanette. For his part, the furious Jeanette was insisting on another shot at the white man. Boston would have nothing to do with yet another meeting between the two heavyweights, but they were matched to fight again in New York.

The return bout was another shocker. Ferguson had done no training for the bout, while Jeanette was determined to avenge the so-called defeat in their last encounter. The white fighter knew that he had no chance against an untrammelled Joe Jeanette, and gave a disgraceful exhibition.

The New York correspondent of *Boxing* was scathing in his condemnation of the way in which Ferguson froze when he saw Jeanette advancing on him with a dreadful anticipatory gleam in his eye, and accused the white fighter of having done most of his training in barrooms. 'Ferguson aspires to the championship title, but by his showing he is more fit for the occupation of cow-puncher between decks. I was told before the fight that Sandy had trained for the contest, but I could guess in two attempts just what the surroundings of his training quarters were, and the elbow-work must have been severe. "Red-hair" got cold feet in the fifth round, but his seconds forced him to continue. The merciful end came in the eighth.'

It was the finish of Ferguson as a White Hope. He fought on, but now he was just a trial horse, cannon fodder for better-managed white heavyweights. He was beaten by Jim Barry, Porky Flynn, Tom Kennedy and even by the elderly Tony Ross. Of this last bout, the *Philadelphia Evening Bulletin* reported, 'Sandy Ferguson, the Boston heavyweight who has frequently been accused of possessing a yellow streak, quit cold in the fifth round.' After this Ferguson tried to redeem himself by writing a plaintive letter to the sports editor of the *Milwaukee Evening Wisconsin* of 12 March 1910:

Just a few lines to let you know that I am on deck again. You can't keep a squirrel off his perch. Some people with a lot of regard for Mr Sam Langford and Mr Jack Johnson, heavyweight champion, have been circulating reports in this neck of the woods that I am all through with the fighting game.

Reason – both are afraid of me and would like to see me out of the way. Johnson I knocked cold in Chelsea, but he was in right and got the decision. Did he ever desire a meeting with me since? Not on his natural!

Rich, isn't it? I am enclosing a doctor's certificate to prove that there is nothing to the reports.

Hoping that you will help me to be right with the public, and thanking you in advance, I am sincerely yours,

Sandy

Of his last twelve bouts Ferguson lost ten, drew one and won only one. His penultimate fight, against Battling Levinsky over twelve rounds in Boston, was a stinker. Driven to distraction by Levinsky's nullifying tactics, Ferguson bit his opponent so hard on the shoulder that Levinsky had to have stitches inserted in the wound after he had won on points. Ferguson was suspended for life. The ban was later reduced to one of six months. It was immaterial. After one more losing fight Ferguson retired. In 1919 he was shot and killed in a barroom brawl. He was 40 years old.

The trouble with all the leading White Hopes up to 1913 was that, with the exception of Luther McCarty, none of them could string together enough successes to be considered a legitimate challenger for Jack Johnson. They kept defeating one another. Bombardier Wells defeated Tom Kennedy but lost to Al Palzer and Gunboat Smith. Palzer beat Wells, Kennedy and Fulton, but was knocked out by Luther McCarty. Porky Flynn knocked out Fred McKay and was decked in turn by Stanley Ketchel and Fred Fulton. Andre Anderson defeated Al Palzer and Boer Rodel but lost to Tom Cowler and Homer Smith. Carl Morris beat Fred Fulton and Battling Levinsky and was beaten in turn by Luther McCarty, Jim Flynn and Gunboat Smith. Smith defeated Billy Wells and lost to Tony Ross and Jack Geyer. Jim Coffey defeated Jim Flynn and Al Reich and was knocked out in the first round by Soldier Kearns. Gunboat Smith defeated Frank Moran, Carl Morris and Arthur Pelkey but lost to Jim Coffey and the extremely faded Tony Ross.

So the carousel went round for three or four years, with no White Hope stepping up as the logical leading contender. In the meantime the public was eager for a title fight.

In 1912, after two years out of the ring, during which he had been living high on the hog, Jack Johnson suddenly agreed to defend his title again. He was to meet everyone's opponent, Fireman Jim Flynn. The attention on the up-and-coming White Hopes wavered as fight fans wondered what the veteran could do.

In the three years that had elapsed since his one-round knockout at the hands of Sam Langford, Flynn had been trudging round the fight circuit, from Los Angeles to Oklahoma City, New York, Toronto and Denver, among other venues, as usual refusing to meet no one in the process. Since his manhandling by Langford, Flynn had notched up another twenty contests. He had won eleven of them and lost only one, a second knockout at the hands of Langford. All the rest had been no-decision bouts. His most recent notable contest was a ruthless demolition of the novice Carl Morris in 1911.

Jack Curley promoted the Johnson–Flynn bout to get in on the White Hope quest. The problem was that the parsimonious Curley was trying to launch a White Hope championship challenge without a real White Hope. Fireman Jim Flynn came cheap. A lifetime of fighting for peanuts had dulled his acquisitive instinct. He was prepared to go in with Johnson for a second time in return for a pittance. This meant that Curley could afford to meet Johnson's financial demands and put on the fight.

As a safeguard to ensure Flynn's cooperation, Curley also became his manager. As a result, the promoter thought he saw a lucrative chance to avoid the long drawn-out process of finding and training his own white heavyweight. Flynn came ready-made, if slightly chipped at the edges. Johnson was only too ready to have an easy fight, and signed up with surprisingly little fuss.

Strangely enough, fight reporters did not rise to the bait. Few of the newspapers heralding the contest referred to Flynn as a White Hope. Perhaps he was too familiar and battle-scarred to justify the epithet. Or perhaps it was just too obvious that he had no chance. Concomitant with being a White Hope came the assumption that the hopeful had to have a faint chance of victory against Johnson.

Flynn did his best to talk up the fight, but no one was paying much attention. At a press conference before the fight the Fireman went through the motions, saying that he was boxing for the honour of whites and that he had given promoter Curley permission to shoot him if he failed to defeat the champion. Johnson also did what he could to promote the bout, but as he admitted years later in his memoirs, it was difficult to find anything complimentary to say about the extremely limited challenger. 'If he had any championship timber in him,' wrote Johnson in lordly fashion in his autobiography, 'I was as eager to find it out as any.'

Curley did his best to publicise the match. Frantically he tried to make Flynn appear to have at least some sort of chance. The promoter was an ingenious man. During the lead-up to the second Gotch–Hackenschmidt wrestling match, which Curley was promoting, the Russian Lion had injured his knee so badly that he could not do any roadwork. In order to fool reporters Curley scoured the streets of Chicago until he found a 21-stone lookalike for the wrestler, and made him go for training runs through dimly lit streets at night.

Flynn, a realist at 33 years old, did so little training for his big chance that his trainer, former middleweight champion Tommy Ryan, abandoned him in disgust, because his charge was overweight and was doing nothing about it except bullying a few untalented sparring partners.

Johnson knew as well as anyone that he would be able to stroll through the fight for the mere $30,000 he had been guaranteed in his title defence. The champion's main problem lay in dealing with the hate mail which descended upon him in shoals as he was going through his perfunctory preparations for the bout. One message, purporting to come from the Ku Klux Klan, informed Johnson that, if he did not lie down in the ring to his challenger, he would be lynched.

Apart from the revolver that was fired into the air during the first round, about the only exciting thing that happened during the fight was announcer Tommy Cannon's vain hope, expressed in the introductions, that as the occasion was being graced by the presence of several hundred ladies, the gentlemen present would moderate their language.

Flynn's game plan, which would explain his neglect of training, was to try to break as many rules as possible in an effort to disconcert the unbothered champion. For nine rounds he tried to butt Johnson into submission, ignoring the plaintive pleas and warnings of the referee. Unfortunately, Flynn was considerably shorter than his opponent and had to leap off the ground with both feet in order to reach the champion's chin, allowing Johnson to take evasive action. Eventually tiring of this tactic, Johnson knocked the Fireman down with a right uppercut. A police captain hovering outside the ring stumbled in through the ropes to stop the fight. Flynn had lasted two rounds longer in his 1907 fight with Johnson.

So poorly was Flynn regarded by fight fans that less than 5,000 people turned up at an arena intended for 17,000. Receipts for the tournament amounted to $35,000. Once Johnson and his opponent had been paid off, Jack Curley was left with a significant loss.

A week after the Flynn fight, Johnson opened the Café de Champion, a Chicago nightclub festooned with portraits of the champion. Its sheer flamboyance further annoyed his detractors. There was a great scandal when, one night in their bedroom over the café, Johnson's wife took a revolver belonging to her husband and fatally shot herself.

Johnson continued to be his own man, stating simply, 'I am not a slave . . . I have the right to choose who my mate shall be without the dictate of any man.' It was all too much for the white establishment, and the authorities closed in on the champion.

Johnson had been much seen in the company of his white secretary Lucille Cameron. He was arrested, after Cameron's affronted mother laid evidence against Johnson, and charged under the newly instituted Mann White Slavery Act of taking her across the state line 'for immoral purposes'. The Act stated that any man who crossed a state line with a woman not his wife and had sex with her was committing a criminal offence. Johnson and Cameron had occasionally travelled together from Pittsburgh to Chicago.

In November 1912, Johnson was first brought before Judge Kenesaw Mountain Landis, a former bicycle racer and the proprietor of a roller-skating rink before he took up law as a profession. Later he became the Commissioner of Baseball in the USA. Landis presided over the federal grand jury, which charged Johnson in a second trial with violating the Mann Act with Belle Schreiber, one of the champion's former mistresses. The Johnson trial was a useful means of obtaining publicity for the judge. Eventually the champion was allowed out on bail.

Johnson married Lucille Cameron but could not shake off the hounds baying at his heels because of his affair with Schreiber. Evidence given at the court hearing in May 1913, before Judge George Carpenter, dealt mainly with the white women in his life. He was fined $1,000 and sentenced to a year and a day in prison. Released on bail, Johnson fled the country with his wife, and was not to return to the USA for seven years.

The year in which Johnson fled to Europe, 1913, was a busy time in the USA. Woodrow Wilson was inaugurated as president; the outstanding Native American athlete Jim Thorpe was stripped of the gold medals he had won at the 1912 Olympics because several years before he had earned a few dollars playing semi-professional baseball; the Brooklyn Dodgers opened their new state-of-the-art stadium at Ebbets Field; while an unknown English comedian called Charlie Chaplin joined the famed Keystone film studio. The fiftieth anniversary of the Battle of Gettysburg was celebrated with a grand parade of the now-aged veterans of both armies. Citizens were taking to the roads in ever-increasing numbers: almost half a million automobiles were produced in the USA in 1913. A grimmer statistic in a nation still divided by race was that 211 lynchings, almost all of them of black men, took place in the same year.

Johnson might have gone, but he still held the title, and there was no let-up in the search for a White Hope to challenge him. And because the feared champion was safely on the other side of the Atlantic, managers could issue empty challenges to him to their hearts' content, building up huge gates for the elimination contests in which the white heavyweights took part.

Writing in the *Ring* in 1930, Billy McCarney, one of the leading managers of the time, described the widespread interest in the search for a white challenger. 'It was back in the period between 1910 and 1915 that every overgrown small town lad who thought he had any ability was signed by big and small time managers, placed in the hands of trainers, with the dethroning of Jack Johnson as the chief objective.'

The Flynn bout had shown that the public would not pay to see Jack Johnson in action against any old plug-ugly. The crowds wanted to see the champion in with an unsullied and attractive white newcomer who would be in with a chance against the black man.

As it happened, there was one on the horizon.

8

THE COWBOY FROM DRIFTWOOD CREEK

By 1913, Al Palzer and Luther McCarty had emerged from the pack as the two most likely prospects among the first White Hopes.

The organisation of boxing in the USA was still haphazard. In many areas, like New York State, public bouts were still banned. Wily promoters got round this by forming private clubs, at which bouts were allowed. These were very popular, especially if the showmen could persuade their members that they were watching embryonic White Hopes in action. For those big men who could actually run up a winning streak of bouts, there were large purses to be fought for.

Luther McCarty had started work in the family snake-oil business as a huckster, helping his father, the 21-stone self-styled White Eagle, touring the small towns of Nebraska to sell his cure-all potions by performing Native American dances to draw the crowds.

It was an era of travelling salesmen in rural areas, peddling bottled nostrums that were claimed to be cure-alls. One of the most notorious was Dr B.J. Kendall's addictive blackberry medicine for stomach ailments. It consisted of 122-proof whiskey reinforced with opium.

These tent shows were often the only forms of entertainment to visit the remoter areas. Nebraska was a hard state. In the first decade of the twentieth century some of the original rancher settlers were still fighting the incoming, would-be farmers, who were spreading across the western part of the area to take advantage of new irrigation schemes and fresh, hardy crop strains.

Young Luther McCarty's main job in the travelling family business was to look after the snakes used in the act while his burly sister Hazel performed what was claimed to be a genuine Native American snake dance. McCarty had taken a few boxing lessons at the Young Men's Christian Association gymnasium, but Hazel was considered the better fistic prospect of the two. Later she earned a living in vaudeville, billed as the world's champion woman bag-puncher.

When he was 15, Luther McCarty ran away from home with some relief and took to the road leading out of Nebraska. This led eventually to the high seas, and for several years the well-built youth shipped out as a deckhand, sailing round Cape Horn in the process. Tiring of this he returned to dry land and worked briefly as an ironworker on high bridges. He gave this up when he fell and broke a leg. When he had recovered he returned to Nebraska and in 1910 took up his life as a cowboy once more. He was still only 18.

In order to supplement his income McCarty had several professional fights in Nebraska during this period. His first bout took place at Swift Cloud, where the young heavyweight received eighteen dollars for his winning effort. But the young tyro did not have things all his own way. Boxing in Sidney against Harry Hollinger, a local tannery worker, McCarty walked into a wild right hand and was knocked out. When he recovered, the local newspaper, the *News*, reported him as saying to the winner, 'You made a dub of me, Harry, but I'm going to stick to this game and show up some of you fellows before I am through.'

Soon after this, McCarty left home again. This time he abandoned a young wife, Rhoda, and Cornelia Alberta, his infant daughter. For a while, in 1911, he boxed around the Midwest under the name of Walker Monahan, perhaps to avoid discovery by his abandoned spouse.

In his first full year as a pugilist, McCarty picked up fights wherever he could find them, racking up a series of knockout victories in the process. Between bouts he filled in with a touring boxing booth, taking on all comers. He fought three times in Fargo, North Dakota, and had another three bouts in Springfield, Missouri, whose civic fathers called the town the 'Queen of the Ozarks'. He continued to have a soft spot for Springfield and visited it as often as possible.

In Culbertson, Montana, McCarty attracted some attention by knocking out an experienced Canadian champion, Watt Adams, in the second round. An impressed Canadian promoter booked the young American to fight 'Iron Man' Joe Grim in Calgary.

Grim was one of the ring's oddities. Born Saverio Giannoni in Italy in 1881, he had been brought to the USA at an early age, and then embarked upon a career as a professional boxer. He made a name for himself as a human punchbag. Grim could not box and did not possess a big punch. He could, however, soak up any amount of physical punishment. Many opponents could knock him to the canvas; few could keep him there. He lasted the distance against some of the most feared punchers of his era. At the end of each bout, the Iron Man would totter to the ropes and, through bloodied lips and broken teeth, boast to the crowd, 'I am Joe Grim! I fear no man on earth!'

Over the course of his ring career, Grim had some 300 fights, most of them of the no-decision variety. He won a pitiful ten, but was knocked out on only three occasions. By the time the Iron Man met the novice McCarty, Grim had doggedly gone the distance with two of the greatest punchers of their era, ex-heavyweight champion Bob Fitzsimmons, who put Grim down seventeen times, and a young Jack Johnson, who downed Grim so many times that the reporters present lost count.

McCarty knocked Grim out in four rounds. Admittedly, the Italian was at the tail end of his career, but even so the young Nebraskan's feat got him noticed by managers on the perennial lookout for White Hopes. The former heavyweight champion Tommy Burns, who had been present at the Grim fight, urged McCarty to persevere.

The former cowboy fought his way as far as Chicago, taking labouring jobs between bouts. While he was training at the McConnell gymnasium he impressed manager Billy McCarney. It was McCarney who had persuaded the gullible Victor McLaglen to spar with Jess Willard for the right to challenge Joe Cox in Springfield, and had made money by charging admission to see the gym bout.

McCarney had been shrewd enough to pass up on an opportunity to handle Jack Johnson, that walking graveyard for unsuspecting white fight managers. As McCarney told it, an impecunious Johnson had approached him in Philadelphia one day after he had won the title and told him that he had decided to appoint the former law-school student as his new manager. 'The combination', Johnson told McCarney cheerfully, 'is Fighting Jack and Manager Billy. We're going to make a mess of money.'

Cautiously McCarney had verbally agreed to the proposed arrangement. Later that same day he received a telephone call from the expansive Johnson, who said, 'Seeing that you're my manager I'm sending a boy over for fifty dollars.' 'It's too late,' retorted a deadpan McCarney without missing a beat. 'I've resigned.'

By the time McCarty had appeared on the horizon, Willard had lost to Cox, and the ever-optimistic McCarney was on the lookout for another heavyweight meal ticket. It was apparent on first sight that McCarty's boyish charm would make him popular with fight crowds, but would his gymnasium form translate into a real action fight? The manager decided to waste no time finding out. He signed McCarty up and at the beginning of 1912 launched his prospect on a series of bouts against good-quality heavyweights, including several White Hopes.

In later years, in an article in *Ring* magazine, McCarney explained his plan of action for his new heavyweight: 'I decided to make of Luther a picturesque, colourful character. I prepared a grand stage setting and the newspaper men, novelists and fight promoters throughout the country aided my cause . . . I gripped the public pulse with the story of this Western cowboy giant, the new "White Hope" who would whip any man in the universe.'

Things were not easy at first, and, as they crossed and recrossed the country, the manager and his huge fighter often had to share a cramped upper berth on a Pullman. However, McCarty handled all his opponents with ease, scoring a series of knockouts, including a 1912 six-round victory over the highly regarded Carl Morris. The spectacular manner of this victory caused leading sports writer W.W. Naughton to enthuse in the *San Francisco Chronicle*, 'A new star has appeared in the pugilistic firmament. He tumbled big Carl Morris and his name is Luther McCarty. Sounds more like the name of a historian or a revivalist than a bruiser, doesn't it?'

McCarney then matched his fighter against his former charge Jess Willard. Willard was regarded as clumsy and lacking in charisma, but he was also beginning to assemble a series of plodding wins over good men and was a definite prospect. The fight was scheduled for New York, the big time for both men and a definite showcase if either had any aspirations to meeting Johnson for the title. It was a tough era and one which produced tough men, especially in New York. Comedian Jimmy Durante, who was just starting his career at the time, later reminisced that in most saloons in the Big Apple you were considered effeminate if you took off your hat. McCarty was dwarfed by the taller and heavier Willard, but outboxed his opponent. He could not put the Arkansas heavyweight away, but at the end of the ten-round, no-decision bout, reporters at the ringside were unanimous in giving McCarty their unofficial decision.

The Nebraskan cemented his new-found fame by ending the year with knockout victories over the still useful Al Kaufmann and the ever-dangerous slugger Jim Flynn in another White Hope tournament. By now the money was starting to roll in, and McCarty decided to make his home in Springfield. Suddenly, Luther McCarty was the man of the moment. There were now only two white heavyweights being talked about – McCarty after his display against Willard, and Al Palzer, the winner of the first White Hope tournament in New York the year before. It was a match made in heaven. When enough money had been dangled before him, Palzer agreed to defend his ersatz World White Heavyweight Championship crown.

The proposed bout aroused a great deal of interest, but almost did not take place. McCarty had badly damaged his left hand in his victory over Jim Flynn, and a few days before his contest with Palzer he broke his right hand on the head of a sparring partner. Tom O'Rourke had had it written into the contract that if either fighter defaulted he would pay his opponent $2,500. Both McCarney and his heavyweight had been living well and could not scrape together that much money.

Luther McCarty was perfectly prepared to enter the ring with his hands injected with a painkilling serum, but rumours of his injuries were going around the fight crowd and there were calls by those who had bet on the Nebraskan fighter to have the bout postponed. To prevent this happening Billy McCarney arranged for his heavyweight to have both fists X-rayed and examined by a specialist.

The doctor gave McCarty a clean bill of health, but only because the wily Billy McCarney had sent Bull Young, one of McCarty's sparring partners, to be examined at the hospital in place of the principal in the bout. The medico, no follower of the prize ring, did not understand that he was running the rule over a ringer.

The bout took place at Vernon, California on 1 January 1913. Despite his sore hands, McCarty won on an eighteenth-round knockout and was recognised, for what it was worth, as the White Heavyweight Champion. The fight attracted great interest. Some 11,000 people paid to see the bout, while another 3,000 milled about outside the arena, trying to get in. One newspaper report said, 'The fight was so one-sided that the referee stopped it . . . to save the reeling Palser [*sic*] from further punishment.' After the bout the referee, Charlie Eyton, told reporters that McCarty was the most promising heavyweight he had seen in years.

For the once highly touted Palzer it was virtually the end of the road as a White Hope. Even his manager Tom O'Rourke disowned the Iowan. In an interview with the American correspondent of *Boxing*, published in the issue dated 1 February 1913, O'Rourke claimed, 'During the two weeks preceding the ring battle Palzer was intermittently a nervous wreck, and would frequently lie at full length on a bench in his training quarters and cry like a baby for hours.'

Failing to recover from the beating McCarty had handed out to him, the Iowan went on to lose on knockouts to several new White Hopes, including Frank Moran and Dan Daily.

As a result of his victory McCarty was offered a two-week vaudeville engagement in New York at $2,000 a week. At McCarney's urging he appeared on stage in cowboy chaps and

Stetson, performing rope tricks. It was the beginning of an era of lavish revues, led by the Follies productions of Florenz Ziegfeld. Beautiful girls and speciality acts supported top-liners in a series of sketches, monologues, crosstalk duos and acrobatic performances. Even the most celebrated performer was on stage for no more than a single twenty-minute spot, and in the leading theatres a showgirl who did little more than stroll across a stage in beautiful clothes could earn $75 a week when the average annual wage was $750. The well-remunerated McCarty used some of his stage earnings to purchase a long-desired specially made silver-studded saddle for $700.

The only event which marred the aftermath of the championship bout for McCarty was when the young heavyweight returned with his freshly acquired diamond-studded belt, valued at $5,000, to his new home in Springfield. A reception which had been planned for him had to be cancelled when several church and civic leaders of the city decided that prizefighting was too ignoble a profession to be honoured in this manner.

This was small potatoes as far as manager McCarney was concerned. He was doing his best to fix up a title match for McCarty against Jack Johnson in Europe. At this time McCarty also received a challenge from an unknown self-appointed White Hope. This was Harry Hollinger, who had knocked out the novice McCarty a few years before. Lacking McCarty's wanderlust, Hollinger had stayed at home and was still working at the local tannery. Seeing a chance for instant fame and a quick buck Hollinger offered to give McCarty a chance to reverse the decision. McCarty ignored him.

White Eagle, McCarty's father, still peddling his snake oil, was also doing well out of Luther's fame, securing a thirty-week vaudeville tour in which he was billed as the only man who had ever given the champion a whipping.

While negotiations were proceeding with Johnson, McCarney arranged a warm-up bout to keep his man in trim. The opponent was a 28-year-old French Canadian White Hope called Arthur Pelkey. Pelkey's fighting career had got off to an uncertain start.

He had drawn his first fight and in 1911, in his second bout, he had been knocked out in the first round by black heavyweight George Christian. Christian was one of those long-distance fighters who provide a faint thread of continuity to the game down the years. Five years later he was being knocked out in the first round by a young Jack Dempsey in Price, Utah. Welterweight fighter and boxing historian Bob Hartley remembers Christian in the 1930s, challenging booth fighters from the crowd at a Midlands fair in Great Britain.

After his loss to Christian, Pelkey had rattled off a string of victories. Records are incomplete, but it is possible that he entered the 1911 New York White Hope tournament won by Al Palzer and that he defeated Al Benedict before being eliminated in a subsequent heat by that habitual loser Sailor White. Since then, without ever scaling the heights, he had knocked out his fair share of opponents and had gone the distance in no-decision bouts with other prospects like Jess Willard, Jim Coffey and Soldier Kearns.

Pelkey, whose real name was Peletier, had been properly noticed when he was matched with fellow Canadian and former world heavyweight champion Tommy Burns. Five years had passed since Burns had lost his title to Johnson at Rushcutters Bay, and the former champion had been keeping a low profile in the interval. He had fought only twice and at the age of 31 had all but retired from the ring. He had been dabbling in promotion and management and, like every other handler, was on a constant lookout for a White Hope, preferably another Canadian.

Burns, who had made his home in Calgary and was running a clothing store, thought that Pelkey might fit the bill. Since his loss to George Christian, Pelkey had remained unbeaten. And as a former fighter Burns had one great advantage over most of his contemporaries: he could actually try out his prospects in the ring.

Burns matched himself against Pelkey and set out to sell the fight to the citizens of Calgary. He appeared at social functions, gave talks and opened public buildings. On the eve of the bout he even held a special Ladies' Day to explain the intricacies of boxing to those members of the fairer sex who had never witnessed a bout.

The two men met over six rounds in a no-decision bout in Calgary on 2 April 1913. The fight was spectacular. Pelkey was knocked down three times while Burns went to the canvas once. Spectators were divided as to which fighter had come out on top, but everyone was agreed that the fight had been an exhilarating one. Shortly afterwards Burns announced that in future he would promote Pelkey's major fights and that he would spare no efforts to guide his White Hope to a world-title shot.

Whether the Burns–Pelkey fight was genuine or merely a glorified exhibition match, designed to enhance Pelkey's reputation and boost audiences for Burns's promotions, has been a matter for speculation. The former champion was no stranger to 'business arrangements', as his encounters with Philadelphia Jack O'Brien had proved. He had once expressed his simple philosophy: 'I went into the boxing business more or less by accident, and have stuck to it because I found that I could make more money in that way than I could in any other.'

Burns was still ostensibly pursuing his claims to a self-promoted return match with Jack Johnson in Calgary. He wrote to a local newspaper, stressing this intention but also insisting that, if he were to fight Johnson once more, the referee must ensure that the breaks were clean, i.e. that both fighters must take a step backwards from a clinch when ordered to do so by the referee. 'A clean break contest', wrote Burns sanctimoniously, 'is absolutely devoid of brutality.'

These wild challenges to Johnson were probably little more than attempts to gain publicity for the tournaments being held at the arena Burns had built on the fringes of the city. Certainly, Burns's next move enhanced suspicions that he was merely beating the drum for his White Hope. He issued a personal challenge for a Burns–Luther McCarty fight, offering the white champion $10,000 – win, lose or draw – to come to Calgary. The *Edmonton Journal* announced with undisguised scepticism, 'Burns is confident he is still in the game.'

Burns's challenge got him a lot of headlines. These grew even larger when the former champion abruptly pulled out of the bout, announcing that McCarty would instead meet Arthur Pelkey in defence of his White Heavyweight Championship. It is probable that the crafty Burns never intended meeting the much younger and bigger Nebraskan, but was merely ballyhooing the fight with Pelkey. It was to be held at the newly constructed Manchester Stadium, in which Burns had an interest.

At this point, Jack Johnson, beset by monetary problems, intervened from France, offering to come to Calgary and defend his genuine world title against McCarty. Burns dismissed this challenge with hauteur. Interviewed by the *Calgary Daily Herald*, the promoter said self-righteously, 'There is absolutely no reason why I should make this match. Johnson has not conducted himself in a gentlemanly manner at all since gaining the title, and now that I am a matchmaker I am only putting on matches which are between men of good character and clean-living fellows.'

The promoter's machinations were extremely effective. Tickets to the Pelkey–McCarty fight were priced from two to six dollars. Burns arranged for special streetcars to take spectators from the city to the arena. Three thousand people packed the stadium on the night. Before the main bout Burns, who was acting as fight announcer, deferred to the Reverend William Walker for a few words before the bell got the championship fight under way. Walker concluded his peroration by gesturing at the heavyweights waiting impatiently in their corners and saying, 'Here are two fine young men. They are in perfect physical condition, ready for their big test. And it should remind all of us always to be ready to meet our Maker when the time comes.'

His words were to prove eerily prophetic. The bout started with McCarty landing a left jab and then going forward into a clinch with Pelkey, which the referee Ed Smith had to disentangle. Then, as ringsider Tommy Burns put it, 'McCarty stepped back and went down very slowly.' Pelkey, who had not landed a punch in the 106 seconds that had elapsed since the bell, looked on in amazement.

There were angry cries of 'Fake!' from the crowd. Smith, as bemused as Pelkey had been, counted McCarty out. He tried to revive McCarty but failed. He then called for a doctor. Two were present in the hall and they did their best to help the stricken heavyweight. By this time Billy McCarney had dashed across the ring and was kneeling at McCarty's side. After another fifteen minutes, with still no response from the boxer, it was decided to carry McCarty outside, in case the fresh air might help revive him. Doctors injected morphine and tried to force brandy past his lips. It was all to no avail. Luther McCarty, aged 21, was pronounced dead.

Pelkey and Burns were both charged with manslaughter by the Royal Northwest Mounted Police but were released on bail. To make matters even worse, the night after the contest the Manchester Arena burnt to the ground, the result, Tommy Burns was always convinced, of an arsonist at work.

An inquest was held. Pelkey, shattered and given to bouts of uncontrollable weeping, was exonerated. The coroner brought in a verdict of accidental death. Medical testimony declared that McCarty had died from internal bleeding brought about by a broken neck. Tommy Burns gave evidence that on the morning of the bout he had spoken to McCarty, who had complained of a stiff neck that he assumed was due to sleeping in a draught the previous night.

The bizarre death of the leading White Hope was marked in headlines across the USA. The *Milwaukee Free Press* of 25 May announced, 'McCarty's body had hardly grown cold when theatrical men from the United States began making Pelkey offers to go on stage. Within five hours after he had become world's heavyweight champion [*sic*], Pelkey had received no less than five offers. He refused all, however.'

Despite the verdict of the coroner's court, the principals in the fight still had to be brought to trial. They appeared before Chief Justice Harvey, who told the jury that they must decide if the contest had been a prizefight, and not an exhibition, and, if so, whether Pelkey was responsible for the death of his opponent.

Billy McCarney was always convinced that McCarty's injury had been sustained in a fall from a horse on the ranch near Calgary which he had used as a training camp. Others pointed out that only a month before the Pelkey bout McCarty had gone ten rounds in a tough no-decision fight with hard-punching White Hope Frank

Moran. It was possible that one of Moran's fearsome right swings had started the trouble with McCarty's neck.

After hearing the reports of witnesses to the fight and the medical testimony, the jury decided that the bout had indeed been a prize-fight, but that it was impossible to tell whether Pelkey had been responsible for the demise of McCarty. Pelkey was released. Burns was told that charges that he had organised the tournament would remain on the register, but nothing ever came of this.

Thousands of people filed passed McCarty's body as it was laid out before his burial in the family plot at Piqua, Ohio, where his father was now living. Some newspaper reports stated that the fighter had left $65,000, which went to his estranged wife and daughter, but it seems more likely that the widow received $10,000.

The White Heavyweight Championship did Arthur Pelkey no good. So badly affected was he by Luther McCarty's death in the ring with him that he never fought well again. The first time he defended his crown, against Gunboat Smith, he lost. Burns remained loyal to his man and continued to manage Pelkey for a while, but then joined the Canadian Army as a physical fitness instructor in 1914, and, apart from several inconsequential bouts and an unsuccessful one-fight comeback in England after the war, Burns, the former champion, drifted away from the game.

Arthur Pelkey fought on until 1920, but he was merely going through the motions in order to earn a living at the only trade he knew. After the ill-fated bout with McCarty he lost a dozen fights by knockouts and departed from the White Hope scene.

9

THE BUSHMAN AND
THE BLACKSMITH

For a short time Australia became one of the centres of White Hope production. The sport had really taken off in the continent in 1880, when former bare-knuckle fighter and convert to the gloved game Jem Mace had paid a brief visit with his boxing booth to Australia and New Zealand.

Not only did Mace discover and encourage a young Timaru blacksmith called Bob Fitzsimmons to leave New Zealand to develop his boxing skills in Sydney, he also taught a tough gymnasium owner called Larry Foley, who went on to develop the world-class heavyweights Peter Jackson and Frank Slavin, and middleweights of the calibre of Fitzsimmons and Jem Hall.

Without exception, however, all these fighters had to quit Australia and make their homes in Europe, South Africa or the USA in order to further their careers. It was not until 1907 that a couple of home-grown heavyweights emerged who were to fight for the world heavyweight championship in Australia.

The first of these was a raw-boned outback slugger known as Boshter (a local slang term for 'magnificent') Bill Squires. He had been born on a sheep station outside the New South Wales bush town of Narrabri. His father had been a bare-knuckle fighter and Squires developed into a useful brawler himself. He engaged in a number of bare-fist encounters while earning a living variously as a miner, shearer and railway navvy. He always claimed that he had taken up boxing with the gloves after he had been persuaded to challenge a touring booth fighter. Squires had knocked out the professional and attracted the notice of a former bantamweight boxer, who took Squires to his Newcastle home and introduced him to some of the niceties of the Marquess of Queensberry rules governing gloved fighting.

Squires proved as adept in the ring with the gloves as he had in the ten bouts he had engaged in as a bare-knuckle fighter, but his early days were not easy. Talking about his initial bouts to a reporter from the *London Free Press*, he said, 'The day after a fight I went back to work in the mines. At one time, when I was new at the game, in order to beat the champion of one of the provinces, I walked 200 miles, trained for two weeks and fought for a fifty dollar purse.' However, after Squires scored a significant victory over the black Peter Felix, a former Australian champion, he was taken up by John Wren, a well-known gambler.

When he was 19 and working in a factory, Wren had gathered together every pound that he could muster and had bet the lot on a champion racehorse called Carbine to win the 1890 Melbourne Gold Cup. Because there were so many runners in the crowded field and the horse was heavily handicapped, Carbine had started at very reasonable odds. The horse had won, giving Wren a profit of £180.

The youngster used the money to launch an illegal off-course bookmaking organisation known as 'the shilling tote'. This proved very popular, as it gave ordinary people who could not get to racecourses an opportunity to back their fancies. Wren soon became rich, owning his own racecourses, boxing stadiums and a theatre.

The entrepreneur took a great pride in his new heavyweight and promised to secure Squires a shot at the world title. For a while it looked as if Philadelphia Jack O'Brien might be persuaded to come to Australia for a championship elimination contest, but the American turned the bout down to fight Stanley Ketchel instead. Disappointed, Wren appointed a puppet manager to look after Squires and arranged for his man to go to the USA to challenge Tommy Burns for his championship there.

Just as Squires was about to leave, in 1907, Jack Johnson turned up on the shores of Australia. He had heard that Tommy Burns might be coming to the continent and intended to challenge the champion when he arrived. There was much newspaper talk of

Johnson meeting Squires before the Australian sailed, but it was too late to make the necessary arrangements.

Johnson made the most of the situation, gaining a great deal of publicity by declaring that Squires had left because he was afraid to enter the ring. The black fighter implied that the same would apply to all other Australian heavyweights.

This impelled the newspapers to take up the cause, demanding that another local big man be brought forward to uphold the honour of his country. The choice fell upon the unhappy Bill Lang, a former blacksmith. He was quite well known in the Melbourne area as an Australian Rules football player and amateur boxer, but at this time he had had only nine professional fights and was little more than a novice. His main achievement had been to hold his own in a couple of fierce training-camp spars with the recently decamped Bill Squires. At this stage in his career he was certainly no match for a man of Johnson's experience.

Johnson warmed up with a one-round knockout of Peter Felix and then, on 4 March 1907, met Lang in the pouring rain in the open air at Melbourne, before a crowd of 15,000. Johnson entered the ring first and then had to wait, sheltering under an umbrella. The absent Lang did not raise the spirits of his supporters when he sent a message to the ring saying that it was too wet to fight.

Eventually Lang was persuaded to enter the ring and the bout got under way. At the end of the first round Johnson asked his seconds when his real opponent was going to put in an appearance, because the man facing him in the ring was just a joke. Johnson toyed with the novice for a few rounds, to give the crowd a show, and then started knocking the other man down. He put Lang on the canvas six times before flooring him for good in the ninth round. Then Johnson sauntered out of the ring and spent the next few months contentedly adding to his ring earnings with judicious bets at hospitable Australian racecourses.

For the time being, Australian fight fans turned their attention away from Lang and transferred their interest to their premier heavyweight, Bill Squires, who had reached the USA. There he had started at the top by challenging Tommy Burns for his title. Believing that he was on to a good thing, the champion had accepted and both men had gone into training. Squires, with his strength, long reach and power of punch, showed up so well in his sparring sessions that many newspapermen tipped him to defeat Burns. The small, self-contained champion was neither popular nor particularly highly regarded by boxing followers. He was widely expected to lose his title to Squires, who was on a winning streak, and he entered the fight an underdog in the betting.

Their bout took place in San Francisco on 4 July in front of a crowd of 20,000. Promoted by Jim Coffroth, it was a short-lived affair but hectic while it lasted. At the bell Squires walked boldly into the champion's arc of fire and was dropped heavily. The Australian was up after a short count, and, as Burns sailed in to finish him off, Squires leapt forward and landed a left hook to the mouth, which made the champion stagger back. Burns said later that it was one of the hardest blows he had ever taken in the ring. Automatically the dazed Burns fell into a clinch, and, as he waited for his head to clear, he bluffed his opponent by asking whether the Australian could fight or not. This disconcerted Squires. He pushed the champion away but did not immediately follow up.

This was all that Burns required. He hit Squires with a bludgeon of a right, felling his adversary again. Once more Squires pulled himself up, but Burns landed another right and it was all over in 2 minutes and 8 seconds of the first round. The referee, James J. Jeffries, walked over and handed the winner $10,000, a sum given to Squires by John Wren for the Australian to bet on himself to win.

The result of the Squires–Burns fight, following upon Lang's defeat at the hands of Jack Johnson, caused a great deal of gloom in Australia. This was deepened when Squires fought the blown-up middleweight Jack Twin Sullivan and was knocked out in the nineteenth round. The Australian was not finished, however. He followed Burns to Ireland, where the champion was defending against the local champion, the tubby Jem Roche. Squires entered the ring before the bout started and challenged Burns to a return fight. Burns, who had knocked Roche out almost before Squires had retaken his seat, expressed his willingness to let the Australian have another title tilt.

Squires stayed on in Ireland for a match with the loser Jem Roche, but, as both men had been knocked out in the first round by Burns, their bout was not well attended. Squires won on a fourth-round knockout and followed Tommy Burns to Paris for their rematch.

The second contest, held on 13 June 1908, was much better than their first abortive effort. However, it almost did not take place, because promoter Hugh McIntosh moved heaven and earth in a vain effort to steal the bout for Australia, where he knew it would draw a huge crowd.

Burns won the Paris fight in eight rounds, though not before he had been sent staggering in the fourth round and then dropped for a short count in the seventh. But, after regrouping, Burns connected with a hard blow to the body and Squires was unable to get up before the count of ten.

McIntosh hurried back to Australia, where he presented the local newspapers with an eyewitness account of the Paris bout, in which, he declared with a straight face, Burns had been most fortunate to win. The reporters fell for his account and used many inches of column space to tell their readers how close the Australian had been to gaining the world championship in France.

When Burns arrived in Australia, he played along with the pre-match publicity, declaring that Squires was a worthy opponent and a credit to his country. For his part Squires averred that the champion had hit him harder than any other man he had met. A large crowd greeted Squires at the station when he arrived in Sydney for his final training sessions, and 15,000 spectators bought tickets for the third meeting between the two, which would be the first contest for the World Heavyweight Championship to be held on Australian soil.

Again Squires fought bravely, but the much smaller Burns was too much for him. The Australian built up a slight lead over the first few rounds and then the champion began closing him down. Burns's style was unspectacular but effective and his body punches had Squires clinching and gasping for breath. In the thirteenth round Burns knocked Squires down three times. The towel was thrown in from the Australian's corner, just as a police inspector at ringside was demanding that the bout be stopped.

Less than two weeks later, Burns fought the ever-optimistic Bill Lang in Melbourne. This time 19,000 hopeful fans crowded the arena. Before the fight could get under way, the canny Burns declared that he had forgotten an essential elastic support for his injured forearm. Lang's handlers let the champion get away with his ploy and the nervous Australian had to wait while one of Burns's men went back to the hotel to fetch the bandage.

When the fight finally started, the big-punching Lang caused a sensation when he floored a casual champion with a heavy left hook. This acted as a wake-up call for Burns. He boxed cautiously until his head had cleared and then dismissed all thoughts of carrying Lang for the sake of his supporters. Burns moved in viciously. He knocked his opponent down four times and, in the sixth round, Lang's seconds threw in the towel.

There followed a momentary pause in the Australian heavyweight scene. Both of their hopes had been beaten by Burns, while Squires had also been hammered by Jack Johnson. In fact, the only bright spot on the Australian boxing horizon in 1908 had been the success of their amateur middleweight champion Reginald (Snowy) Baker in the London Olympics. Baker had won three fights in a single day to reach the final, where he had been matched against an England cricketer, J.W.H.T. Douglas. Baker had lost a thrilling bout on points to win the silver medal, but back home it was regarded as a moral victory, as the referee for the contest had been Douglas's father.

For the two Australian heavyweights a certain amount of cautious consolation was considered necessary before they were launched upon the world scene once again. When the furore following the Jack Johnson–Tommy Burns fight at Rushcutters Bay had died down, the rebuilding of the local big men got under way. In the following year Bill Lang was matched against former world heavyweight champion Bob Fitzsimmons. The Englishman was brought to Australia by Hugh D. McIntosh, who took over the mantle of Fitzsimmons's manager for the duration of his stay, while Tommy Burns was recruited as the Englishman's chief second.

Fitzsimmons was 47 years old. He had been boxing professionally for some twenty-eight years and had practically given up the sport to concentrate on his variety tours. Even so, *Boxing* optimistically gave the veteran a chance, pointing out Lang's comparative lack of experience: 'he has only been in the game since 1905'.

The bout was held at the Rushcutters Bay arena on 27 December 1909. It was scheduled over twenty rounds and billed as a fight for the heavyweight championship of Australia. In front of 12,000 people, the former world champion established a slight lead over the first few rounds but then succumbed to Lang's power of punch. By the twelfth round Fitzsimmons was reeling around the ring, cut and bleeding. A hard blow sent the Cornishman reeling back to the ropes. He dropped his guard and Lang hesitated, unwilling to strike a defenceless man, but the proud Fitzsimmons beckoned him in.

Reluctantly, the Australian approached and hit his semi-conscious opponent with a light tap to the jaw. It was sufficient to send the English fighter to the ground, where he remained until the count had been tolled over him.

When he had recovered Fitzsimmons walked unsteadily to the ropes and addressed the sympathetic crowd. 'I'm through,' he declared. 'I will never box again.'

The *Philadelphia Evening Star* of 27 December wrote sympathetically of the loser, 'Though Fitz trained faithfully he lacked his old punch and cunning. Had it not been for the fact that Lang was a trifle awed in meeting a man of Fitz's reputation, he would have finished the old man in half the time.'

A week later Bob Fitzsimmons was the guest of honour at another Sydney boxing tournament. Between bouts he was summoned into the ring and presented with a gold card case by Bill Lang on behalf of the local boxing fans. Fitzsimmons made a gracious little speech in which he wished Lang well for the future. Later that night the veteran sat up late in his hotel room with the young Australian heavyweight and Billy Williams, his manager, reminiscing about his fighting career and showing the younger fighter his favourite punches.

Although the Fitzsimmons bout was a meaningless one, it rehabilitated Lang in the eyes of his followers. Australian fans pointed out that he was still only 25, had never fought abroad, and that his two defeats had been at the hands of Johnson and Burns, the best men in the world at the time. Lang, it was decided, was definitely a White Hope and should be groomed for another shot at Jack Johnson.

These hopes suffered a blow in April 1910, when Tommy Burns made a comeback and was matched in Sydney with Lang for the British Empire Heavyweight Championship. Again Burns defeated Lang, this time over twenty rounds.

However, the ex-blacksmith reinforced his supporters' hopes for him when he three times knocked out Bill Squires to assert his claim as Australia's leading heavyweight. Apart from one abortive comeback attempt years later in 1916, Squires retired from the ring. He lived on to a hearty old age, dying in 1962 at 83 years old.

Lang was taken up by the ever-hopeful McIntosh, who escorted his White Hope to the USA, boosting him as the fighter who had beaten one former world champion, the elderly Fitzsimmons, and put up stern fights against two others, Burns and Johnson. However, the Australian's putative attempt to establish himself as a slightly passé contender soon foundered. In fact, Lang's main claim to fame on his visit to the States lay in being an unwitting central figure in a fistic scandal.

He was matched with former middleweight champion Stanley Ketchel, now a burnt-out case at the age of 24 and increasingly reliant on his manager Wilson Mizner putting the fix in with potential opponents. There was an uproar when Ketchel suddenly pulled out of the bout, claiming a sore foot. The *New York Telegraph* caused a scandal when it published an interview with Lang's manager, Hugh D. McIntosh, in which the latter claimed that he had refused to post a bond of $5,000 guaranteeing that Lang would not attempt to knock Ketchel out.

The article in the *Telegraph* killed any thoughts of a Lang–Ketchel bout. Instead, the Australian was matched against Al Kaufmann in Philadelphia. This was almost exactly a year after the San Francisco heavyweight had been humiliated by Jack Johnson in their ten-round, no-decision bout. Since then, Kaufmann had been outclassed in a couple of no-decision contests against Philadelphia Jack O'Brien and had the ignominy of being recruited as one of Johnson's sparring partners in the champion's preparation for his title bout with James J. Jeffries in Reno.

No one considered the shot Kaufmann to be a White Hope any more, but merely a trial horse for aspirants to the cherished inner circle of good white big men. Lang was expected to knock out his tall opponent with little trouble. Instead he struggled over the course of a turgid six-round, no-decision bout with the Californian giant. True to prizefighting form, the Australian blamed his poor showing on an injured hand. In an interview with the *Police Gazette* of 21 January 1911, Lang claimed, 'An injured hand prevented me from beating him. I almost had him out in the second round and could have finished him if I had been able to use my right hand. He saved himself by clutching me around the neck until the bell rang.'

When it became evident that Lang would not draw flies in the USA, McIntosh decided on one more throw of the dice in an effort to establish the Melbourne man. He took him to England and matched the Australian with the wildly eccentric Irishman, Petty Officer 'Nutty' Curran, for the Heavyweight Championship of the British Empire. Curran was a battered adherent of the Iron Hague laissez-faire school of training who boasted that he had never met an opponent who could get past his face.

Lang knocked Curran down in the first round but was disqualified when his follow-up blow struck the dazed Irishman while he was still in the act of rising from the canvas. But he redeemed himself slightly with a knockout win over American Jack Burns, and McIntosh decided to give his increasingly tarnished White Hope one last chance. In 1911, he matched Lang against Sam Langford at Olympia in London. Sports writer Trevor Wignall, present at the bout, described the build-up to the fight in his book *The Story of Boxing*. 'The contest was boomed to such an extent that it was the only thing talked about for weeks. Lang had arrived in London with the reputation of being a world-beater.'

McIntosh did his best to publicise the fight by writing a letter to the *Baltimore American* of 14 January: 'I have just matched Sam

Langford and Bill Lang, and I will endeavour to match the winner against Johnson. I will give it as my opinion now that Lang is the man destined to meet Jack Johnson for the championship of the world, and you can place me on record that Bill Lang will be the next world's champion. I feel certain of this. He has improved out of all recognition.'

Sam Langford and Bill Lang went into training in London, but neither was of much use to their promoter when it came to building up their contest in advance. Langford had good reason to be wary of too much contact with white people and refused to attend any social functions with them, while Lang was too bashful to do more than utter a few non-committal grunts when interviewed by the press. Andrew Soutar, a sports writer who tried to interview the Australian, gave up in disgust when Lang would only reply with the words 'Oh, yeah!' to any question.

Nevertheless, the promotion was the most glamorous boxing tournament ever seen in England up to that time. Aided by ex-lightweight Jimmy Britt, who interrupted his vaudeville career to undertake publicity for the contest, McIntosh pulled out all the stops. On the night of 14 February the ringside glittered with men in dress shirts and white ties and bejewelled women in evening gowns. Stewards, many of them old fighters, looked incongruous in tight white linen jackets with gilt buttons, while pretty girls sold programmes.

To help the film cameras and hopefully enhance the visual effect, Langford had been issued with a set of white boxing gloves. The black fighter was extremely suspicious of this departure from the norm, but as usual philosophically went along with his white boss's whims. A military band played both men into the ring.

During the preliminaries Lang, at 6ft tall and weighing 14 stone, towered over his opponent, outweighing Langford by 2 stone. From the first bell, the Australian was nowhere in the fight. Andrew Soutar, watching from ringside, wrote of Lang in his autobiography *My Sporting Life*, 'He was like a rabbit fascinated by a stoat. The little black walked straight up to him arms down by his side . . .' Lang tried to keep his smaller opponent at the end of his left jab, but did not have the experience to deal with Langford's in-fighting style. Totally outclassed, Lang was knocked down in the second round and again in the third and the sixth. James Butler described Lang as spending the best part of each round bent almost double in an attempt to escape Langford's punches. At one point Langford even dropped his arms to his sides and stuck out his chin invitingly. Lang struck him on his unprotected jaw with no fewer than four consecutive blows. Langford only laughed and turned to wink at his seconds.

Towards the end of the sixth round Langford moved in for the kill. He swung his right, overbalanced and fell to the floor. Lang lashed out automatically in return. His glove slid across the top of his fallen opponent's skull. It was a travesty of a real punch, but the referee Eugene Corri stepped forward and disqualified the Australian for hitting his opponent while he was down. Afterwards Corri said that he was only too pleased to have an excuse to bring the bout to an end before Lang got seriously hurt. He may have been right, for Lang collapsed in his corner before he could leave the ring. Langford chatted idly with his seconds and before he returned to his dressing room ostentatiously smoked a cigar.

As a fight it had been too one-sided to be interesting. Censoriously, Trevor Wignall reported from the ringside that Lang 'was scared stiff when he entered the ring, and his display would not have done credit to a schoolboy'.

There was an aftermath. During the bout, Sam Langford had been puzzled by his opponent's apparent durability. Time after time Langford had toppled Lang with vicious blows, only to see the Australian doggedly get to his feet again. Langford was sure that he had struck Lang as hard as any man he had fought, seemingly to little effect. When he got back to his dressing room, he recounted years later, he split the gloves open with a knife. He discovered that the padding had been stuffed with the fur of a rabbit, to render it ineffective as a striking weapon and give the Australian an extra advantage. To all intents and purposes Langford might have been hitting his opponent with pillows.

Langford took the offending gloves to the promoter's office and threw them on the desk. 'Oh, Mr. McIntosh,' he said sadly, 'you are a wicked man.'

It was a bad night for the wealthy occupants of the ringside seats as well. As they left the arena, gangs of masked thugs were lying in wait to rob them.

Lang received such a bad press for his inept showing against Sam Langford that he was no longer considered a White Hope. McIntosh, disillusioned with his man's showing, drifted out of boxing, preferring to put on theatrical productions. Lang returned to Australia. Unfortunately, it was at a time when decent American fighters, sensing good purses and easy pickings, were visiting the continent on a regular basis. The black American Sam McVey knocked Lang out in two rounds in Sydney, while Tom 'Bearcat' McMahon dispatched the Australian in five rounds. In 1913, Dave Smith, who was little more than a middleweight, took the Australian title from Lang and the latter gave up boxing in favour of keeping a hotel.

1 0

FRENCH CONNECTIONS

Boxing was late coming to France, but by 1913 *la boxe* was one of the country's most popular sports. This was mainly due to the efforts of the precocious Georges Carpentier and his manager François Descamps. Since Descamps had started coaching the 13-year-old and three years later had steered him to the French lightweight title, the handsome and hard-punching Carpentier had become the sporting idol of his country. Before the end of his career he would go on to win the welterweight, middleweight, light-heavyweight and heavyweight championships of France and to become the light-heavyweight champion of the world.

On his way up, Carpentier did not have it all his own way. As a 17-year-old he was thrashed by two tough American middleweights in Frank Klaus and Billy Papke. Unfortunately, Papke could not hang around for a return match, though he did also fight fellow American Willie Lewis while he was in Paris. At the weigh-in for that fight, someone in the crowd milling around the scales mentioned that Stanley Ketchel was the world's middleweight champion. This was a sore point with Papke, who considered himself to hold the title. Believing that the remark had been made by Lewis's manager, Dan McKetrick, Papke took a swing at him. The *Milwaukee Free Press* took up the story: 'The act caused a small riot . . . and Papke would have been badly mauled if he had not taken it on the run.'

The fine black heavyweight Joe Jeanette also defeated the Frenchman. Carpentier's manager, Descamps, was shrewd enough after this to employ Jeanette to take a hand in the training of his protégé. As a result, by 1913, Carpentier was considered capable of beating any European heavyweight and was being groomed for a shot at the world light-heavyweight title, with a tilt at the heavyweight championship to follow.

There were three major boxing halls in Paris alone, each one paying much higher purses to the right fighters than any in England or the USA. This led to a major migration of foreign boxers into the country. In addition, unlike the USA and England, there was no discernible colour bar in France. Jack Johnson himself made his home in exile there for a time, while Sam McVey was so popular in Paris that he settled there, and as a sign of his acclimatisation announced that from then, in homage to his adopted nation, he was to be billed as Sam McVea. In the three years he stayed in the capital he made so much money that he was able to stroll along the boulevards dressed in a frock coat, top hat and striped trousers as his daily attire. He lost only one of more than thirty fights in Europe, and this was in a thriller with his old adversary Joe Jeanette. McVey knocked his opponent down at least twenty times, but in the process shipped so much punishment that he had to retire in the forty-ninth round.

Joe Jeanette arrived in Paris with his manager, the shrewd Dan McKetrick, ex-editor of the *New York World*, and opened a boxing school in the French capital before undertaking a number of fights there. In 1909, his fight with the sturdy Canadian White Hope Sandy Ferguson caused a sensation, especially in the thirteenth round, when both heavyweights landed their best shots simultaneously and each went tumbling to the canvas. They beat the count and the black boxer went on to win on points. Their first bout was so popular that the two men met in France on three other occasions before they went home for a summer holiday.

France was undergoing a sporting renaissance, particularly in the air. In 1908, the Michelin brothers, André and Edouard, created the Michelin Grand Prix, with an award of 20,000 francs for any aviator who could achieve a flying distance of at least 20 kilometres. The prize was won by Wilbur Wright, the famous pioneer, with a distance of 125 kilometres. The competition became an annual one, with each year's winner asked to fly at least twice as far as the previous winner.

France also had its own early version of kick-boxing, which did not catch on in Great Britain. In an article in *C.B. Fry's Magazine of Sports and Out-of-Door Life* in 1905, an English visitor to a French School of Arms in Paris wrote reassuringly, 'The kick which the Frenchman introduces so nimbly into his sparring matches does not in the least constitute a reason for writing him down as an ass . . . They are not bred of an uncontrollable desire to turn his back on his opponent. They are matters of rule.'

Some American big men who were a little past their best also settled for a while in France, claiming to be White Hopes in transit. The wily Kid McCoy, inventor of the corkscrew punch and one-time disputed claimant to the world light-heavyweight title, was 39 and had recently been declared bankrupt when he turned up. The USA had become a little too hot for him when his bout with former heavyweight champ James J. Corbett was declared to be fixed, practically ending boxing in New York for a while.

Despite his advancing years, McCoy was still good enough to outpoint PO Nutty Curran in Nice. His victory was watched by a local resident, the poet, playwright and Nobel Prize-winner for Literature Maurice Maeterlinck, a boxing enthusiast. He took the American under his wing. The two men became friends and companions. McCoy taught the writer how to box, in preparation for a charity exhibition bout between Maeterlinck and Georges Carpentier. For his part, the American fighter learned French and tried to read his host's books. The sardonic, witty and totally unscrupulous McCoy had always attracted the interest of writers. In 1904, when he was training for a fight with Philadelphia Jack O'Brien, he had been visited at his training camp by the humorous novelist P.G. Wodehouse. The usually gentle and retiring Wodehouse had even volunteered to box a round with McCoy, but the fighter's then wife (he was married six times) arrived and bore off her husband, a fact for which Wodehouse was to express his gratitude in later years.

French interest in Carpentier as a White Hope grew when he was matched against Bombardier Wells in Nice on 1 June 1913. The bout was scheduled as part of the Ghent Exhibition and was billed as being for the European Heavyweight Championship, although Carpentier weighed less than 12 stone. Wells was 3in taller and more than a stone heavier than his younger opponent. There was a certain amount of feeling between the two men. Four years earlier, when Carpentier as a welterweight had been preparing for a fight at Leigh on Sea in Great Britain, he had sparred with Wells and had resented it when the much bigger man had not pulled his punches.

The Ghent fight seemed an odd one for Descamps to agree to. Wells's defeats by Americans had almost ruled him out as a White Hope, yet he appeared to be much too big and strong for his opponent. The French manager, however, thought that a decisive victory over the British heavyweight champion would cement Carpentier's claim to being the best in Europe.

Descamps told the 19-year-old Carpentier to stay close to Wells from the off. Carpentier did his best to snuggle up to the big man, but he was knocked down heavily in the first round and seemed fortunate to survive to the bell. Acting on his corner's instructions, the Frenchman alternately clinched and ran in the second and third rounds. By the fourth round he was all right again, while Wells's confidence was beginning to trickle away at the sight of his adversary apparently none the worse for wear. Then Carpentier moved in and knocked out the passively resigned Wells with a right to the head and a left to the body.

Back home in Great Britain, many fans refused to believe that their champion could have run out of steam again. The National Sporting Club rematched the pair for a purse of £3,000 and side-stakes of £300. The hall was crowded, with onlookers anticipating a decisive win for the English fighter on his home turf. Wells did his best to psych out his opponent. He kept Carpentier waiting for five minutes in the ring, and then caused a further delay by complaining about the bandages on the hands of the French fighter.

When the fight finally got under way, this time Wells lasted only 73 seconds. The French fighter sallied towards his apparently transfixed opponent, battered him around the ring and knocked him out with a one-two to the body. As the heavyweight lay wretchedly prone on the canvas, the brilliant Welsh featherweight Jim Driscoll broke all the club rules by racing to the ringside and berating Wells furiously, calling him a spineless coward. The Welshman was ordered away from the ring, but some distinguished members of the club had also joined in and were by now hissing, 'Fake!' The *New York Times* of 9 December reported, 'Wells finally rose, and attempted to make a speech, but his voice was not audible above the excited hubbub, and anyway the spectators were in no mood to listen to explanations from their fallen hero.'

Wells never recovered from these two defeats, but the victories fast-tracked Carpentier into the leading ranks of the White Hopes. Descamps, who was never averse to taking a gamble if the potential rewards seemed high enough, challenged Gunboat Smith to come to Europe to defend the White Heavyweight Championship of the World against the young Frenchman.

The lean and rangy Smith had been making steady progress since leaving the US Navy. He had gained valuable experience early on by acting as a doughty sparring partner for Jack Johnson when the champion had been preparing for his title defence against Stanley Ketchel. Johnson's system of counterpunching had proved too much for the inexperienced Smith, but the ex-sailor had persevered and had secured a great deal of favourable newspaper publicity when, during a sparring session, he had staggered the champion with a potent right-hand punch. After this incident Smith went on to build an impressive record as a hard-punching and resourceful heavyweight contender. He defeated such big names as Frank Moran, Fireman Jim Flynn and Jess Willard, before going on to cause a significant upset by outpointing Sam Langford over twelve rounds in Boston. There were some, however, who thought that Langford, who was still hoping for a title shot, boxed gently with his white opponent in order to persuade Jack Johnson that he would be easy meat.

When Smith defeated Al Pelkey, still shell-shocked by the ring death of his opponent Luther McCarty, he also won the White Heavyweight Championship, for what it was worth. In Europe, with Carpentier emerging fast after his defeats of Wells, it was worth quite a lot. A number of European promoters submitted offers to stage a match between the two men for Smith's unofficial championship.

To Descamps's disappointment the bout did not take place in France. A British promoter, Dick Burge, a former British lightweight champion now promoting at the Ring in the East End of London, secured the contest with the offer of a large purse and hired Olympia as the venue.

A huge crowd met Smith at Paddington station. The American fighter trained at Harrow, where the atmosphere in the camp was light hearted. One visitor saw Smith's trainer, one-time leading black heavyweight Bob Armstrong, encouraging a goat to charge at his fighter. One night Smith attended a tournament in London. Not impressed by the attitude of one British fighter who showed no appetite for conflict, the American heavyweight remarked scornfully that if the bout had taken place back home the offending boxer would have been shot so full of holes that he would not be able to swim for a year.

It was a sign of the influence still being cast over the scene by Jack Johnson in exile, and the respect extended to him even by the leading White Hopes, that, when Gunboat Smith was asked off the record when he was going to fight the black champion, the white heavyweight paused reflectively and then said curtly, 'Johnson will wait, and the longer the better.'

When asked for his plan of campaign against Carpentier, Smith said, 'I have never seen that French guy but when I meet him at Olympia, I shall bring a right hand punch over from my hip, and if I land he will think Olympia has fallen in.' When asked for his intentions should he lose, the pragmatic Smith answered grimly, 'Fight again! And after that, more fighting, for that is how I live.'

The contest, held on 16 July 1914 before a sell-out crowd, was exciting and controversial. Early on Smith was floored and saved by the bell, but he came back into the fight and, with his extra weight and strength, was beginning to back Carpentier up. In the sixth round, Carpentier missed with a powerful right hand, overbalanced and tumbled to the ground. At the same time Smith threw a counterpunch. The Frenchman was on his knees and in the act of rising. Smith's punch grazed the top of Carpentier's head.

The impact was minimal and the blow was obviously unintentional, but technically it was a foul. Descamps was too experienced to let such a golden opportunity for victory pass him by. The manager tumbled into the ring, screaming 'Foul!' and protectively cuddling the head of his bewildered and embarrassed heavyweight. The referee, Eugene Corri, at once disqualified Smith for striking his opponent while he was down. Later he wrote sternly in his autobiography, 'It was no use discussing whether Smith intended to foul him or regretted having fouled him. The fact remains that he contravened the rules of the Ring by hitting his opponent when he was down.'

There was uproar in the hall. Smith's manager, Buckley, rushed over and screamed (in questionable taste, as the referee mildly remarked), 'How much, Mr Corri, did you have on Carpentier?' Fred Dartnell, who covered the match for his newspaper, later wrote in his book *Seconds Out*, 'I always thought that Mr Corri was rather bluffed by the French party.'

It was too late for recriminations. The fight was over and Carpentier could now claim to be the White Heavyweight Champion. A disappointed and resentful Smith returned to the USA, where salt was rubbed into his wounds when, in a return bout with Sam Langford, the black man, fighting with much less restraint than in their previous encounter, knocked out his white opponent. Smith, as he promised, fought on, but his time as the leading White Hope had come and gone.

Carpentier came back to Paris an even greater hero. He took on Tom Kennedy as a sparring partner and the Paris newspapers were full of the prospects of the handsome Frenchman fighting Jack Johnson for the latter's world title. It never materialised. The canny Descamps realised that his charge, weighing little more than 12 stone and still only 19 years old, was not yet ready to concede 2in in height and 1½ stone in weight to the greatest defensive heavyweight the world had so far seen. Threatening noises were made by the French manager in the newspapers, and vague challenges were thrown out, but in the event Carpentier had only one more minor fight before enlisting in the French Air Force.

The French heavyweight did, in fact, take part in another unrecorded bout before his war service. In 1914, Carpentier received an unexpected challenge from a young Yorkshire amateur called George Mitchell. Disgusted by the fact that Bombardier Billy Wells had only managed to last 73 seconds against the French champion, Mitchell mentioned to a friend that he was sure he could elude Carpentier in the ring for longer than that.

The remark reached the ears of a family friend, a textile executive with business contacts in France. Boldly, he challenged Carpentier on Mitchell's behalf. To the amazement of just about everyone, and the consternation of George Mitchell, the French heavyweight accepted.

Matters snowballed. Almost before he knew what was happening, Mitchell found himself smuggled into Paris to face Carpentier before a secret gathering of society men and women. Five Bradford businessmen raised a purse of 3,500 francs to compensate Mitchell for the beating he was about to take. It was now too late for Mitchell to back out, much as he regretted his original boast. While the crowd looked on with great enjoyment, Mitchell sustained a beating at the hands of the humourless Carpentier, for whom fighting was a serious matter.

Things got off to a bad start when, at the first bell, the Frenchman crossed the ring with his left arm extended in his customary pawing manner. Mitchell, who had never seen his opponent box, thought that Carpentier was holding out his glove for a handshake. Instead, Carpentier whipped his left into Mitchell's body and followed this with a right to the jaw. Mitchell went down heavily.

Altogether, Carpentier knocked the Englishman down four times while their bout lasted, but Mitchell, although groggy, lasted 22 seconds longer against the Frenchman than Wells had done. Honour satisfied, Mitchell's seconds threw in the towel. Later the adversaries shared a bottle of champagne before parting.

Mitchell was one of two English amateur White Hopes of the period. The other was an all-round young athlete called John Hopley. As a heavyweight boxer, F.J.V. Hopley had won the public schools' heavyweight championship in 1899, and then had represented Cambridge successfully against Oxford; he'd been picked as a fast bowler for the university cricket team, and, while playing for Blackheath, had won several rugby union caps for England. English newspapers played up his boxing background and claimed that the strapping young man was already good enough to fight Jack Johnson for his title.

Later, sanity prevailed when it was pointed out that Hopley had not even been good enough to consider entering the Amateur Boxing Association championships. The furore died down and Hopley departed from a boxing scene he had never even been particularly interested in inhabiting.

With Carpentier reluctant to meet Jack Johnson in anything other than a social context, more credible matches were being made in Paris. Johnson, a hedonist in a hedonistic city, was enjoying himself thoroughly but at the same time was rapidly running out of money.

He was happy to be living in France and continued to be aggrieved by his treatment in the USA. In an interview in *La Boxe et les Boxeurs* on 16 July 1913, he complained, 'I can say that I have been the most persecuted man in the world. The Americans who definitely cannot accept my victory against Jeffries, the relatively important sums of money I have won nor my lifestyle, seem to have committed themselves to my downfall or at least my financial ruin.'

He was living in a luxurious furnished apartment and attending cabarets and nightclubs almost every night. By the end of 1913, he had not fought seriously for seventeen months, since his knockout of Fireman Jim Flynn in Las Vegas the year before. He engaged in several, probably fixed, boxer–wrestler encounters and was then forced to break his self-imposed rule of not fighting other black boxers by accepting a match against Battling Jim Johnson, a second-rate heavyweight who had once earned his living in a circus, feeding the lions and cleaning out their cages. It was the first gloved fight between two black heavyweights in which the world title was at stake.

Jim Johnson was one of the peripatetic circus of black boxers who kept meeting one another all over the world. He fought Joe Jeanette eleven times, Sam Langford on ten occasions and Sam McVey seven times. Jack Johnson was out of condition but his opponent was too limited to take advantage of the fact. After ten dull rounds the bout was declared a draw when Johnson announced that he had broken his arm and could not continue. For once the champion was lucky. Technically, with Jack Johnson refusing to box on, the bout and his title could have been awarded to his little-known opponent.

Many believed that Johnson had abandoned the fight for no good reason, but a doctor declared that the champion had suffered a slight fracture of the radius. Certainly Battling Jim, who fought out of a low crouch, had a reputation for causing his opponents to break their hands on his skull. Earlier that year in Paris, the English heavyweight Jewey Smith had been forced to retire when he fractured his knuckles hitting the bobbing head of Jim Johnson, and years later an outstanding black fighter called Harry Wills also had to retire with a broken arm when he took on Battling Jim. No one, however, had suggested that Smith or Wills should have been given a draw as a result.

Jack Johnson needed a big-money fight against a White Hope. As it happened, one of the best was currently plying his trade in Europe. This was the cheerful, libidinous red-haired American Frank Moran. Moran had spent some time in the United States Navy, serving President Teddy Roosevelt as quartermaster on the presidential yacht *Mayflower*, and he had also been a deckhand on the luxury yacht of the millionaire J.P. Morgan. Upon his discharge he had also spent several weeks as a student at a dental school at the University of Pittsburgh before deciding that there was more money in knocking teeth out than extracting them scientifically. His brief sojourn in the classroom had been enough to earn him the sobriquet of the 'Fighting Dentist' when he turned professional in 1910.

Moran was a hard-punching, handsome happy-go-lucky wanderer and ladies' man, who numbered among his girlfriends the Hollywood serial queen Pearl White. In the ring he garnered a lot of newspaper publicity by naming his potent looping right 'Mary Anne'. Moran was being managed, in a condition of mutual antipathy, by former newspaperman Dan McKetrick, who was promoting bouts in Paris. Moran always felt that his manager had little regard for him compared with McKetrick's star heavyweight Joe Jeanette.

There were a number of other points at issue between the fighter and his manager. One of the main ones was Moran's refusal to sign a contract with a man he considered was cheating him and would continue to do so.

The disgusted McKetrick retaliated by saying, in the manner of managers down the ages, that he would never employ Moran again, unless he needed him. Unfortunately, the cash-strapped Jack Johnson was willing to fight Moran or any other White Hope. McKetrick could not bear the thought of merely taking the promoter's cut of the gate when he could appropriate a quarter of Moran's purse as well.

As a result, McKetrick, against his better judgement, went ahead and organised the tournament, hoping to talk Moran out of his cut when the time came to settle up. The American employed a French frontman, Theodore Vienne, to handle the details. Johnson trained in a ballroom. The French public disparaged Moran's chances. *L'Auto* of 22 June 1913 asked, 'Why did America put its hopes in this new champion of the white race whom it put on the path on which the Negro had already found Tommy Burns and Jeffries and reduced both of them to nothing?'

Nevertheless the hall was packed for the event. Another selling point was the fact that Georges Carpentier had been persuaded to referee the bout. When the Frenchman entered the ring, to the loudest cheer of the night, it was noticeable how slim and frail he seemed next to the burly Jack Johnson.

The fight itself, held on 27 June 1914, was an absolute frost. Jim Brady, who had managed two heavyweight champions in James J. Corbett and James J. Jeffries and who knew his big men, covered the event for the *New York American*. He was scathing in his condemnation of the fighters' feeble efforts.

It was a second-rate exhibition between two mixed-ale fighters. That's my opinion. Johnson and Moran were misnamed fighters tonight. Had the fight been held in New York the spectators would have stopped the disgraceful bout in ten rounds. Not one effective blow was struck by either man during the entire contest. There was never a suspicion of a jar, much less a knockdown. The spectacle of a world's champion, superior in weight, science, experience and strength, clinging to a smaller antagonist, expressing in every move and appealing glance his yearning for the final tap of the gong – this was Johnson in the last three rounds.

Johnson was now 36 years old and as usual had not trained hard. Nevertheless he had done enough to be awarded the decision on points by Carpentier. Many disgruntled spectators believed that this was just another cynical example of Johnson's disregard for his audience and that the black fighter had just coasted his way through the bout as easily as possible. Reporter Fred Dartnell, present at ringside, thought otherwise. He believed that the hitherto-invincible world champion was beginning the long slide down the far side of the hill. 'I got into the ring and cut the gloves away from his wrists, which were so swollen that it was impossible to untie the gloves. Johnson was dead tired, and although he assured me with a kind of distrait, far-away look in his eyes, that he had enjoyed the fight, I think the disillusionment of life was then already beginning to tell upon him.'

Even worse was to come for both fighters. McKetrick was so disgusted by his rows with Moran and the disagreements he had had with Jack Johnson before the bout that he saw to it that neither fighter got paid. The profits of $36,000 were paid into a French bank, while McKetrick tried his hand at litigation. He claimed that Moran owed him money for training expenses and that this should be handed over before either fighter received his due.

A bruised Moran managed to catch up with the promoter at a racecourse the day after the fight. Reluctantly the promoter handed over 200 francs. It was all that the heavyweight was to see, and 200 francs more than Johnson ever pocketed from the bout. On 4 August 1914, war broke out in Europe and no banking transactions took place. The money was still there, vainly claimed by Johnson and Moran long after hostilities had ended.

No one in France was now interested in professional boxing matches. Raymond Poincaré, the President of the French Republic, made a public appeal to his countrymen to form a sacred union, *L'Union sacrée*, to face the Germans. Many of the American sporting immigrants hurried back home as quickly as they could. Only those whose high life had cost them all their money were forced to stay on.

For a time Jack Johnson was among those who stayed, unwilling to return to the USA and face the prison sentence hanging over him. However, as the war grew closer he left, in July 1914, for Russia; from there he went on to Spain, where he settled for several years.

In 1915, Frank Moran also was still in Paris. With the advancing Germans almost within earshot, there were no more boxing tournaments being held in the capital. An almost destitute Moran swallowed his pride and approached McKetrick again. He told the promoter that he wanted to get back to the USA for some easy fights. The unforgiving McKetrick told him that, as far as he was concerned, the only way Moran would get home would be by walking across the Atlantic.

Fortunately, Moran managed to get a bout with Bombardier Billy Wells in London, where fights were still being staged. By this time the British heavyweight had lost all credibility as a White Hope and was in bad odour with the public for his perceived reluctance to rejoin the colours when less fit men were fighting and dying in France.

Even so, a knockout victory over the still formidable Moran might have revived Wells's fistic career. There was no chance of this. Wells entered the ring in his usual state of fluttering distress. The fact was picked up by Moran's veteran second, Birmingham-born Charlie Mitchell. Mitchell went back a long way. Twenty-seven years earlier he had fought for over three hours to a thirty-nine-round bare-knuckle draw with world champion John L. Sullivan in the pouring rain at Chantilly in France.

A genuine hard man, Mitchell was contemptuous of Wells's temperamental approach to the business of boxing, and saw a chance to win the fight for Moran almost before it had started. Both fighters had to wait in their corners while a bulldog was auctioned from the ring for war charities. Mitchell took the opportunity to encourage his fighter in loud stage whispers designed to reach the ears of the quaking English champion. 'Look at him,' sneered Mitchell, indicating the boxer in the other corner. 'He wants his mama, doesn't he? Come on now, get the bull pup sold and send for an undertaker and a coffin!'

Moran's second kept up his stream of vituperation until the bell sounded to start the fight. Wells's left jab was in evidence early in the bout, but his dogged opponent wore the Englishman down and knocked him out in the tenth round, earning enough money for his passage home to the USA.

Wells fought on for another ten years, retiring in 1925, but he was never again regarded as a prospect for world honours. In his book *Boxing and Physical Culture*, his one-time trainer, strongman Thomas Inch, wrote of the heavyweight, 'I was asked to take over his training at a difficult time in his career [1911] and found him a particularly pleasant person to deal with. Handled in rather different fashion throughout his career he might easily have met with far greater success.'

11

THE LAST HOPES

In 1913, the USA once again became the centre of the White Hope campaign. By this time most of the major overseas contenders, like Bombardier Billy Wells and the Australians Lang and Squires, had had their chances and lost them. Carpentier was biding his time in the hope of putting on more weight. Other aspiring heavyweights never really had what it took. But still new young giants were imported by American managers unable to find home-grown prospects. Most of the fresh batch proved no better than their predecessors.

All the same, American newspapers and the public were still optimistically demanding the emergence of a white heavyweight to defeat the world champion. From France Jack Johnson issued a defiant challenge, telling the sports editor of the *Defender* on 10 August 1913 that he was prepared to fight any white challenger for $30,000.

Johnson showed no sign of wanting to leave the relative tranquillity of France. He was probably wise to stay where he was. The year 1913 was not an easy one for the black population of the United States. By the end of the year, forty-five black males had been lynched there, many of them in the Southern states of Mississippi and Georgia. The pretexts for these examples of summary mob rule were mostly accusations of murder or rape. More and more black boxers with reputations left for Europe, where they could pursue their violent craft in relative peace. At the same time, an increasing number of European heavyweights were imported into the USA to meet the need for a credible White Hope.

One of these shooting stars was Irishman Con O'Kelly, Cork-born but a resident of Hull on the east coast of England. O'Kelly,

6ft 3in tall, weighing nearly 16 stone and with a chest measurement of 50 inches, certainly looked the part of a White Hope. The former policeman also had the distinction of having won a gold medal in the freestyle heavyweight wrestling class at the 1908 Olympics. This feat had been all the more impressive because a few months before the Games had started, O'Kelly had been hospitalised after being buried by a falling wall when helping the fire brigade to effect a rescue.

After winning his gold medal, O'Kelly had resigned from the police force to turn professional and tour the musical halls. The minutes of the Hull Watch Committee noted that PC 249 O'Kelly was leaving 'to enable him to wrestle with Jose Levette, the champion of Spain'. However, his enthusiasm was dampened slightly when he was thrown all over the stage during a ring encounter with the famous George Hackenschmidt, the Russian Lion.

Realising that he would never make much headway in wrestling as long as Hackenschmidt was around, the pragmatic O'Kelly changed sports and became a professional boxer. He rattled off a series of victories and in 1909 was matched in Hull with the American White Hope Tom Kennedy. By this time the Irishman had built up a considerable following, and the purse of £750 was said to be the largest so far offered for a boxing match in the north of England.

Kennedy had been in France at the time and knew nothing about O'Kelly when he signed up for the match. The American was the first to enter the ring, and, in order to psych out his opponent, Kennedy did not turn round when the local hero came down the aisle to a tumultuous storm of applause. 'I figured I'd scare him to death by ignoring him,' explained the American.

It was a ploy that was to rebound on Kennedy. When the referee called both men to the centre of the ring for their pre-match instructions, Kennedy made a leisurely turn and saw Con O'Kelly for the first time. He goggled at the giant glowering at him from the other corner. 'I had never seen such a monster,' he recalled with awe, 'and when he stripped, the chills ran up my back. He had arms like steel bands. His chest was the chest of a Jeffries!'

It was a case for quick thinking, and Kennedy was equal to the occasion. He realised that to win the fight he would have to gain the upper hand psychologically in the few seconds left before the fight started. As the referee started his preamble, Kennedy suddenly whipped his right hand into the solar plexus of the unsuspecting O'Kelly, doubling the Irishman up. 'That sort of punch won't be called a foul, will it?' asked Kennedy casually.

The referee was so amazed that he could only shake his head dazedly. O'Kelly's seconds, equally dumbfounded, helped their stricken man, still bent over in agony, back to his corner. The bell went and Kennedy raced eagerly across the ring as the half-paralysed O'Kelly turned feebly, and started pummelling his Irish opponent. Kennedy kept on top throughout the contest, and also showed the Irishman one or two other tricks of the trade he had not experienced before.

After being butted particularly painfully by the American in the third round, O'Kelly responded in kind. Unfortunately, Kennedy had disguised his use of the head by waiting until O'Kelly's broad back obscured the view of the official. O'Kelly's illegal rejoinder was seen by everyone in the hall and the scandalised referee disqualified him at once. 'What about him?' wailed O'Kelly to no avail. 'That guy nutted me!'

It was considered that, under the circumstances, O'Kelly had done well enough against Kennedy while their fight had lasted to justify his being exported to the USA to join the ever-swelling ranks of White Hopes. He made his base among the Irish expatriates of Boston, and was even advised for a time by former heavyweight champion Bob Fitzsimmons. Fitz recommended the heavyweight to manager Tommy Ryan, the one-time middleweight champion and opponent of Stanley Ketchel. Ryan took on the huge O'Kelly and for a time entertained high hopes for his charge.

O'Kelly was promised a dozen fights in the USA at about $500 a time. This was not a bad return for his efforts. At about the same time Jim Thorpe, the great Native American athlete, had just been recruited by the New York Giants for $7,500, a year after being stripped of the gold medals he had won at the 1912 Olympics for the pentathlon and decathlon because it was discovered that as a youth he had once earned a few summer dollars as a semi-professional baseball player.

The better American college footballers were also being offered increasingly tempting rates to turn professional. Willie Heston, a graduate from Michigan, was paid $600 for his first game for the fledgling Canton squad. Unfortunately he broke his leg early in the game and never played again.

The biggest money, however, remained in prizefighting. In the year that O'Kelly started his North American tour, former champion Tommy Burns, well past his best years, still took home $5,000 tax-free after his bout with Arthur Pelkey. A good or even promising white heavyweight could still earn the big bucks.

The 24-year-old O'Kelly started off well by winning his first five bouts in the USA. Then he was put in with the ageing fighter Hank Griffin. Griffin was coming to the end of the road, but back in 1902 he had twice drawn with a young Jack Johnson. Johnson always said that the 6ft 4in Griffin had been the hardest puncher he had ever faced.

Ryan figured that a victory over the veteran black fighter would justify O'Kelly's claim to being a White Hope. Unfortunately, Griffin proved too experienced for the Irishman and knocked him out in five rounds. Ryan decided to stake everything on one throw of the dice and matched O'Kelly with Griffin in a return fight. The Irish heavyweight had one of his best nights and knocked Griffin out in the fifth round.

This result gained O'Kelly plenty of publicity, and in his next fight, against another black boxer, Jeff Madden, in January 1911, the Irishman was billed as 'the new White Hope'. O'Kelly secured a creditable draw against a good heavyweight and went on to outpoint the durable Porky Flynn.

One problem faced by O'Kelly was the fact that he had been a police officer in England. There was a great deal of anti-English feeling among the Irish population in the USA, and large crowds gathered, hoping to see the former guardian of the law defeated.

Even hardened reporters were beginning to wonder whether O'Kelly might have something, and there were many demands in the sports pages for the visitor to be matched against a top man. He was put in with Jim Barry, apparently on the downslope after defeats by Al Kaufmann and Porky Flynn. Barry, a one-time friend and sparring partner of middleweight champion Stanley Ketchel, had once been considered a White Hope himself, but had fallen on hard times. The son of an Irish father and a French mother, he was one of the few white heavyweights willing to meet the leading black fighters, but Sam Langford, who fought the white boxer on at least eleven occasions, had once unkindly speculated that this was because Barry was often so incapacitated by drink or dope that he could hardly make out the shape, let alone the colour, of his opponent.

On this occasion the fuddled American soon proved to be much too good for his opponent. He gave the game O'Kelly such a dreadful thrashing that the ringsiders called for the bout to be stopped.

It was virtually the end in the USA for O'Kelly. Before he left for England he twice defeated Jeff Madden in return fights, but it was reckoned that if an over-the-hill heavyweight like Barry could toy with the Irishman, he had no future as a White Hope, even though he had won nine, drawn one and lost only one of his fights on his tour. Barry, a notorious hellraiser, was shot and killed in a saloon brawl in the Panama Zone in 1913.

O'Kelly had a few more fights in Great Britain, but was badly beaten by the black American Battling Jim Johnson, who was based in Paris. The Irishman used his ring earnings to take over a pub in Hull. There was talk of a northern promoter matching O'Kelly with Bombardier Wells for the British title, but the outbreak of war put an end to the proposal. In 1914, at the age of 29, O'Kelly retired from the ring.

Another White Hope who tried his luck in the USA was George Rodel, a South African. Born Lodewikus van Vuuren in the Free State village of Smithfield, he had a successful run as an amateur heavyweight in his home country. Rodel came to England in 1911 to try his hand at the professional game. He won a few fights, and then attracted some notice by beating the wild PO Nutty Curran three times. Admittedly, two of these wins were the results of his opponent's disqualifications, almost inevitable where Curran was concerned, but the other seemed genuine enough. Rodel decided that he was ready for a better class of opponent. He was then misguided enough to go into the ring with the great black fighter Sam McVey, who knocked him out in the first round. This was followed by an eleventh-round stoppage at the hands of big Joe Jeanette.

The South African was sure that these setbacks would finish his career, but he did not appreciate the machinations of boxing. Bombardier Billy Wells, the British heavyweight champion, was in the process of rebuilding his career after a three-round knockout at the hands of Al Palzer at Madison Square Garden. His connections were looking for an easy opponent for their man before he took on the much more formidable Gunboat Smith.

With the early exit against McVey on his record, Rodel was an attractive prospect for Jim Maloney, Wells's manager. The South African fought Wells at the King's Hall in London on 6 December 1912, living down to Maloney's expectations by going out in the second round.

There was little left in England for Rodel, so he did what many White Hopes had done before him and crossed the Atlantic to try his hand in New York. Here he had a rare stroke of luck. A devout man, Rodel encountered a priest who was a boxing enthusiast. The man of the cloth urged the South African to try to persuade manager Jimmy Johnston to handle his affairs.

Rodel managed to get into Johnston's office, forcing a way past the chancers, gamblers and assorted low life who formed the bantam-cock Englishman's regular entourage, and put his case to the tiny ex-Liverpudlian. Johnston listened sceptically. He had tried as hard as any manager to find his own personal White Hope and was beginning to wonder if he would be forced to rely on smaller fighters to keep him in comparative luxury. Certainly the South African looked big enough, and Rodel had the sense not to mention his quick-time defeats at the fists of McVey and Wells.

Johnston sent Rodel off to the local gymnasium to be tried out by some of the perpetual losers who hung around there, hoping to earn coffee-and-cakes money. An hour later his trainer returned to the office, shaking his head and reporting that the South African had been knocked all round the ring by several of the resident patsies.

That should have been the end of the matter, but Johnston, who was not a religious man, had nevertheless been flattered by the fact that a priest had considered him worthy of building Rodel's career. He also had the germ of an idea. Instead of showing the battered Rodel the door, Johnston put on his hat and took him round to the office of sports writer Bob Edgren. He had fed Edgren a number of stories for his column in the past, and, while the writer was not a gullible man, Edgren had been known to go along with a weak story as long as it was interesting enough.

The one pitched to him by Johnston that afternoon was worthy of any sports writer's attention. Indicating the shy, broad-shouldered South African, the manager announced proudly that not only was Rodel a fine White Hope in the making, but that he had been a hero of the Boer War.

Even the blasé Edgren took notice of this. He started scribbling as Johnston went on to inform him glibly that, in the conflict between South Africa and Great Britain, Rodel and his older brothers had been fearless commandos operating behind the British lines. As Johnston rattled on, improvising madly, Rodel slumped in a chair, paying little attention to what was being said as he recovered gratefully from the maulings he had taken in the gym that morning.

The next morning the exploits of the hastily rechristened 'Boer Rodel' formed the main story in Bob Edgren's influential column. Adhering to the proud traditions of the press, other writers freely purloined Edgren's copy and by the end of the week Rodel was being hailed as a fitting contender for the world's championship. To keep his fighter in the public eye, Johnston ordered Rodel to parade up and down Broadway in an army greatcoat.

Then, after providing his charge with a couple of set-ups in Art Nelson and Tim Logan, Johnston had to kill the goose that lay the golden egg by actually matching the South African against some reasonable opponents. The manager did not want to do this, but there was no money in matching his prospect with any more pork-

and-beaners. To make matters worse, several sports writers had worked out that 'Boer Rodel' would only have been 12 years old when the South African war had ended, a trifle young to be a sharpshooter.

To deflect the growing tide of resentment among the writers, in 1913 Johnston hastily matched Rodel against the hard-punching Irishman Jim Coffey, managed by Billy Gibson. Coffey did the Boer's cause no good by knocking him out in nine rounds. Johnston was not going to give up yet. For his next fight he put Rodel in with the leading White Hope, Gunboat Smith.

Even hardened fight fans regarded this as overmatching to the highest, or lowest, degree. It was plain that the master of ceremonies shared their views. Having introduced both fighters, he added that the bout would take place over ten rounds. He then glanced at the apprehensive Rodel and added caustically, 'Or less!'

As it happened Rodel put up a brave show. He even managed to break his opponent's nose. Despite all his enraged efforts, Smith was unable to put the dogged South African away and had to be content with the almost unanimous decisions of the newspapers at the end of their no-decision bout. After the bloody battle, the *Milwaukee Free Press* of 12 April 1913 congratulated the South African on his courage. 'Rodel, a big, awkward fellow, came back after he had been knocked down ten times and in the last three rounds outgamed, outgeneraled and outfought the leader of the white hopes.'

Only one newspaper declared that Rodel had easily defeated Gunboat Smith. This was one in which the sports writer had not turned up at the arena, preferring to spend an evening of passion with his girlfriend. Blinded by lust, the hack had even believed Jimmy Johnston when the manager telephoned him after the bout to swear that Rodel had given the Gunboat a merciless beating over ten rounds. With his mind on other things, the hack had scribbled his report of the fight based on Johnston's version. This was the solitary cutting that the handler used when trying to book more fights for Rodel with promoters.

Johnston might have been able to get his heavyweight bouts, but Rodel could not make the most of the opportunities presented.

In a return bout with Smith he was knocked out in three rounds. He won only one more fight in 1913, and that was against an unknown on a foul. Over the next few months the fearless Johnston put the South African in with such big punchers as Fireman Jim Flynn, Jack Geyser and the up-and-coming former ranch hand Jess Willard. Most of these bouts were no-decision affairs, but Rodel was adjudged to have come off second best in the majority of them.

Only against the gigantic Jess Willard was Jimmy Johnston able to display his true managerial skills. This was Rodel's first bout with the gigantic Kansan heavyweight. Willard was going through a bad time. In a recent fight with Bull Young, he had hit his opponent so hard that the other fighter had died.

Johnston, as callous as ever, did his best to take advantage of Willard's distress. He managed to convince the credulous giant that Rodel had a faulty heart. If Willard should hit the South African too hard, declared the manager, Rodel might suffer the same fate as the unfortunate Bull Young. Willard accepted the story. On the night of the fight he treated his opponent with such reverent care that Rodel not only lasted the ten-round, no-decision bout, but was also declared the winner by a number of sports writers in attendance.

The preamble to the bout was too good a story to be kept a secret. The way in which Willard had been duped became common knowledge in New York, and the angry giant demanded a rematch. Rodel, ignoring the rumours that his manager had tricked Willard, believed that he had won the first fight on merit and that he could do so again. He was mistaken. In a return match Willard flattened him in six one-sided rounds.

Rodel had a few more fights and even managed to beat those two professional losers Fred McKay and Sailor White, but he knew that his brief time in the sun was over. He was knocked down so many times that he began to be known as the Diving Venus, after a well-known aquatic stage performer. He retired from the ring in 1914, at the age of 25. Jimmy Johnston started looking for a White Hope more worthy of his efforts.

For a few weeks he thought he had found one in 'Agile' Andre Anderson from Chicago, whose real name was Fred Roesenilern. The heavyweight's career did not get off to a good start when, in his first important contest, he was knocked out in five rounds in Lexington, Kentucky by the much lighter Jack Dillon. However, Anderson was barely out of his teens and New York fight followers did not much care what happened in Kentucky. Johnston had the tall youth brought to New York and ran his eye over him in the gym. The manager liked what he saw and gave the Chicago fighter a spot on a promotion he was organising.

The selected opponent was the doughty black fighter Battling Jim Johnson. Johnson was coming to the end of his career and suffered badly from arthritis in his shoulders. Jimmy Johnston paid a visit to the black fighter's dressing room and found him huddled in a blanket, praying out loud that his shoulders would not seize up during the contest.

This was all that the manager-cum-promoter needed. Always in search of an edge for his fighters, he tiptoed away with Johnson's second and bribed the latter to throw ice-cold water liberally from a bucket over Battling Jim Johnson's upper body between rounds.

The hireling did as he was told. At the end of each round, when the perspiring Johnson returned to his corner he was greeted by a tub of iced water being thrown over him enthusiastically by his traitorous handler, who then refused to towel the black heavyweight down. Johnson protested long and loud at this cavalier treatment. On one occasion after the bell, he even remained sullenly in the middle of the ring and had to be ordered back by the referee to face his freezing deluge.

Even so, the experienced Johnson was able to drop Anderson three times in the first five rounds. Then the inter-round water treatment began to take effect. Johnson, suffering agonies, found it increasingly difficult to lift his arms. By the ninth round, tormented beyond endurance and with his gloves dangling at waist level, he was finding it almost impossible to defend himself. With Johnston screaming dementedly at him from his corner, Anderson moved forward and knocked his opponent out with a roundhouse right.

It was a triumph of managerial chicanery, but one Johnston found it almost impossible to repeat. Anderson's next opponents were almost distressingly fit and well, without a hint of sciatica among them, a fact made abundantly clear when the young Chicago heavyweight was knocked out by Fred Fulton and Charley Weinert.

Anderson was given one last chance to redeem himself when he was matched against an unknown heavyweight from the Midwest called Jack Dempsey. Dempsey was starving and giving away 3 stone in weight to his much taller opponent. However, he had a friend. A young reporter called Gene Fowler had seen Dempsey fight in the sticks and had given the young heavyweight a letter of introduction to a friend of his, the famous New York sports writer Damon Runyon.

Fowler had asked Runyon to help Dempsey get started on the New York fight scene. Against Anderson this was not going to be easy. Briefly the writer considered bribery, but said to a friend, 'We can put handcuffs on Anderson, but that'll cost too much money.' Instead, Runyon decided in advance to cast his newspaper's decision in favour of the newcomer.

For a while it looked as if this would prove difficult. For the first few minutes Anderson raised Jimmy Johnston's hopes when he smashed Dempsey twice to the canvas. This turned out to be a big mistake. Dempsey got to his feet, weathered the storm and finished the fight strongly. All the same, most onlookers thought that Anderson had done enough to win the unofficial decision. But Runyon swung the weight of his newspaper, the *New York American*, behind Dempsey, and naturally that counted for much more than the unbiased opinions of a few hundred genuine fans.

Dempsey had one more fight in the capital, sustained a couple of broken ribs but linked up with a new manager in Doc Kearns who, three years later, was to steer Dempsey to the world title. Anderson was less fortunate. The newspaper attribution of a loss to the unknown Dempsey dented his confidence and caused Johnston to lose interest in his White Hope. After the loss to Dempsey, Anderson lost four contests on first-round knockouts and won only four more fights over the next five years.

It was getting hard to see the wood for the trees. So many huge lummoxes were claiming to be White Hopes, or else to have been White Hopes, that it became difficult to sort them all out. To have been one of the contenders for Jack Johnson's title was always worth newspaper space in a subsequent career, and many made use of this fact.

A typical example was the Californian Edgar Kennedy, a film comedian later to become famous for his 'slow burn', in which he reacted almost in slow motion to an on-screen insult. Kennedy claimed to have been a White Hope, who had won the Pacific Coast championship in 1912, and to have gone the distance with the up-and-coming Jack Dempsey. There is no record of Dempsey ever meeting an Edgar Kennedy, but admittedly this was during a period when the young heavyweight would ride the rods into town, go to the nearest saloon and challenge any man in the house to fight for a few dollars or a collection to be taken after the bout.

The story went that Kennedy turned up in Hollywood on the Mack Sennett studio lot in 1913, when he was 23, and when asked what he could do said he could lick anyone on the lot. This proved to be the case and Kennedy got a job from fight fan Sennett. The actor's claims to have been a White Hope emanated from the studio publicity department, as did the erroneous claims that Edgar was the brother of true White Hope Tom Kennedy.

A more genuine claimant was Australian heavyweight Colin Bell. He came to Great Britain in 1914, supposedly the winner of over thirty contests and never having been knocked out. Actually, a year earlier he had been stopped twice inside the distance back home by Sam McVey, but McVey was so ferocious and such a scourge of white fighters that a loss to him hardly counted. Soon after his arrival in England, Bell lost on a foul to Petty Officer Nutty Curran. Again this was largely dismissed by the boxing public. If you fought Nutty, either he would foul you early on or he went so crazy that he railroaded you into fouling him, if only to get out of the ring as quickly as possible.

Eleven days later, on 4 May 1914, Colin Bell went in with the outstanding black American Joe Jeanette. It was taken as a sign of

Jeanette's confidence that only two nights earlier he had knocked out Kid Jackson in seven rounds in Paris. Everyone expected the Australian to go under early in the fight. Instead he fought doggedly and went the distance, and there were even cries of dissent when the American was given the decision after twenty rounds.

Bell's display was so good that in June 1914 he was matched with Bombardier Billy Wells at Olympia. Wells was making one of his almost annual comebacks, this time after being stopped in the first round a few fights before by the Frenchman Georges Carpentier. The tournament was the first to be promoted by the flamboyant, well-known showman C.B. Cochran.

True to his theatrical roots Cochran made a great show of the production, with no expense spared and a well-oiled publicity machine set in motion beforehand. He gained acres of newspaper publicity when he announced that the master of ceremonies for the evening would be a parish priest wearing full canonicals. Bell was boosted as the greatest heavyweight ever to emerge from the colonies. It all worked, because on the night 10,000 seats were sold at prices ranging from five shillings to five guineas.

Bell showed no sign that he was fit to be in the ring with even a faded White Hope like Billy Wells. The Australian was knocked out in two rounds. Spectators wondered out loud how a man who could push Joe Jeanette all the way could have crumbled so quickly before the Bombardier. The answer came some time later from hints dropped by an indiscreet Joe Jeanette. The black fighter let it be known to friends that he had been paid to make Bell look as good as possible in their contest, to build up interest in a Wells–Bell bout. Whether the bribe came from C.B. Cochran or Wells's connections was not made clear.

The man who did best out of the bout between Bell and Wells was not C.B. Cochran, who soon followed Hugh D. McIntosh into a disillusioned exit from boxing promotion, but a Liverpool comic called Harry Wheldon. For years afterwards he toured the halls in a sketch called White Hope. Wheldon appeared as a gormless heavyweight, together with a stooge acting as his manager, challenging 'any lady . . . any lady . . .?' in the hall to a contest.

197

Should any virago show any signs of accepting the challenge, Wheldon would cower behind his manager and implore him, 'Tell 'em what I did to Colin Bell!' Then he would add in a stage whisper, 'But don't tell 'em what Colin Bell did to me!'

Something of a laughing stock in Britain, Bell decided to abandon ferocious European heavyweights and snide comics and, like so many others, try his luck in North America. He did little better there, being on the receiving end in no-decision bouts with Porky Flynn and Battling Levinsky in New York and Gunboat Smith in Montreal. Bell then abandoned his ring career and returned to Australia, presumably in the fervent hope that Harry Wheldon was not contemplating a world tour.

After Colin Bell, with the political situation changing in Europe, fewer expatriate White Hopes landed on the shores of the USA. Trench warfare in France was killing tens of thousands of soldiers. In 1915 the Allies abandoned Gallipoli to the Turks, leaving Australia with a permanent distrust of Britain and a growing sense of disillusionment about the future of the Empire. In the same year, Ernest Shackleton's attempt to cross the Antarctic literally lost most of its momentum when his vessel the *Endurance* became trapped in pack ice. It drifted slowly with the ice and then, in November, disintegrated, spewing twenty-eight men over its sides. In the field of science the first direct transatlantic radio-telephone call was transmitted from Canada to France.

And the White Hopes plodded on. A big Irishman, Jim Coffey, the Roscommon Giant, made an impression for a time, but he had already emigrated to New York before he turned professional. He worked for a time as a motorman, driving a trolley car for eighteen dollars a week, but was then lured from his trade as a garage mechanic by the shrewd manager Billy Gibson, and rattled off a series of knockout victories, including one over Gunboat Smith, until two defeats at the hands of Frank Moran destroyed the Irishman's hopes of a tilt at Jack Johnson's title.

Coffey's first encounter with Moran was almost cancelled. The American was still smarting from his unpaid Paris encounter with

Jack Johnson, when the purse had been impounded by the courts. For some reason, minutes before the scheduled start of his bout with Coffey, Moran still had not received his payment. Obdurately, the former seaman sat it out until the promoter hastily assembled the cash in notes from the box-office takings. Boxing legend has it that Moran then had the money stuffed into a bucket and carried to the ringside, where he could keep an eye on it while an obliging friend sat on the bucket until he had concluded his demolition job on the Irishman.

However, Coffey by now was getting $6,000 a bout. This news reached the ears of one of his brothers, a Dublin policeman, who promptly announced his intention of joining his brother as a pugilist in the USA. 'I could always lick that kid,' he told the *Beloit Daily News* of 3 June 1915. 'If he can get six thousand iron men for licking some sucker over there, it's up to me to go over and get some of that coin.'

Shortly after his announcement, the *Lusitania* was sunk just south of Queenstown in Ireland with great loss of life by the German submarine *U-20*. The action precipitated the entry of the USA into the war but disconcerted Coffey's brother. Abruptly the policeman changed his mind about travelling. 'I'll tackle no submarine,' he told the same newspaper with a shudder. 'Jim can clean up all he likes undisturbed by me!'

In the USA Jim Coffey's training sessions attracted some attention in the newspapers. Before a number of his contests the 6ft-3in Irishman would repair to the Roman Catholic Maryknoll Seminary, near Ossining in New York State, and get into shape by joining in the daily tasks of the priests, rising before dawn for a day spent ploughing the fields.

For all his size and strength, Coffey, like most of his peers among the White Hopes, was reluctant to tangle with the diminutive but waspish managers and promoters who inhabited the New York fight scene. On one occasion Coffey and fellow Hope Jess Willard tried to gatecrash one of feisty Jimmy Johnston's promotions. They wanted to see the latest heavyweight prospect, Al Reich, the Adonis, in action against Gunboat Smith. Coffey and Willard, with a combined weight of nearly 30 stone, tried to force their way through the turnstiles without paying. However, when the courageous gatekeeper told the two boxers that former bantamweight Johnston was on his way down to deal with them, Coffey and Willard paid for their seats as meekly as lambs.

When Coffey was knocked out by Jack Dillon, a fighter 3½ stone lighter than the Irishman and known as 'Jack the Giant Killer', he began to be written off as a White Hope. The *Washington Post* of 18 February 1916 declared judiciously of the Irishman, 'He's weak below the waist. That's his trouble. His legs are bad. His legs go first and he can't stand up to fight.'

In 1917, in the throes of an unsuccessful comeback, Coffey found himself also in contention with the law. On 11 October, he appeared in a New York courtroom to defend a $50,000 breach-of-promise lawsuit brought against him by Miss Mamie Hughes, who claimed that she had consented to continue her relations with the boxer only on the understanding that he would marry her.

Probably with some relief, in 1918 Coffey broke off from his fighting career and Miss Hughes by enlisting in the US Navy. Upon his return from the service he had only a couple more fights before retiring from the ring.

By 1913, about the only major manager who had not found his own personal White Hope was that man of a few thousand words, Dumb Dan Morgan, commonly acknowledged to be the most garrulous of all the managers of his time. Morgan was doing fine with the lighter weights, but he felt it as a slight that, unlike Johnston, Gibson and all his colleagues and rivals, he did not have the boasting rights to a simpleton giant.

Eventually one came along. One morning as Morgan was sitting with his feet on the table perusing a sports sheet and pencilling in his bets for that afternoon, a fighter whose given name was Barney Lebrowitz turned up begging for an audience. For six or seven years Lebrowitz had been boxing out of Philadelphia under the ring name of Barney Williams without attracting much public interest. He was a dogged and skilful, if totally unspectacular, boxer who had been making very little money and hoped to do better on the East Coast.

Morgan could see at once that his caller was more of a light heavyweight than a behemoth, but at least Lebrowitz was bigger than some of the flyweights the manager had been handling lately.

Shrewdly Morgan asked his visitor to describe his boxing style. He hoped that Lebrowitz was going to tell him that he was a banger with a jaw of granite. Instead the truthful fighter confessed that his usual style was to circle his opponent cautiously and then shuffle forward to tie him up in frequent clinches.

It was not the answer Morgan had been hoping for, but at least Lebrowitz's honesty gave rise to the hope that he was also naive and would not be too insistent in any future dealings on receiving a detailed breakdown of any fight purses Morgan might secure for him. In order to test his potential White Hope's ability and lack of common sense, Morgan agreed to take on the fighter on a trial basis.

First there had to be changes. The *nom de ring* 'Barney Williams' had to go in case it reminded people that under this name, in 1912, the fighter had taken part in twenty contests without winning one inside the distance. Morgan informed his man that from then on he would be known as Battling Levinsky. The first name would give the crowds the impression that he was a slugging attacker, instead of a soft-punching, back-pedalling cutie. Levinsky was selected to appeal to the ethnic sensibilities of ticket buyers, as at that time only Irish and Jewish fighters were drawing really good metropolitan crowds.

Morgan threw Battling Levinsky in at the deep end. Callously he accepted a last-minute substitute fight for his heavyweight against Porky Flynn, on 30 July 1913. Flynn had been in with almost everyone and acquitted himself well against the best. His nickname came not from any excess of weight but because he was inordinately fond of pork scratchings. Surprisingly, Levinsky had not heard of him and accepted Morgan's duplicitous assurance that he would be going in with a no-hoper.

The manager did, however, provide his new heavyweight with a fight plan. Morgan informed Levinsky that when the bell rang to start the first round, Flynn usually remained facing his own corner post, rippling his back muscles in order to intimidate his opponent, before turning to start fighting. Morgan instructed Levinsky at the bell to cross the ring swiftly but stealthily and to be standing within punching range of his opponent as the heavyweight turned.

Levinsky obeyed orders to the last detail. When Flynn had completed his muscle-flexing act and whirled round to race to the centre of the ring and open fire, Levinsky was already standing facing him. The Philadelphia man promptly let fly with his best shot. If the Battler had been a puncher, the whistling left hook that he sent over might have disposed of the rugged Flynn in record time. As it was, the punch staggered the big man and closed one of his eyes.

At ringside, Dumb Dan sighed contentedly. 'Run!' he shouted to his new charge. Levinsky needed no such encouragement. He went on the retreat and boxed the stunned Flynn silly for the rest of the night. At the end of the ten-round, no-decision bout, Levinsky was given the unanimous decisions of the sports writers and Morgan had himself a White Hope.

In Levinsky the manager discovered that he had a workaholic, prepared to fight as often as Morgan could book him into a stadium. In 1914, the Battler had thirty-five contests, while in the following year he entered the ring on twenty-eight occasions. These were just Levinsky's recorded bouts. With substitute appearances and the odd moonlighting fight the total could well have been much higher.

The Battler barred no one. He survived no-decision contests with such White Hopes as Fireman Jim Flynn, Jim Coffey, Tony Ross, Gunboat Smith, Tom Cowler, and many others. Morgan capitalised on the boxer's known willingness to fight by issuing all sorts of completely untrue press releases about Levinsky's crowded schedule. One flyer, for example, claimed that the heavyweight had engaged in three fights on one day on 1 January 1915, in Brooklyn in the morning, Manhattan in the afternoon and Connecticut in the evening. Equally lacking in foundation was the story featured in many newspapers that Levinsky had been whisked out in the first act of a show he had been attending with his wife to box as a substitute a few blocks away, had lasted the distance and had rejoined Mrs Levinsky before the final curtain.

Nevertheless, the Battler's genuine schedule was impressive enough. For most of his career no one could put Levinsky away, but unfortunately his boxing style was so negative that he never got a shot at the World Heavyweight Championship.

Even here Dumb Dan Morgan was able to swing matters his fighter's way. The World Light Heavyweight Championship had rather fallen into abeyance with the retirement of Philadelphia Jack O'Brien. One day the manager of a fighter called Jack Dillon, who had knocked the gigantic Jim Coffey out of contention as a White Hope, was bemoaning the fact that his fighter was too light to secure lucrative bouts in the heavyweight class and that he needed a gimmick to attract promoters. Naturally, Dumb Dan took this as a professional challenge. He hired a couple of typists for a day and got them to write to every major sports writer in the country, announcing that Jack Dillon was now the light-heavyweight champion of the world. 'You just announced it,' he said matter-of-factly afterwards. 'That was all there was to it.'

The ploy worked. Dillon became universally recognised as the new light-heavyweight champion. This boosted his standing and as a result he was able to secure lucrative bouts with Gunboat Smith and Fireman Jim Flynn, among others. This sudden success for Dillon and his manager began to rankle with Dumb Dan. After all, it had been his idea to claim the light-heavyweight championship for Dillon. It was time that Levinsky, his own fighter, got onto the gravy train.

Some years later, in 1916, Dumb Dan challenged Dillon to defend his title against Battling Levinsky. Dillon agreed without giving the matter a lot of thought. After all, he and Levinsky had already met in at least five no-decision contests and one draw without harming one another. In fact they had also fought a no-decision bout as far back as 1911, when Levinsky was still fighting out of Philadelphia as Barney Williams. So the two men met again, this time for the championship. Levinsky won and was able to claim the light-heavyweight title as his own.

His new championship came as something of a sop to Levinsky. He still went in with the major heavyweight White Hopes, though the newspaper decisions were beginning to go against him as he aged. But he placidly continued to be true to his style of circling, retreating and tying up all comers and thus avoiding major damage. Altogether he fought from 1906 until 1929, taking part in over 300 contests.

12

THE POTTAWATOMIE GIANT

Slowly, almost by default, a White Hope emerged to make a serious challenge to Jack Johnson. His name was Jess Willard and he was a giant of a man. He had been born in St Clere, Kansas, in 1881, the youngest of four brothers. His father, a Civil War veteran, had died at the age of 37 from the long-term effects of wounds sustained in battle. Willard had grown up on his stepfather's ranch, but his ambition to become a cowboy had to be abandoned when he grew to an enormous size.

Instead he had earned a living for a time by breaking in and trading horses, often obtaining his wild mounts from the local Pottawatomie Native Americans and selling them on to ranchers. For a time he became a teamster, transporting goods in wagons. When times were hard the big man had settled down to a general labouring job among horses in a stable. On 28 March 1908, Jess Willard got married and started thinking about better ways of earning a living. This led him to a gymnasium and a boxing career.

He had shown no natural aptitude for the sport, and when he had first tried out as a boxer in Oklahoma City in 1910, he was completely outsmarted by a welterweight, who had spotted Willard a hundred pounds and still driven the big man in confusion from the gym. Later, after he had taken a hard punch in a fight against Joe Cox, Willard suddenly stopped fighting, pushed the referee in front of his opponent and stood behind the official, quitting on the spot, claiming that he had been warned by gangsters that it would be unsafe for him to continue. As in his previous contest Cox had been knocked out in two rounds by Fireman Jim Flynn and was to be stopped by Luther McCarty in six in his next bout, Willard's actions were regarded with contempt in fight circles.

Nevertheless, the gigantic heavyweight managed to build up a successful record, mostly in and around Oklahoma, although his purses were small because he was such an unexciting fighter. Oklahoma had only been a state since 1907, and Oklahoma City had a population of about 65,000, so Willard was not exactly fighting at the centre of the fistic universe. He lost his first bout on a foul to Louis Fink on 15 February 1911, but after that built up a string of victories until his bizarre retirement against Joe Cox.

There was no doubt that Willard was an immensely strong man. He stood 6ft 5in tall, although his publicists claimed that he was an inch taller, had a reach of 83 inches and weighed 18 stone. He had a long, hard left jab, and, when he wanted to use it, a crushing right hand. He was, however, a cautious, unimaginative man and not a natural fighter. Unless he was roused to action, his bouts tended to be dull.

Once he had obtained the services of a good manager and publicist, and had been carefully guided through the ranks of the White Hopes, all sorts of stories were spread about how the big man came to take up boxing. One of them was that he had beaten up a couple of feared gunfighters in a saloon brawl and decided that fighting for cash would be a cinch. Another was that he had been spotted tossing huge bales of hay weighing 500lb each onto a cart and had been persuaded to adapt his strength for the boxing ring.

Willard's grandson said that the more likely reason was that Willard saw his first professional bout at the Union Athletic Club while on a visit to Oklahoma City and had heard that there was money to be made from the fight game, especially for white heavyweights. As a poorly paid livery-stable worker with a wife and family to support, the prospect appealed to Willard and he decided to explore the possibilities.

Years later, he wrote of his feelings at the time: 'I knew that I was a big fellow and powerful strong. I just sat down and figured out that a man as big as me ought to be able to cash in on his size and that was what started me on the road to boxing.'

First he approached Billy McCarney, the leading promoter and manager in the area. After running his eye over Willard in the gym and witnessing his less-than-glorious display against the welterweight, McCarney at first passed on the opportunity to back the young giant. For a time Willard was passed from handler to handler. They were all impressed by his size but put off by his clumsiness and lack of enterprise in the ring. Then a manager called Brock had to flee from the law, leaving Willard unpaid from a bout and almost starving, and he was taken over by Jimmy Bronson.

Halfway through 1911, Willard started training at Billy McCarney's gymnasium for the fight with Joe Cox. It was then that the conniving McCarney persuaded the touring Victor McLaglen to fight Willard in the gym and charged fifty cents a head for the spectators to watch Willard demolish the music-hall performer.

Any reputation that Willard might have earned in his unofficial bout with McLaglen was destroyed when he quit against Joe Cox on 16 July 1911. McCarney and Jimmy Bronson both decided that there was too much dog in the huge man for him ever to become a successful White Hope.

Almost in despair Willard went to Chicago. Here he persuaded Charles Kid Cutler to manage and train him. Cutler was an old heavyweight who had been managed by John L. Sullivan until he had been knocked out in one round by Jack Johnson, and then taken on as a sparring partner in Johnson's music-hall act. Cutler did his best to instil a little skill and determination into his new heavyweight, and even took Willard into his home to feed him up.

Cutler taught Willard well and in 1912 the giant won a couple of fights and looked quite good in the process. In fact he performed a little too well, because at this juncture another manager stole Jess Willard from Kid Cutler. It amazed onlookers that anyone would want the Kansan heavyweight, but he was big, and any giant had some sort of chance in the current spate of no-decision bouts with newspaper verdicts delivered by venal, easily bribed sports writers. As White Hope Frank Moran remarked wryly, 'When you go near a pressman in America you've got to make a noise like soft money.'

The man who wanted to take on the Kansan was Tom Jones, a bald, one-time Illinois barber. He seduced Willard away from Kid Cutler by promising to take him to New York, where the big money was to be had. The ungrateful Willard agreed and tiptoed away from Cutler into the night, without bothering to look back. This defection was regarded as unethical even by prevailing boxing standards, and Willard was forced to justify his flight in the *Milwaukee Free Press* of 13 April 1913. The giant told a reporter, 'Cutler and I are not only old friends but good cronies. I like him and he likes me, but just the same we have not made much progress as a team. This is a time when I should be getting matches and making money and I find myself idle most of the time. I need someone who knows the managerial game and who can further my interest as well as his own.'

The chicanery had its repercussions a few years later when the Kid caught up with Jones in a Chicago bar, floored the manager with one mighty punch and made him pay $5,000 for the big man's contract.

There was no doubt that the cunning and well-connected Jones was the right manager for Willard at this stage of his career. The *Milwaukee Free Press* of 13 March 1913 acknowledged this: 'If there is any class to Willard at all, Jones will have him in the top flight, where the plums hang lowest, in a very short time.'

Willard took some time to settle down but slowly began to make headway. He knocked out Sailor White in the first round, and in a bout with Soldier Kearns he hit his opponent so hard that ringsiders swore that the soldier had been lifted inches off the ground by the blow.

Meanwhile, Tom Jones did his best to build up Willard's reputation. He made the heavyweight don a ten-gallon hat and wear boots with lifts in order to emphasise his height. Wearing this attire Willard was introduced from the ring at big tournaments as the former cowboy who had abandoned his spread to win back the heavyweight title. All the same, those in the know bemoaned Willard's lack of aggression. Timekeeper George Bannon, who worked several of Willard's New York fights, summed up the opinion of many when he said simply, 'I don't think he liked to fight. I think he only fought for the money that was in it.'

Not everything went according to plan. In 1913, Willard lost on points over twenty rounds to White Hope Gunboat Smith in San

Francisco. In the process the ex-cowboy managed, not for the first time, to drive his handlers to distraction. The *Milwaukee Free Press* of 1 June 1913 reported, 'there was friction in the Kansan's corner . . . poor Willard was the victim of conflicting instructions. Some of his henchmen were yelling to him to "go in" and others to "keep away". During the hubbub, Manager Tom Jones grabbed one of the aids by the hair and nearly succeeded in making him as bald-headed as Jones is himself.'

Worse was to come. On 22 August 1913, Willard was matched with the journeyman fighter Bull Young, billed as the Wyoming Plainsman, in Vernon, California. Halfway through the bout Young stung Willard with several sharp blows. Jolted out of his lethargy Willard fought back with unaccustomed spirit. By the eleventh round he was landing some very hard right hands, punching for once with all his weight. Bull Young suddenly collapsed beneath Willard's onslaught. He lapsed into a coma and died. Willard, his manager and the promoter were all arrested for manslaughter but were acquitted. The *Philadelphia Inquirer* of 27 August 1913 described the result of the trial. 'The death of "Bull" Young was "unintentional" by Jess Willard according to the verdict of a coroner's jury . . . The death was caused, the verdict said, "by contusion of the jaw due to a blow on the chin delivered by Jess Willard".'

These events had a traumatic effect on the big heavyweight and he seldom punched his full weight again. This led to a temporary slump in his record, compounded when Jimmy Johnston persuaded the nervous Willard that his fighter Boer Rodel had a bad heart, so that Willard treated the South African in the ring with the greatest of care until Rodel connected with a knockout punch in the tenth round. Later Willard tried to explain his philosophy: 'I never hurt any of my opponents before the eighth round because not one of them was able to hurt me much before the eighth round, and when they did hurt me I got real mad and just swung on them and settled matters as quickly as I could.' Unfortunately, he could not harm the better White Hopes even when his dander was up. However, the ghoulish fact that he had killed a man in the ring was used in

Willard's publicity build-up and was one of the factors which finally secured him a shot at the world title.

In Europe, after the financial fiasco of his bout with Frank Moran, Jack Johnson was almost broke and desperate to fight again. It was 1914, and there were newspaper calls for the world champion to join the French Army and fight for the nation which had given him shelter. His finances were so low that Johnson was even reduced to contemplating fighting Sam Langford again. He had received none of the $14,000 he had been promised for fighting Frank Moran, he was still living expensively, and bookings for his not-very-good music-hall act had all but dried up.

Promoter Jack Curley got to hear of the champion's plight, and in 1914 he cabled Johnson, who was in Moscow, and the two men agreed to meet in Paris. However, the war was now raging in France and their meeting took place in London instead. The two men had got on quite well when the promoter had put on Johnson's last title defence in the USA, against Fireman Jim Flynn in 1912, but the black fighter was willing to consider propositions from almost anyone.

Curley's first suggestion was dismissed by the champion as being too fanciful. The promoter had come up with the idea of a title defence in Mexico, sponsored by none other than the rebel leader Pancho Villa. Johnson refused on two grounds. On the one hand, an area swept by rebellions and counter-insurgencies might not be the most stable as far as receiving the purse money was concerned. On the other, if the region were to enter a period of stability then the authorities might like to curry favour with the USA by handing Johnson back across the border.

Jack Johnson told Curley that he was all in favour of a title defence, but that the promoter would have to go away and come up with a more likely venue and a suitable opponent. The bout could not be held in the USA because the champion would be arrested as soon as he tried to return home. It was agreed that Johnson would receive $30,000, an additional $1,000 expenses and a share of the motion-picture rights. The challenger would practically have to buy his chance of the title, receiving half of what was left after Johnson had been paid and all expenses were taken care of. Curley also hinted that he would be able to bring influence to bear in certain quarters to allow Johnson back into the USA and to gain him a federal pardon. The promoter then left to put the wheels in motion.

When the news reached the USA that Johnson was up for a title defence, it caused a flurry of excitement among the White Hopes and their backers. It was generally agreed that, after the death of Luther McCarty, the two leading contenders, almost by default, were big Jess Willard and Gunboat Smith. Smith had the edge on the other man by virtue of an easy victory over Willard and a superior record. On the other hand, on several occasions Smith, a former sparring partner of the champion, had seemed reluctant to go into the ring on serious terms with Johnson. There was also the matter of Smith's odd defeat at the hands of the Frenchman Carpentier and the more convincing crushing he'd received at the hands of Sam Langford.

Willard's record was by no means bad. By this time he had had thirty fights, with twenty-one wins, including eighteen knockouts, four losses, and a number of no-decision bouts. There was no doubt, either, that Willard had the connections. By 1914, the Kansan was almost overmanaged. Others had weaselled their way in to give Tom Jones immoral support, and it was estimated that now the big white heavyweight owned only 25 per cent of himself. The rest of his purses went to his backers.

Jack Curley secured the financial backing of businessman Harry H. Frazee and arranged a secret meeting with Jess Willard. Curley took a train from New York, while the boxer travelled from Pasadena. In July 1914, the two men met at night on an almost deserted railway platform at Kansas City. They sat on a baggage cart and hammered out the financial details before Willard agreed to challenge Jack Johnson for his title.

With the chance of a lucrative title fight on the horizon, it was definitely time to keep Jess Willard in cotton wool. The White Hope's entourage came up with a simple method of ensuring that their man did not suffer any embarrassing ring losses while negotiations with Johnson were under way. They ordered Willard not to fight anyone.

This suited the big man down to the ground. After a six-round knockout of the obliging Boer Rodel in Atlanta in 1914, leading contender Jess Willard did not enter the ring again in anger for a year. He lived a sybaritic life in California, where he made a one-reel film entitled *The Heart Punch* and waited without undue anticipation for the call to arms.

When Willard's name was run before Johnson, the black champion let it be known that it was a matter of complete indifference to him. He had barely heard of Willard and what he did know about the leading contender hardly filled Johnson with dread.

The venue was altogether a more interesting matter. Jack Curley had now come up with the idea of using the Cuba Oriental Racecourse, ten miles outside Havana. The date of the fight was to be 5 April 1915. Early in 1915, some nine months after making his agreement with Jack Curley, Johnson left Europe for Cuba, using the $1,000 expense money to pay the fares for his small party. He travelled by way of South America and set up a training camp in Cuba.

Willard had started training in Texas for the proposed Mexican title challenge, but when the venue was changed to Cuba, he moved to a training camp close to Havana. Manager Jones made sure that the gigantic Willard was in the shape of his life. After his twelve-month layoff Willard's weight had ballooned to over 21½ stone. By the time he entered the ring he had reduced it to 19 stone. Willard was extremely apprehensive about the forthcoming bout and started casting about for propitious omens. He claimed to have found one when he saw a black seagull fall from the sky, exhausted after battling strong winds. This cheered Willard somewhat, and he went into his battle with the champion in a better frame of mind.

There were 16,000 spectators at the racecourse, including many women, cabinet ministers and provincial governors, as well as many American tourists. One odd sight was a detachment of uniformed Cuban cavalry soldiers seated on their horses in perfect formation throughout the fight. The 32-year-old Willard entered the ring in a long robe with a ten-gallon sombrero on his head.

Jack Johnson had won the title on a cloudless day outside Sydney on Boxing Day 1908. He was to lose it on an equally beautiful day outside Havana, 6 years and 3 months later. Johnson may have been 37 years old but he made the running from the start. In the earlier rounds he outboxed his much larger opponent and on one occasion in the seventh round even rushed him into the ropes and scored with heavy right-hand punches.

By the fifteenth round Willard was beginning to get on top. As usual he fought methodically behind his telegraph pole of a left hand, seldom getting involved in exchanges of punches. The *New York Times* reporter at ringside wrote approvingly, 'Willard played a game in the ring that was declared necessary to beat Johnson, namely, to make the latter act as aggressor.' After twenty rounds Johnson was showing signs of exhaustion. By the twenty-fifth he sent a message from his corner to his wife Lucille, telling her to leave the stadium.

In the twenty-sixth round Willard landed a fierce right to his opponent's jaw, knocking him to the canvas. Johnson rolled over, lay on his back and raised an arm to shield his eyes from the rays of the sun as he was counted out.

The *Anaconda-Montana* of 6 April 1915 reported the closing moments of the fight. 'Jess rushed in again, forcing the Negro into Willard's corner, where the finish came. Johnson was slow in guarding and his strong, youthful opponent hooked a swinging left to the body. The fading champion's legs quivered and again the towering giant feinted for the body. Johnson dropped his guard and Willard won the title with a quick hard swing to the exact point of the jaw.'

Johnson's seconds helped their man to his feet and supported him back to his corner. Johnson sat there for almost five minutes before he seemed to have recovered enough to stand up again. Some excited spectators tried to invade the ring, but they were beaten back with the flats of machetes wielded by rural guards.

The wisdom of Willard's backers in holding out for a forty-five-round distance for the championship was exemplified when the

Philadelphia Tribune interviewed referee Jack Welsh immediately after the bout. He agreed that he would have declared Johnson the winner on points after the twentieth round. 'I think that Johnson put up one of the most masterful battles that I have ever witnessed,' he said. 'He couldn't have lost in the shorter route.' Johnson accepted his defeat gracefully at the time, saying, 'Willard was too much for me. I just didn't have it.'

There was little sympathy for the fallen champion. The *Philadelphia Tribune* of 10 April 1915 summed up the feelings of many whites when it said of Johnson, 'He has done the African people in all parts of the universe more injury since Reno, 4 July 1910, than any other living man.' The *New York Times* of 6 April 1915 congratulated Jess Willard, the new champion, for having restored fistic white supremacy.

13

THE CAPTAINS AND
THE KINGS DEPART

With big Jess Willard enthroned as Heavyweight Champion of the World, the search for a White Hope could be abandoned. The participants in the crusade mostly went on to other things.

A year after the Cuban fight, Jack Johnson caused something of a stir when he claimed to have been bribed to lose to Willard by Jack Curley, the promoter. The former champion said he had been offered $50,000 and a promise that he would be allowed back without penalty into the USA. Curley denied the charge hotly.

Opinion was divided as to the validity of Johnson's claim. Many said that he had been old and fat at the Cuba Oriental Racecourse and had been defeated on merit by a bigger, younger and stronger opponent. On the other hand, an expert of the calibre of Ted Kid Lewis, the English future Welterweight Champion of the World, had trained with Johnson in Havana and always said that a Johnson fighting flat out would have beaten Willard.

Whatever the truth of the matter, Johnson returned to Europe and had a few desultory fights around the world. In Spain in 1916, he engaged in a bout that was bizarre even by his standards. He went into the ring against Arthur Cravan, an extremely minor English poet who for a time had been editor of an avant-garde Parisian magazine called *Maintenant*. Cravan had fled from France upon the outbreak of war and dared not return to Great Britain in case he should be called up to serve in the armed forces.

Like much of the human flotsam drifting around war-torn Europe, Cravan ended up in Spain. Here, in 1916, he met an equally penniless Jack Johnson. In a desperate effort to raise money the two men agreed to fight one another, Cravan claiming to be a leading

British heavyweight, although he had never before entered a boxing ring. In an effort to gain fistic credibility he was billed, quite erroneously, as the nephew of Oscar Wilde.

A large crowd turned out in Barcelona to see a visibly shaking Cravan knocked out in the first round without throwing a punch. The crowd rioted, demanding its money back. Fires were started in the stadium and Johnson had to be locked up in a local police station overnight for his own protection. Cravan, an altogether wilier character, had had the foresight to demand his purse in advance and used it to purchase a steamship ticket to the safety of the USA. The poet was on the high seas before Jack Johnson had even been released from his cell.

The former champion hung on disconsolately in Barcelona, going through his savings. He pestered influential American visitors, begging them to help him return home. In 1918 he encountered Fiorello La Guardia, a future crusading mayor of New York City, in a Barcelona barber shop. La Guardia was a wartime officer in the US Army Air Service, present in Spain on a military mission. In his autobiography *The Making of an Insurgent*, La Guardia recounted how Johnson begged to be allowed to join his country's army. He followed up their meeting with a pathetic letter in which he said, 'There's no position you could get for me that I would consider too rough or too dangerous. I am willing to fight and die for my own country.' La Guardia did what he could but was told that Johnson was too much of a diplomatic hot potato for his request to be entertained.

Finally, in 1920, Johnson returned wearily to the USA and surrendered to the federal authorities. He was sentenced to a year and a day in Leavenworth Penitentiary, where he helped out with the boxing programme. Upon his release he attempted a ring comeback, and indeed he only finally retired from boxing at the age of 50.

For the rest of his life he toured with theatrical shows, gave lectures and worked in a flea circus. He met up once more with Jess Willard. This was in Los Angeles in 1944. The two men sat side by side in a sideshow booth where, for the price of a 25-cent ticket, spectators could ask them about their controversial title fight in Havana. Two years later, Jack Johnson died in a car crash.

The White Hopes went down various paths. The very first to fight Johnson after he had won the championship had been the Briton Victor McLaglen. After he retired from the ring, boxing continued to be good to him. Some time after his retirement, at a loose end, he was hanging around the National Sporting Club, a meeting place for wealthy and influential patrons of the noble art. Here he happened to bump into I.B. Davidson, a film producer who was looking for a brawny, tough-looking character to play a prizefighter called Alf Truscott in a 1920 silent costume melodrama entitled *The Call of the Road*. McLaglen, with his battered features, certainly looked the part and was never one to turn down a challenge. To his surprise, not only did he enjoy making films, he was actually rather good at it.

He was cast as an action hero in a number of British films and was then recruited by Hollywood, where he became a considerable hit in silent movies. His career in talkies was given a boost when he won an Oscar as Gypo Nolan, an informer betraying a comrade for the price of the boat fare to America, in the 1935 film *The Informer*, set in Ireland. McLaglen's life had been so varied and interesting that it was probably inevitable that, unlike more cosseted actors, more than once he would appear to re-enact episodes from it. In *Klondike Annie* (1936), for example, he supported Mae West by playing a hard man engaged in the Alaskan gold rush, which must have brought back memories of his own prospecting days in the mining camps of Ontario. Similarly, in *The Lost Patrol* (1934), he commanded a group of soldiers besieged by tribesmen in the desert, an echo of his own infantry-fighting days in Mesopotamia.

Victor McLaglen spent more than 30 years acting steadily in Hollywood, ending his days as a blustering character actor, often in westerns directed by his old friend and mentor John Ford. After he had become a wealthy man he did not forget his hard times as a down-and-out. It became his practice from time to time to tour Skid Row in Los Angeles, round up a gang of drunks and throw a party for them, often lasting several days, at the lofty Hollywood Roosevelt Hotel.

Another of the early White Hopes had been Jack O'Brien. In his retirement, the Philadelphia Irishman was often sought out by other fighters eager to learn his tricks of the trade. In 1924, when O'Brien was 45, he was hired by François Descamps to show Georges Carpentier, who was about to fight Gene Tunney for the light-heavyweight title, how to counter his prospective opponent's antisocial ploy of jabbing his thumb into the other fighter's eye.

The veteran was only too pleased to pass on his knowledge of the more nefarious aspects of the fight game. Unfortunately for the Frenchman, O'Brien's demonstrated counter consisted of smashing his fist into Carpentier's Adam's apple. The blow knocked the pride of France down, and it was days before he could speak above a whisper. O'Brien then embarked upon a lucrative career in passing on his ring knowledge as a New York boxing coach. He specialised in giving gentle, well-paid workouts to middle-aged businessmen who wanted to boast that they had been in with a former world champion.

James J. Jeffries, who had engaged with Johnson in the 'Fight of the Century' in Reno, went through a bad period after losing to the black champion. For a time he started drinking heavily and roistering. He came close to death in an automobile accident when a car driven by racing champion Barney Oldfield in which he was a passenger went off the road at high speed. This seemed to give Jeffries pause for thought, because soon afterwards he went back to his ranch and its peaceful alfalfa. Later he lost a great deal of his fortune in the stock-market crash. At the age of 50, bald and fat, he was forced to tour giving sparring exhibitions with an old opponent, Tom Sharkey.

In 1932, he converted a barn on his property into a fight hall and became a fairly successful boxing and wrestling promoter, putting on bouts much patronised by Hollywood stars in the stadium known as Jeff's Barn. He died in 1953, at the age of 77.

The First World War brought a hiatus to the careers of many European White Hopes. Georges Carpentier became a hero, flying a small aircraft on scouting missions at low levels over the German lines. He was twice wounded and decorated, winning both the Croix de guerre and the Légion d'honneur. Between 1915 and 1918, he fought in the ring only three times. After the war he resumed his ring career and won the Light Heavyweight Championship of the World, although there were suspicions that the champion, Battling Levinsky, had gone down rather quickly in order to boost his opponent's American record. Carpentier's judgement, when earlier he had refused to fight Jack Johnson – namely, that he was too small to go in with the really top-class heavyweights – was proved accurate when he fought Jack Dempsey for the World Heavyweight Championship in 1921. The Frenchman fought bravely but was knocked out in four rounds in the world's first million-dollar gate. Fittingly, Carpentier retired from competitive boxing in 1926, by then a wealthy man.

Other fighters did not survive the war as successfully as Carpentier. Iron Hague, the first English White Hope, joined the Army and was badly gassed in the trenches at Ypres in 1915. As a result he remained in poor health for the rest of his life. After the war he worked in the Mexborough steelworks, dying penniless in 1951. Shortly before his death he commented sadly, 'I have never asked for anything in my life, but things are a little hard sometimes.' The only possessions of value that he left were the boxing gloves with which he fought Sam Langford, with several dried spots of Langford's blood on them.

George Mitchell, who had challenged Carpentier to a private bout in Paris, became a lieutenant in the Black Watch and was killed in France by a grenade. John Hopley, the rugby international touted briefly as an amateur White Hope, won a DSO in action and was then put in charge of physical training at Sandhurst, where world flyweight champion Jimmy Wilde was one of his non-commissioned officers.

Bombardier Billy Wells also became a forces' physical-training instructor and boxed on for a time after the war, losing his British title. He then worked as a small-part actor in British films and was the muscular athlete who beat the gong before the credit titles

219

in Rank films. For all his fame Wells had never earned really big ring purses, and he ended his working life as a security guard at a film studio.

The careers of some of the American White Hopes had unusual endings. Tom Kennedy, the so-called 'Millionaire Boxer', who lost to Wells, made enough money to retire from the ring and open a bar in New York. One night he witnessed a gangland killing in his saloon and was warned not to give evidence when the case came to trial. Never slow to take a hint, Kennedy fled to the West Coast, where he picked up work as a personal trainer to Douglas Fairbanks Senior, the leading movie action star of his day.

Impressed by his instructor's physique and tough appearance, Fairbanks urged him to enter motion pictures and gave him a few introductions. Kennedy secured work as an extra, and a few walk-on parts, and slowly emerged as one of the film capital's most dependable character actors, embarking upon thirty years of portraying dumb cops or the menacing henchmen of crooks. Never a star, one of his most memorable and typical roles was as a confused officer on board a ship chasing the Marx Brothers around a deck in *Monkey Business*.

Frank Moran, the possessor of the notorious 'Mary Anne' punch, followed his friend Kennedy to Hollywood, but had to be content with small parts. He survived a minor conviction for smuggling bootleg booze during Prohibition. The hulking Al Kaufman also drifted out to the West Coast and secured minor roles in such movies as *Daredevil Jack*, a serial starring Jack Dempsey.

After Al Palzer had lost his White Heavyweight title to Luther McCarty in 1913, disconsolately he returned to his parents' farm in Fergus Falls, Minnesota. As a 12-year-old, Palzer had run away from home to start an itinerant life, but after achieving fame in the ring had become reconciled with his family. After his return home in 1914, one day his 60-year-old father Henry, after a day of heavy drinking, picked a quarrel with his wife. He then produced a gun and started shooting wildly. Mrs Palzer received two bullet wounds in her arms. Al Palzer tried to wrestle the weapon from his father. It went off again and Palzer was shot in the stomach. Bleeding badly, he ran a mile and a half to the local hospital. He died there the next day, on 25 July 1914, fourteen months after the death in the ring of Luther McCarty. His father was sentenced to five years' imprisonment for manslaughter.

Lantern-jawed Arthur Pelkey, who had first been spotted and taken up by Tommy Burns after fighting a draw with Kent Salisbury in Boston in 1910, never won another fight after the death of McCarty in their Calgary bout. He died at the age of 37 of sleeping sickness. To the end he suffered from nightmares featuring the lifeless form of McCarty at his feet. His manager Tommy Burns, who inadvertently had sparked off the White Hope campaign by losing his title to Jack Johnson at Rushcutters Bay, had his last fight in 1920 at the age of 39. Flabby and out of condition, he used a frontman to promote a fight against the English champion Joe Beckett. Burns was stopped in seven rounds but cleared £4,000. He used part of the proceeds to buy a public house in Newcastle upon Tyne in the north-east of England. Later he operated a speakeasy in New York. He lost most of his money in the American stock-market crash. In the 1930s he became an itinerant minister of religion in California, calling himself 'a paratrooper of the Lord'.

To the end the Canadian fired off indignant letters to the press in an attempt to correct the impression that Johnson had outclassed him during their Sydney bout. He died a pauper in 1955.

The massive and cheerful former Olympic wrestling champion Con O'Kelly opened a gymnasium in his adopted home of Hull. For years he could be heard exhorting his young charges, 'Come on, lads, learn and train hard! It's good for the soul!' In the 1930s he accompanied his son, Con Junior, also a heavyweight and a former Olympic wrestler, on a tour of the USA. Con Junior had a reasonably successful career and then abandoned the fight game to become a priest, to the enormous pride of his father.

O'Kelly's fellow countryman Jim Coffey, the Roscommon Giant, saved enough money from his bouts to be able to return to his beloved Ireland, where he purchased a farm and lived out his life in contentment. His 1959 Associated Press obituary stated accurately enough, 'Jim Coffey, an amiable giant whose skill in the ring never matched his courage and determination, was one of the prize-ring figures who came close to the top but never made it.'

The South African Lodewikus van Vuuren, better known as George 'Boer' Rodel, was not as fortunate. He remained in New York after retiring from the ring, where the best work he could obtain was as a longshoreman. Perhaps even this was preferable to being paraded up and down a roadway in an old army greatcoat as a war hero by the scheming and unscrupulous Jimmy Johnston. Rodel died in 1955, at the age of 67.

Gunboat Smith, another former White Heavyweight title-holder, went on too long and lost his last two fights on first-round knockouts. One of these summary defeats was to Harry Greb, known as the 'Human Windmill'. Greb gained an unfair advantage at the opening bell by promptly sticking his thumb into the Gunboat's eye, and while his opponent was temporarily blinded he brought over a crushing right hand to finish the bout and Smith's boxing career. The big man then became a top-class referee.

One bout at which he officiated was between his former opponent, Harry Greb, and Tiger Flowers for the world middleweight title. When both fighters came out to receive their pre-match instructions from Smith in the centre of the ring, Greb said cheerfully to the referee, 'Hello, Gunboat, old pal!' Smith, remembering the illegal thumbing incident, growled, 'Where do you get that "old pal" stuff?'

Greb returned to his corner in a chastened mood, fully expecting to get the worst of any forthcoming decisions. At the end of the bout the two judges voted for Flowers. Gunboat Smith decided in favour of the man who had almost blinded him.

Tom Cowler, who had so impressed James J. Corbett when the latter saw him fight on one of his theatrical tours of Canada, never recovered from a beating by Jack 'the Giant-Killer' Dillon, who gave the Cumbrian 6 inches in height and almost 3 stone in weight and finished him off in two rounds. Cowler returned to England after the war, had a few more contests and died at the age of 59.

Jim Flynn, 'the Pueblo Fireman', who fearlessly fought them all, from Johnson to Dempsey, over an incredible 27-year period from

1903 until 1930, drove a cab in Phoenix when he gave up the ring. He would never be drawn on accusations that a destitute and desperate Jack Dempsey had gone into the tank in their first encounter in 1917, when Flynn had surprisingly won in the first round. After his retirement the Fireman suffered problems with his eyesight and died a poor man, at the age of 55, in 1935.

George Hackenschmidt retired from the wrestling ring, became a naturalised French citizen and lived to a great age. He wrote books on philosophy and became a guru on healthy living. In his eighties he was still working out with weights and running 7 miles several times a week.

Jess Willard, the White Hope who finally defeated Jack Johnson, did not have an easy time of it as champion. Not long after winning the title he was in the headlines for all the wrong reasons when he went to see the escapologist Harry Houdini perform at the Orpheum Theatre. When invited to come down onto the stage to represent the audience as an observer, the heavyweight champion sullenly refused to do so. This led to an altercation between the two men. It ended with Houdini, relishing the publicity he knew would ensue, shouting prophetically to the giant from the stage, 'Remember this, I will be Harry Houdini when you are not the heavyweight champion of the world.'

Willard fled the theatre. Houdini's agent started telephoning the newspapers. The next morning the headline of the *Los Angeles Times* read, '2000 Hiss J. Willard. Champion Driven From Theatre by Hoots and Calls'.

Willard made money touring with circuses and Wild West shows and in 1916 fought ten rounds with Frank Moran at Madison Square Garden in New York. The one unusual feature of this exercise in tedium was that it was the only World Heavyweight Championship bout in which no official decision was rendered. Willard received the newspaper verdicts, but Grantland Rice summed up the feelings of most present when he wrote that if the Willard–Moran bout was supposed to be brutal, 'then dancing should be stopped on account of its innate cruelty and savagery. There are times when even an expert cannot tell which of the two sports is under way.'

Willard was an unpopular champion. Not only did he refuse to join the armed forces at a time of war, but he would not even box exhibitions for the troops. In 1919, he defended his title for Tex Rickard, making a comeback as a promoter. In their bout at Toledo, Ohio, the champion was slaughtered by Jack Dempsey, the best fighter around. Willard was floored seven times in the first round by the savage challenger, but lasted until the interval after the third round, when he retired. After the bout, clad in his baggy street clothes, alone and forsaken by his backers, Willard emerged from his dressing room into the almost empty stadium. Still semi-conscious and half-blind, he felt his way along the wooden fence, looking for a way out. He was discovered by reporter Charles MacArthur, later a Broadway playwright. Tenderly McArthur guided Willard to a taxi and took him back to his hotel.

The ex-heavyweight champion made a comeback four years later and was knocked out in eight rounds by South American Luis Firpo, who was then being groomed for a tilt at Dempsey's championship. Later Willard abandoned ranching and went into real estate, earning extra cash by refereeing fixed all-in wrestling matches. He died in 1968 at the age of 86.

Many of the promoters and managers involved in the White Hope campaign remained unscathed in boxing for many years, but Hugh D. McIntosh, who had promoted the Jack Johnson–Tommy Burns bout in 1908, was not one of them. The Australian became disillusioned with the politics of boxing. In 1913 he gave up his lease on the Rushcutters Bay stadium. For a time he became a theatrical impresario and then opened a chain of milk bars in Britain. Eventually everything went wrong and he died in straitened circumstances.

Tex Rickard linked up with the new star, Jack Dempsey, and went on to become the leading promoter of his day, taking over Madison Square Garden. He survived a messy and highly publicised court case, being found not guilty of a charge of the rape of a 15-year-old girl. He died in 1929, at the age of 58, following an operation for appendicitis.

A character witness at Rickard's trial had been Anthony J. Drexel Biddle, the millionaire banker who had backed Philadelphia Jack O'Brien. He remained on the periphery of boxing. At the age of 41, in 1917, he joined the Marine Corps and persuaded the authorities to include boxing in the basic training programme. He remained in the Marine Reserves, and, a decade after O'Brien's fight with Johnson, Major Biddle enjoyed his finest hour before the Willard–Dempsey title match when he led a squad of Marines in an enthusiastic display of arms drill in the ring before the main bout. Biddle and his Marines' heavy boots caused so much damage to the floor that the canvas had to be replaced before the bout could get under way.

Later, Biddle used his connections to obtain a post teaching unarmed combat to FBI agents. He also published a book on the subject, entitled *Do or Die*. Soldiers who had actually fought for their lives in the trenches said that the manual was virtually useless.

He became the subject of a stage show and a subsequent 1967 Walt Disney film, *The Happiest Millionaire*, in which he was portrayed by Fred MacMurray as a bumbling, well-meaning but ineffectual head of a wealthy household.

Jimmy Johnston kept on wheeling and dealing, but he never found his heavyweight hope. Instead, he managed a slew of champions at lighter weights, including middleweight Harry Greb, welterweight Ted Kid Lewis, and Johnny Dundee at featherweight. Perhaps his greatest moment came when he capitalised on the enthusiasm for boxing in Chinatown and persuaded an Irish fighter called Patrick Mulligan to have a pudding-basin haircut, dye his skin yellow and fight as Ah Chung, the lightweight champion of China.

Wilson Mizner remained an enthusiastic ringside spectator, but managed no more fighters, finding none who could give him the same charge that wild Stan Ketchel had done. He filled the gaps between his major activities of gambling and drinking by being a card sharp on transatlantic liners, collaborating in the writing of several successful Broadway plays, engaging in a major real-estate scam in Florida and supplying dialogue to order for Hollywood gangster movies.

Jack Curley made little money from organising the Johnson–Willard championship bout in Cuba, and when Rickard took over the reins of New York boxing promotion he drifted out of the game and back into professional wrestling. He scored a minor victory over Rickard when he succeeded in a legal injunction to prevent the Texan putting on wrestling matches at Madison Square Garden, because these would compete with Curley's own New York promotions. He upset other competitors by ingratiating himself with the wealthy philanthropist Mrs William Randolph Hearst, co-staging charity tournaments with her to provide pasteurised milk for poor children, and securing the backing of her influential husband's newspapers. In time, Curley was eased out of the wrestling scene by younger, and even more ruthless, competitors. He died in 1937, a wealthy man, on his Long Island estate.

Billy McCarney, who had managed Luther McCarty and had turned down the opportunity to handle Jack Johnson as soon as the champion started asking for loans, continued in boxing for many years. As late as the 1930s he was still wheeling and dealing. At an age when most men would have been enjoying retirement, he was observed trying to steal future world champion Max Schmeling from his rightful German manager, probably just to keep his hand in.

Gabby Dumb Dan Morgan remained a part of the boxing scene until he was in his eighties, outliving his White Hope Battling Levinsky by many years. In the Second World War he discovered his niche, touring military camps, sometimes in tandem with Jack Johnson, giving talks on the history of the fight game to enlisted men. He had a low opinion of modern heavyweights compared with the giants of the White Hope era. His view was shared by Johnson. On one occasion the old manager asked the ageing ex-champion why he did not abandon his flea circus to train and manage a modern heavyweight. Johnson shook his head in disgust. 'These fleas can think better than the heavyweights around today,' he snorted. Dan Morgan died in 1955, at the age of 82. Until his last years he was still being employed by promoters to ballyhoo their shows.

Tom O'Rourke had promoted the very first White Hope tournaments in 1911 and had managed the winner, Al Palzer. He died at the age of 84 on 19 June 1936, in the dressing room of Max Schmeling just before the German's first bout with Joe Louis. O'Rourke had been visiting Schmeling, when he simply collapsed and died. His body remained shrouded in blankets on the rubbing table in the dressing room while the phlegmatic Schmeling went out to defeat Louis. Immediately before his death, O'Rouke had sued the New York Boxing Commission for depriving him of his judge's licence on the grounds that he was too old.

Jack London, the writer whose racist diatribe after the Burns–Johnson fight had helped to start the whole White Hope campaign, died at the age of 40, probably by his own hand. He had become the highest-paid writer in the world and had lost all interest in both boxing and the class struggle.

But it was the boxers who truly epitomised the White Hope campaign. Their heyday was a short one and when it was over most of them were discarded and ignored. Many of them went back to labouring, mining, vagrancy or whatever else they had been doing before they had been plucked from obscurity to strut before the screaming crowds. Only a few of them managed to hang on to their ring earnings.

Yet even the least-educated and most self-absorbed former White Hopes knew that for a brief hour they had been involved in a crazy, often sordid, but absorbing period of boxing history. The feelings of them all were summed up by the very first White Hope to enter the ring with champion Jack Johnson, back in 1909. Victor McLaglen's finest hour came many years after he had left the fight game behind him, when, at the age of 49, he had been presented with the Best Actor Oscar at the 1935 Hollywood ceremonies.

The award was to prove a professional lifeline to the former soldier of fortune, but he never regarded it very highly. 'Acting never appealed to me, and I was dabbling in it solely as a means of making money,' he observed. The bishop's son had better things to remember. Towards the end of his long and rather incredible life, he once went on record as saying rather wistfully, 'The only thing which ever thrilled me was boxing.'

EPILOGUE

The reign of Jack Johnson left one significant legacy to the sporting world. For more than twenty years after he lost his title no black fighter was allowed to compete for the World Heavyweight Championship, until Joe Louis won the crown on 22 June 1937.

There had been black world champions at the lighter weights before the advent of Jack Johnson and there were to be many more after he had left the fistic scene. But for over two decades no black athlete was allowed to fight for boxing's supreme prize – the heavyweight title.

There were certainly black contenders worthy of a championship bout – George Godfrey, Harry Wills and Larry Gaines among them – but they were all frozen out by the promoters running the sport. Gaines was an outstanding Canadian heavyweight who actually beat two future world champions, Max Schmeling and Primo Carnera, before they won their titles. For a short time in Paris he was managed by a young would-be writer called Ernest Hemingway. Gaines became so embittered by his ostracism that he called his biography *The Impossible Dream*, writing, 'Like every man who ever laced on gloves, I dreamed of becoming the heavyweight champion of the world. But, for me, it was always the impossible dream, the unreachable star. The politics of the day were against it. The bar was up.'

Few white men wanted another Jack Johnson to claim equality in or out of the ring. Tex Rickard, who was to become the world's leading promoter between 1919 and 1929, set his face against employing black heavyweights. The riots after the Johnson–James J. Jeffries bout, which he had promoted in 1910, had convinced him that he wanted no further part in mixed-race matches.

Jess Willard, the successful White Hope who had dethroned Jack Johnson, lost his title in three rounds to the dynamic former hobo Jack Dempsey in 1919. The day after he had won the championship Dempsey made it plain that he, too, would observe a colour bar. The *New York Times* of 5 July 1919 stated, 'Jack Dempsey announced today that he would draw the colour line. He will pay no attention to Negro challengers, but will defend his title against any white heavyweights as the occasion demands.'

Some years after boxing had been legalised in New York State in 1920, the Boxing Commission insisted that Jack Dempsey should defend his title against the black Harry Wills. Promoter Rickard at first stalled, and then he refused, threatening to take his money-spinning operations out of the state. To make his point, in 1926 he matched Dempsey against the white challenger Gene Tunney in Philadelphia.

Those black heavyweights who followed in Johnson's footsteps either had to 'throw' fights to white opponents or were forced to revert to the same poorly paid chitlin'-circuit matches against one another, which had characterised the careers of Sam Langford, Sam McVey and the other great black fighters of Jack Johnson's era.

The situation was no better in Great Britain. The National Sporting Club, which effectively controlled big-time boxing in the country, had been mortified when Johnson had reneged on his promise to fight Sam Langford at the club. His portrait was taken down from the wall and Johnson himself was refused admittance to the club when he later revisited London.

Even more important from the point of view of British and Commonwealth black heavyweights, the NSC refused to let them fight for British titles, which the club controlled through its system of Lonsdale belts, at any weights. 'Peggy' Bettinson, who ran the club, declared, 'We have no prejudice against the fighting Negro, but we would not run the risk of having to suffer another Jack Johnson.'

In 1929, when the British Boxing Board of Control took over the administration of boxing in Great Britain, it retained the colour bar, its secretary stating, 'It is only right that a small country such as ours should have championships restricted to boxers of white parents – otherwise we might be faced with a situation where all our British titles are held by coloured Empire fighters.' Black boxers from the Commonwealth were allowed to fight only for British Empire titles.

In France, too, in 1922, there was a furore when a black Senegalese boxer called Louis Phal, who fought under the name of Battling Siki, knocked out the national hero Georges Carpentier in six rounds in Paris. An effort was made to save Carpentier's world light-heavyweight title for the whites by disqualifying Siki for alleged rough fighting, but this caused such an uproar that the result was rescinded and the black fighter was allowed to keep his newly won championship.

However, when a proposal was put forward to match Siki against the British heavyweight champion in London in the same year, the Home Office stepped in and forbade the bout from taking place. The *Sporting Chronicle* of 10 November 1922 passed on the official government line, saying that white men should not fight coloured boxers because their temperaments were incompatible, and that under the prevailing conditions in the British Empire it was against the national interest for whites to fight blacks in case passions should be aroused.

Ironically, in 1923 Siki then fought a six-round exhibition contest in Quebec with the ex-champion Jack Johnson, who was in the throes of an unsuccessful comeback. By this time Johnson himself was on the chitlin' circuit and was finally taking on other black boxers for peanuts. Battling Siki made his home in New York, neglected his training and in 1925 was murdered in a street brawl.

It was not until 1934, when a sensational young black amateur heavyweight called Joe Louis Barrow, whose ring name was Joe Louis, turned professional, that the thoughts of the white establishment began to turn to the prospect of a black fighter challenging for the world title.

Louis was carefully handled by an all-black team. His managers were John Roxborough and Julian Black, while he was trained by the former lightweight Jack Blackburn. At first the latter refused to coach Louis, saying that it would be a waste of time even trying to bring a black heavyweight along. Blackburn had sparred with Jack Johnson in his heyday and had not enjoyed the experience. He believed that the champion's behaviour had ruined the chances of any other black heavyweight being given an opportunity. It was not until Blackburn was offered $35 a week that he joined the entourage.

Louis's first professional bouts were so sensational that even white promoters began to take an interest in him. Veteran Jimmy Johnston, who briefly had taken over promoting boxing at Madison Square Garden after the death of Tex Rickard, contacted Louis's managers and offered to get him fights in New York, as long as Louis realised that as a black boxer he would occasionally have to lose bouts to order.

John Roxborough refused the offer. The manager believed that Louis's fighting record would take him into the big time, as long as the heavyweight's behaviour allayed the fears of white spectators. To that end, Roxborough concentrated on building up Louis's reputation as quiet, introverted and non-threatening, except in the ring. As a public-relations exercise he even issued a list of rules, which he claimed Joe Louis would adhere to at all times. His fighter would never: have his picture taken with white women; enter a nightclub alone; participate in soft or fixed fights; denigrate or gloat over an opponent. But he would always remain impassive before the cameras; live and box in a clean manner.

Joe Louis's backers also took good care to keep him away from Jack Johnson and the emotional luggage that the former champion brought with him. The self-absorbed Johnson had never been regarded as a leader of the advance of black rights, even at the peak of his fame, and years later when he tried to approach Louis at the latter's training camp the former champion was turned away.

Roxborough's careful guidance worked. Louis won fight after fight, with only one loss on the way to his championship bid. On 22 June 1937, Joe Louis won the Heavyweight Boxing Championship of the World by knocking out the holder James J. Braddock in eight rounds in Chicago. He retained the crown for thirteen years, until his defeat by another black fighter, Ezzard Charles, on 27 September 1950.

Joe Louis's long reign as champion was untroubled by scandal. The uncontroversial black fighter's shy, deadpan disposition and willingness to fight all challengers won the hearts of boxing followers everywhere and paved the way for the many black heavyweight champions who followed him. Before Louis, there had only been one black heavyweight champion, Jack Johnson. Since his retirement from the ring, almost thirty black heavyweights have won one version or another of the world heavyweight title, and no other White Hope campaign has ever been launched.

In Great Britain matters took longer to adjust. It was not until 1947 that the British Boxing Board of Control withdrew its colour ban, following a statement by the colonial secretary of the then Socialist government, representing the views of a country in which black and white citizens had fought side by side throughout the Second World War, that he regarded the bar as completely unjustified.

In the following year Dick Turpin, the son of a father from British Guiana (now Guyana) and an English mother, who had served in the war in the British Army, won the British middleweight title by outpointing Vince Hawkins over fifteen rounds at the Aston Villa football ground. For the rest of the century he was followed by dozens of British-born black fighters who went on to win British and in some cases world championships.

BIBLIOGRAPHY

Books

Angle, Bernard J., *My Sporting Memories*, Holden, 1925
Batchelor, Denzil, *Jack Johnson and his Times*, Phoenix, 1956
Bell, Leslie, *Bella of Blackfriars*, Odhams, 1961
Bettinson, A.F., *The National Sporting Club, Past and Present*, Sands, 1902
Biddle, Cordelia, *My Philadelphia Father*, Doubleday, 1951
Buggy, Hugh, *The Real John Wren*, Widescope, 1977
Burke, John, *Rogue's Progress*, Putnam, 1975
Butler, Frank, *A History of Boxing in Britain*, Barker, 1972
Butler, James, *Kings of the Ring*, Stanley Paul, undated
Brady, William, *The Fighting Man*, Bobbs-Merrill, 1916
Burns, Tommy, *Scientific Boxing and Self-Defence*, Health and Strength, undated
Cantwell, Robert, *The Real McCoy*, Vertex, 1971
Carpentier, Georges, *Carpentier*, Hutchinson, 1955
Chidsey, Donald Barr, *John the Great*, Chapman and Hall, 1947
Clark, Norman, *All in the Game*, Methuen, 1935
Corri, Eugene, *Refereeing 1000 Fights*, Pearson, 1919
Dalby, W. Barrington, *Come In, Barry!*, Cassell, 1961
Dartnell, Fred, *Seconds Out!*, Laurie, undated
Dearment, R.K., *Bat Masterson*, Oklahoma University Press, 1979
De Coy, Robert H., *Jack Johnson, the Big Black Fire*, Holloway, 1969
Diggelen, T. von, *Worthwhile Journey*, Heinemann, 1955
Doherty, W.J., *In the Days of Giants*, Harrap, 1931
Early, Gerald, *The Culture of Bruising*, Ecco Press, 1994
Farr, Finis, *Black Champion*, Macmillan, 1964
Fleischer, Nat, *The Heavyweight Championship*, Putnam, 1949
——, *Black Dynamite*, 4 vols, Ring, 1938
Fountain, Charles, *Sportswriter*, OUP, 1993
Goodwin, Jack, *Myself and My Boxers*, Hutchinson, 1924
Griffin, James, *Wise Guy*, Vanguard, 1933
Harding, John, *Lonsdale's Belt*, Robson, 1994
Herbert, Michael, *Never Counted Out*, Dropped Aitches Press, 1992

Bibliography

Hietla, Thomas R., *The Fight of the Century*, Sharpe, 2002

Inglis, William, *Champions Off Guard*, Vanguard, 1932

Isenberg, Michael T., *John L. Sullivan and His Times*, Robson, 1988

Jackson, Stanley, *The Life and Cases of Mr Justice Humphries*, Odhams, 1952

Johnson, Alexander, *Ten and Out!*, Ives Washburn, 1927

Johnson, Alva, *The Incredible Mizners*, Hart-Davis, 1953

Johnson, Jack, *In the Ring and Out*, Proteus, 1977

Kahn, Roger, *A Ring of Pure Fire*, Harcourt-Brace, 1999

Kearns, Jack (Doc), *The Million Dollar Gate*, Macmillan, 1966

La Guardia, F., *The Making of an Insurgent*, Lippincott, 1947

Lardner, John, *White Hopes and Other Tigers*, Lippincott, 1947

Liebling, A.J., *A Neutral Corner*, Simon and Schuster, 1992

Lynch, Bohun, *Knuckles and Gloves*, Collins, 1922

Mace, Jem, *The Story of Jem Mace*, McInnes, 1989

Mills, Freddie, *Forward the Light Heavies!*, Stanley Paul, 1956

Moir, Gunner, *The Complete Boxer*, Health and Strength, undated

Morgan, Dan, *Dumb Dan*, Tedson, 1953

Myer, Patrick, *Gentleman Jim Corbett*, Robson, 1998

Palmer, Joe, *Recollections of a Boxing Referee*, Bodley Head, 1927

Power, Bob, *The Les Darcy American Venture*, Lambton, 1994

Preston, Harry, *Memories*, Constable, 1928

Roberts, Randy, *Papa Jack*, Robson, 1983

——, *Jack Dempsey*, Robson, 1987

Rose, Charlie, *Life's a Knockout*, Hutchinson, 1953

Sammons, J.T., *Beyond the Ring*, Illinois University Press, 1990

Samuels, Charles, *The Magnificent Rube*, McGraw-Hill, 1957

Shipley, Stan, *Bombardier Billy Wells*, Bewick, 1993

Smith, Toby, *Kid Blackie*, Wayfarer, 1987

Soutar, Andrew, *My Sporting Life*, Hutchinson, 1934

Sugden, John, *Boxing and Society*, Manchester University Press, 1996

Tregarthen, Clive, *Fighters of the Old Cosmo*, Mumford, 1975

Ulyatt, Michael E., *The Fighting O'Kellys*, Hutton, 1991

Wells, Bombardier, *Modern Boxing*, Ewart, Seymour, undated

Wells, Jeff, *Boxing Day*, Harper Collins, 1998

Wignall, Trevor, *The Story of Boxing*, Hutchinson, 1923

Academic Papers

Green, Jeffrey P., 'Boxing and the "Colour Question" in Edwardian Britain: The "White Problem" of 1911', *International Journal of the History of Sport 5*, 1988

Bibliography

Hutchison, Phillip, 'The Media, Motives, and Jack Johnson: A Narrative Analysis of the Search for a "Great White Hope"', American Journalism Historians' Association Second Annual Rocky Mountain Regional Conference, Brigham Young University, 9 March 2002

Wiggins, David, 'Peter Jackson and the Elusive Heavyweight Championship: A Black Athlete's Struggle Against the Late Nineteenth Century Color-Line', *Journal of Sport History*, Summer 1985

Article

Bennett, Lerone, 'Jack Johnson and the Great White Hope', *Ebony 49*, April 1994

Newspapers

Baltimore American
Los Angeles Times
Mexborough and Swinton Times
Milwaukee Evening Wisconsin
Milwaukee Free Press
National Police Gazette
Nevada Magazine
New York American
New York Post
New York Times
New York Herald Tribune
Ohio State Journal
Philadelphia Evening Bulletin
San Francisco Chronicle
Seattle Mail and Herald
The Sporting Life
Tacoma Daily Ledger
Topeka Capital-Journal
Washington Post

Magazines

Boxing
New Yorker
Ring

Bibliography

Court Transcript

State of Minnesota, County of Otter Tail, District Court Seventh Judicial District, *the State of Minnesota vs Henry Palzer*, 26 July, 1917, at the town of Gorman.

INDEX

Index

Index

Index